STOPPING THE CLOCK

STOPPING THE CLOCK

Why many of us will live past 100—and enjoy every minute!

DR. RONALD KLATZ
President, American Academy of Anti-Aging Medicine

DR. ROBERT GOLDMAN
President, National Academy of Sports Medicine

KEATS PUBLISHING INC. NEW CANAAN, CONNECTICUT

Library of Congress Cataloging-in-Publication Data

Klatz, Ronald, 1955–
    Stopping the clock : why so many of us will live past 100 and
enjoy every minute of it! / Ronald Klatz, Robert Goldman.
        p.   cm.
    Includes bibliographical references and index.
    ISBN 0-87983-717-9
    1. Longevity.   2. Dietary supplements.   3. Hormone therapy.
I. Goldman, Bob, 1955–   . II. Title.
RA776.75.K63   1996
612.6'8—dc20   96-172
                                                            CIP

Printed in the United States of America

Keats Publishing, Inc.
27 Pine Street (Box 876)
New Canaan, Connecticut 066840-0876

96 97 98   6 5 3

Acknowledgments

Managing Editor: Lisa B. Song
Medical Editor: Vincent Giampapa, M.D.
Editorial Assistant: Torye A. Mullins

In addition, we wish to thank the many people who contributed to making *Stopping the Clock* an informative text that will provoke new thought as well as stimulate the creation of the next paradigm of health care, **Anti-Aging Medicine**. We especially wish to recognize:

Frances Kovarik, Ph.D.
Debra Battjes, M.S.
Steven Novil, Ph.D.
Kim Bardley
Gregory Fahy, Ph.D.
Louis Habash
Ben Weider, Ph.D.
Joe Weider
Eric Weider
Thomas W. Allen, D.O.
Thomas Deters, D.C.
Bob Delmonteque, N.D.
Saul Kent
Richard Cutler, Ph.D.
William Regelson, M.D.
Michael Fossel, M.D., Ph.D.
Dharma Singh Khalsa, M.D.
Roy Walford, M.D.
Denham Harman, M.D., Ph.D.
Julian Whitaker, M.D.
John Abdo
GK Goh

Gus Alevizos
Phil Broxham
Glen Braswell
Rafael Santonja, Pharm. D.
Paul Chua
Darryl and Josie Burleigh
Richard Bizarro
Tony Little
Marilyn Hennessy
William Faloon
Jack LaLanne
Tom Purvis, L.P.T.
Phil Santiago, D.C.
David and Betty Siegel
Leong Wah Kheong
Edwin Soeryadjaya
Andy Handayanto
Chan Boon Yong
Yew Lin Goh
Jake Steinfeld
Ron Ooi
William J. Little

Byron Kline
Anthony Barone
William Berridge
Carol Ann Rojc
Kenny Wong
Russ Stewart
T.T. Durai
Barry Datloff
L. Ellen Yarnell
Justine Schmidt
Jim Lorimer
Thomas Miller
Thomas Nelson
Richard Orenstein
Mitch Simon
Don Kleinsek, Ph.D.
Robert Morin, M.D.
Richard Latchaw, M.D.
Loren Martin, Ph.D.
Adam Eilenberg
Mark Abrahams
Neil Spruce
Mark Slavin, D.C.
Ali and Ben Berman
Steven Speigle
Cliff Wertheim
Robert Bram
June Colbert
Perris Calderon
Leslie Cohen
Mike Crohn, D.C.
Thomas Morgan
Thomas Caprel
Cory and Allen Dropkin
Will and Norm Dabish
Eve Magnet
Paul and Mark Goldman
Alice and Arnold Goldman
Goldie Klatz
Harold Hakes, Ph.D.
Alex Thomson
William Louey

Joy Knapp
Mitch Kaufman
Gary Vogel
James Manion
Michael McNulty, Ph.D.
Ian McDonald, M.D.
Mark McCormack
Glen Pollock
Jeff Plitt
Lori White
Howard Ravis
George Rizzos, D.C.
Linda Gioni
Roseann Swain
Royalyn Aldrich
Leeann Chen
Jenifer Stuffen
Silvia Garcia, M.D.
Irene Nathan
David Steinman
Gail Ross
Thomas Nelson
Carol Kahn
Jack Scovil
Thom Hyde, D.C.
Amy Sklar
Joe Schultz
Larry Strickler
Martin Silverberg
Ann Sobel
Gary Strauch
Tom Merridith
Allan Tamshen
Jay and Tracy Tuerk
Pamela Kagan
David Kravitz
Thomas Stauzenbach
Don Owen, Ph.D.
Ronald Lawrence, M.D.
John Butterfield
Ralph Paffenberger, Ph.D.
Stedman Graham

Special thanks to the membership of the American Academy of Anti-Aging Medicine and the National Academy of Sports Medicine for their support and encouragement in this important new specialty of medicine.

The publishers wish to express their thanks to Elizabeth A. Ryan for her early work in the preparation of this book.

Disclaimer

Reader please note: Medicine is referred to as the "practice of medicine" because it requires constant re-education and re-evaluation to maintain proficiency and accuracy. The data presented in this book include research on anti-aging therapeutics written by the best and brightest minds and published by some of the most authoritative texts and journals in the world. But in less than five years from now we will know twice as much about anti-aging medicine and biomedical technology as we do today, and 10 years from now we will have more than five times as much knowledge of this subject.

Because of the ever-expanding knowledge of medicine, the most any author can hope to do is to wisely and prudently put forth theory and practice as best as it is currently known. In preparation of this book, the editorial staff reviewed scores of published reports, hundreds of books, and interviewed many of the worlds leading anti-aging researchers and scientists. However, do not assume the material in this book to be 100 percent correct or safe. It is *not*! This book is not intended to provide medical advice nor is it to be used as a substitute for advice from your own physician. At best, this book is meant to be an educational resource to guide your personal quest toward enhanced health and longevity. If you wish to initiate any of the programs or therapies described in this book, *you must* consult and work in partnership with a knowledgeable physician before doing so.

Perhaps some day, as Woody Allen wrote in the movie *Sleeper,* we will find that the true keys to health and longevity are hot fudge sundaes and smoking cigars. But for now, we can only rely on the vast preponderance of research, scientific opinion, and clinical experience of the individuals whose groundbreaking work has helped to fill the pages of this book.

For important updates and corrections of the information within, consult World Health Network on the Internet at http://www.worldhealth.net or call (312)528-4333 for a recorded message update.

Contents

STOPPING THE CLOCK

Chapter 1

Who Wants to Live to Be 150?

The banquet hall was filled with 1400 of the world's most respected scientific minds in medicine and biotechnology. They had assembled at the 3rd Annual International Conference on Anti-Aging Medicine and Biomedical Technology at the Alexis Park Resort in Las Vegas on December 10, 1995. Dr. Marvin Minsky of the Massachusetts Institute of Technology, the man credited with the invention of artificial intelligence, posed this question to the audience: "Who here wishes to live to the ripe age of 500?" Eighty percent of hands in the room rose with little hesitation. "Well," said Minsky, "now at last we're ready for the next millennium."

Aging is not inevitable! The war on aging has begun! So says the official slogan of the American Academy of Anti-Aging Medicine (A⁴M), founded in 1993 by a small group of physicians and scientists dedicated to slowing, and eventually halting, the aging process. The science of anti-aging medicine is creating a new paradigm of health care and is taking a new approach to aging and to medicine, showing us a new reality for mankind, an adulthood free from the fear of disease, infirmity, and lingering death of old age. In three short years, A⁴M has grown from a concept to the dominant medical and scientific society of clinical anti-aging medicine, representing the interests of more than 700 specialists from 30 countries worldwide.

To understand the concept of anti-aging medicine, realize that with the exception of infection and some childhood disorders, the vast majority of degenerative disease shares but one common characteristic, aging itself. Alzheimer's disease, most cancers, heart disease, non-insulin dependent diabetes, osteoporosis, autoimmune disorders, stroke, death by pneumonia and influenza, arthritis, Parkinson's disease, and the myriad of maladies linked to advancing age commonly afflict only those over the age of 40—the age of lost youth and the portal to seniority.

In the United States, our trillion dollar-plus yearly medical budget is spent almost exclusively on late-state disease-focused chronic care and heroic interventional medicine. If we could only slow the onset of aging as a degenerative process, we could also push back the onset of disease, saving hundreds of billions in health-care costs yearly as well as both improving the quality of life for our increasing elderly population and adding healthy, productive years to their lifespan.

Even without research directed at aging itself, man has for the past 200 years realized as an unrecognized benefit of advances in sanitation, nutrition, early detection and treatment of infectious diseases, an increase in average lifespan of almost 50 years!

The very definition of what is in fact old is changing daily, and the treatments that are giving so many people added years of life are the new interventions and therapeutics of anti-aging medicine—a combination of hormone replacement therapy, nutritional supplements, high-dose antioxidants and vitamins, a custom-designed exercise/rehabilitation program, and a revolution in personal attitude.

Contrary to a commonly held misconception, the purpose of anti-aging medicine is not to extend life in order to live a longer period of time as an "older" person, but rather to delay the onset of the aging process and give everyone a greater num-

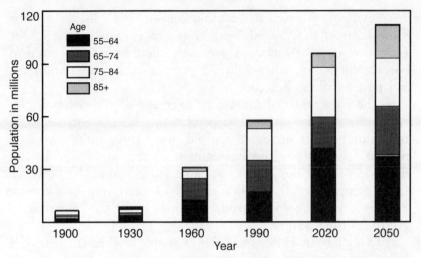

Actual and projected growth of U.S. population ages 55+, 1900–2050.

ber of those middle, healthy years. Who wouldn't want to be as fit and vital at age 75 as he or she was at 45?

> The silent revolution of anti-aging medicine is so gradual yet pervasive that many of us have not even noticed that aging "ain't what it used to be."
>
> • in 1796 — the average lifespan was but 25 years
> • 1896 — average lifespan almost doubled to 48 years
> • 1996 — promises a healthy, productive average lifespan of almost 80 years for most Americans, with many reputable anti-aging scientists predicting average lifespans of 120-150 years before 2046.

We have entered an era when older people make up the greatest proportion of America's population. When the first U.S. Census was taken in 1790, half the population was under the age of 16. In 1990, less than one-fourth the population was under the age of 16. The median age had doubled in 200 years! **In fact, the U.S. Census Bureau predicts that by the year 2025, there will be two 65-year-olds for every teenager!**

Living to 65 used to be a big deal—that's why the government thought that Social Security was a bargain in the 1930s. Only one in 10 Americans ever saw their first Social Security check. Not today, when fully 75 percent of the population will sail past 65 without a care.

The percentage of Americans over age 65 today has tripled from 1900 to 1990 from four percent to 12.5 percent, while the total number has increased tenfold, from three million to 31.6 million. The fastest-growing segment of the population is over 85. Other senior populations are also growing quickly, however. If we compare 1900 to 1991, the 65-74 age group had become 8 times larger, the 75-84 group 13 times larger, and the over 85 group 25 times larger.

Every day in 1990, some 6,000 people celebrated their 65th birthdays. Almost everybody who turned 65 in 1990 was expected to live an average of 17.3 years. In 1900, it was unusual to reach 65 in the first place, and those who did could only expect to live an average of 11 years more.

> Americans aged 80 years and older can expect to live up to a year longer than their counterparts in England, France, Japan, and Sweden.

Look around today, it's not uncommon to see people who are still healthy and vibrant in their eighties and nineties. It used to be miraculous for a person to reach their hundredth birthday healthy, vital and intact. This is no longer true. Most people reading this can fully expect 100+ lifespans *now*. In fact, within the next 30 years, we can expect to see lifespans of 120-130 years in people with their physical states sound and intact, and with their mental faculties sharp and acute. From a historical standard, we are rapidly approaching a state of virtual immortality for the human race!

> There are 70,000 centenarians today. By conservative estimates, the year 2004 will hail 140,000 centenarians, and by the year 2050, we can predict well over a million centenarians.

AGING IS A TREATABLE MEDICAL CONDITION

The dreaded deterioration and vulnerability to the "diseases of aging" can be slowed, prevented and potentially even reversed: memory loss, fatigue, heart disease, circulatory problems, arthritis, stroke, Alzheimer's disease and cancer. The time has come: we *can* stop the clock.

Memory loss and Alzheimer's disease can be successfully slowed and often reversed via new metabolic and nutritional approaches. Medical science today has been able to reduce heart disease by 25 percent, and stroke by 40 percent since the 1950s. Blood screening for biochemical DNA damage will soon make early cancer detection a reality rather than a promise. This will translate to an over 90 percent cure rate for almost all causes of cancer.

THERE IS A DEMAND FOR ANTI-AGING MEDICINE

The baby-boomer generation (those born between 1946 and 1964, now aged 32 to 50), are to be congratulated for driving this new approach to aging and the modern-day reality of longevity and rejuvenation. For the first time in recorded history, an entire generation has decided it has better things to do than sit around and get old. The proven benefits of exercise and a balanced diet have been embraced. From the "Boomers" came the fitness movement, which history will record as being the forerunner of anti-aging medicine. They have made the commitment to be very good at what they do—and they want to keep active for as long as possible.

Boomers believe that age is irrelevant; it's function and ability that matter and they expect to live practically forever. Boomers have an innate desire to stay healthy, fit, and mentally alert because they know that their lives will not only be fuller and more enjoyable because of it, but longer and filled with greater opportunity. This is the generation that has said "*yes*" to anti-aging medicine.

Many political analysts have raised disturbing questions

about the demographics of the progressively elderly U.S. population. They point out that traditionally people over 65 have required far higher levels of social services than their younger counterparts. Particularly as they enter their eighties, they may need assistance with transportation, shopping, home maintenance, and other basic life tasks. Older people also tend to require ever-increasing levels of health care, since age almost always brings with it a lowered immune system and a greater vulnerability to a variety of diseases.

Who then, the politicians ask, will pay for these increased services? Traditionally, the younger portion of the population has supported the elderly, whether directly, through family care, or indirectly, through publicly funded services. Indeed, some commentators have noted that to the extent that we have elderly relatives, we all benefit from Social Security, Medicare, and other programs that serve senior citizens; individuals do not have to assume so great a burden for their own relatives as in the past.

But many analysts fear that as the proportion and number of elderly increases, society will become less willing or able to provide needed services. On the other hand, successful anti-aging medical therapies resulting in an extended and enhanced life span will have a profound impact on the economics of health care in many startling new ways.

For example, when anti-aging medicine is able to delay admission to nursing homes by just one month, the U.S. healthcare system will see **$3 billion** in savings a year! The National Institute on Aging recently reported that if the onset of Alzheimer's disease could be delayed by five years, the nation would save **$40 billion** per year! The healthy elderly population is the wealthiest segment of our population and will undoubtedly continue to pump money back into the economy. This can be seen by the baby boomers being the largest, richest, and biggest-spending segment in the history of American marketing.

Not only will longevity research pay off in great dividends, but fears of the graying of America simply will not materialize, thanks to the anti-aging advances already proven to work in the lab. These advances will forever alter our very notion of age, life, disease and death. Modern medical science has already demonstrated advances that would have been material only for science-fiction writers a few short decades ago.

The U.S. Center for Health Statistics reported that 47,000 people under the age of 44 had heart attacks in 1993, and only 17 percent of those who died of heart disease in hospitals were under age 65.

The future of anti-aging medicine promises the elimination of the disability, deformity, pain, disease, suffering and sorrow of old age on a wholesale basis. Older people today should be cherished as one might appreciate a vintage automobile or historic painting. In a few decades, the traditional enfeebled ailing elderly person will be but a grotesque memory of a barbaric past, just as we sadly recall the millions who suffered horrible deaths to the then nontreatable diseases such as tuberculosis, smallpox, whooping cough, and dysentery.

Three Leading Causes of Death in the United States

- 1896 — influenza, diarrhea, pneumonia
- 1996 — heart disease, cancer, stroke
- 2046 — suicide, homicide, aerospace accident

Just as computer technology is accelerating so that every 18 months power and speed double, making supercomputers compact and affordable enough for every college student to own, so too, biomedical information is doubling approximately every 3.5 years. For instance, who in 1946, just 50 years ago, would have believed it possible to implant neural tissue into the brains of patients suffering from Alzheimer's and Parkinson's disease in order that lost brain and nervous system tissue could be rebuilt? Who would have believed it possible to construct artificial hearts, ears, pancreases, kidneys? Today, all of this and much, much more is ho-hum and commonplace.

Near-term advances in biotechnology have already demonstrated in animal studies that spinal cord injuries can be repaired with cell grafting techniques, and we can expect human spinal cord injuries to be totally repairable in the near future as well. We are regrowing damaged knee cartilage to reverse arthritis in athletes and it's working *today*. Therapies are currently being used to repair and rebuild immune systems in the elderly, preventing the onset of the many diseases of aging: cancer, autoimmune diseases, diabetes and deadly infections.

> Medical science today has been able to reduce heart disease in the population by 25 percent, and stroke by 40 percent since the 1950's.

Research has shown that scientists have already succeeded in producing human-equivalent lifespans of 150-180 years in animals. Technologies will almost certainly be available to enable everyone to enjoy an added 30 to 50, even 100 years of healthy, youthful lifespan. Thus, it is not unreasonable that with medical information doubling every 3.5 years, in the year 2016, just 20 years from now, we will know 64 times more about aging and how to reverse it!

It isn't necessary to wait decades for the benefits of anti-aging medicine, however. It is improving the lives and health of thousands of people right now. In this book, you'll read about the latest developments in the new science of anti-aging medicine. You'll learn about hormone treatments, nutritional supplements, diet, and exercise programs that can help prolong the pleasures of youth. There are multitudes of 70-year-olds performing, thinking, and feeling every bit as well as when they were 55. If you follow the suggestions outlined in this book you, too, can expect one or more of the following benefits:

- an enhanced immune system
- improved memory and cognitive function
- remodeling of body musculature and reduction of total body fat
- enhanced sexual function
- an increased rate of wound healing

> The treatment of aging has less to do with turning back the clock than with the systematic revitalization of a multiplicity of discrete functions. This is a less magical, more clinical definition of what human growth rejuvenation actually is.
> —Vincent Giampapa, M.D., F.A.C.S.,
> Director of Research, Longevity Institute International

- increased aerobic capacity

Does this all sound too good to be true? In fact, these goals are well within your reach. The physicians and scientists of anti-aging medicine believe not only in longer lives but *better* lives. We stress that old age need not be the gateway to degenerated health and diminished vigor, but rather a time of renewed opportunity, a time of renaissance when we have the energy to make use of a lifetime of accumulated wisdom and experience.

If you're willing to make some simple lifestyle changes and work with a doctor who can prescribe appropriate anti-aging treatments, and commit yourself to a longer and healthier life, *you too* can stop the clock. Read on to find out how. Your very life depends on it!

Who will want to live to be 150? You will . . . the day after you celebrate your 149th birthday!

Rules for Immortality

The first and most important rule of Anti-Aging Medicine is DON'T DIE!

The second rule of Anti-Aging Medicine is DON'T GET SICK!

The third rule is DON'T GET OLD! Everyday you stay healthy and alive is another day medical science comes closer to finding the ultimate cure to aging.

* Drive a big car—2800 pounds or more—the survivability in a potentially fatal accident between the largest and the smallest automobiles can differ 10 fold.

* Avoid stress and depression. They are major causes for premature aging.

* Exercise daily. It is your number one defense against the infirmites of old ageism.

* Limit fats in your diet. It is directly associated with an increased risk of both heart disease and cancer.

* Sleep seven to eight hours a night. Quality sleep is essential for rejuvenation and repair. If you're like the 20 million Americans that suffer from insomnia or other sleeping problems—get help!

* Consume little or no alcohol. It is neurotoxic.

* Don't smoke. It stains your teeth, smells bad, and kills more Americans than all foreign wars *combined*. With every minute you smoke, a minute of your life is taken away.

* Try to keep your weight at or even five percent below ideal body weight (IBW). Mortality increases significantly at 20 percent or more above IBW and 10 percent or more below IBW.

* Maintain optimum antioxidant vitamin blood levels. Animal studies indicate a 20 percent increase in longevity with optimum supplementation.

* Early detection is the key to a cure for both heart disease and cancer— get blood tests and comprehensive anti-aging physical exams yearly.

* If age 55 or older, consider hormone replacement therapy if needed by a knowledgeable physician.

* Drink adequate purified or bottled water. As much as 70 percent of municipal water systems surveyed were polluted with potentially toxic amounts of flourine and chlorine. According to recent Environmental Protection Agency reports, these chemicals have been associated with an increased risk of urinary tract cancers.

* Think young, Aging is as much a state of mind as it is a state of physiology. Lie about your age (especially to yourself). Keep young friends around to remind yourself what "youth" feels and thinks like.

* Do not accept "just getting old." Fight tooth and nail to remain youthful and vigorous. At least 40 marvelous anti-aging drugs now exist and hundreds more are under development for everything from bone loss, Alzheimer's treatments, wrinkle reduction and gray hair. Find an anti-aging doctor and get started on a program *now*. If you can't locate an anti-aging doctor, call the American Academy of Anti-Aging Medicine at (312) 622-7401.

Chapter 2

Theories of Aging

We are forever in search of the cure for old age. Dozens of theories have been proposed, yet science has not produced a universal theory of aging. Generally, scientists believe that aging is a mechanism installed in the human body to insure the continued survival of the species. From the species' point of view, the most important time of our lives is our period of fertility, the years during which we're able to create new life. While it's socially functional for some people to live longer than that, to pass on the accumulated wisdom that might help the young survive, from nature's point of view, we are not that useful after the age of around 40.

As a result, many bodily functions begin to decline, with ever-accelerated losses of function continuing in each succeeding decade.

Why do we age? Current theories of aging at the cellular and molecular level generally revolve around two themes: aging is programmed and aging is accidental. Programmed aging theories are based on the idea that from conception to death, human development is governed by a biological "clock." This clock sets the appropriate times for various changes to take place. The changes in vision, loss of calcium in the bones, decreasing hearing acuity and lowered vital capacity of the lungs are all examples of programmed aging. Accidental theories of aging rely on chance—the notion that organisms get older by a series of random events. Examples are DNA damage from free radicals or just the wear and tear of daily life.

Before we embark on these different theories of aging, it is important to recognize the underlying assumptions that theoretic gerontology uses for the basis of aging:

Aging is developmental As we age, we become more mature adults, growing older developmentally, not chronologically. A 60-year-old chronologically may have the physiologic age of a 45-year-old person, or a 50-year-old may have the diseases and ill health paralleling the physiologic decline of an 80-year-old person.

Normal aging and pathologic aging are different Pathologic aging, such as adult-onset diabetes or arthritis, which may later bring on cardiovascular disease or osteoporosis, is not considered "normal" aging. These conditions are due to heredity or lifestyle. Whereas developing cataracts is "normal" aging, because if you live long enough you will get them.

Living longer is a gift of 20th-century science and technology The discoveries of vaccinations, insulin, antibiotics, new surgical techniques, hormone replacement therapies and treatments for life-threatening diseases all contribute to staying older longer.

Here are the four principal theories of aging, each of which accounts for some aspects of the process.

1. *The "Wear and Tear" Theory*

Dr. August Weismann, a German biologist, first introduced this theory in 1882. He believed that the body and its cells were damaged by overuse and abuse. The organs—liver, stomach, kidneys, skin, and so on are worn down by toxins in our diet and in the environment; by the excess consumption of fat, sugar, caffeine, alcohol, and nicotine; by the ultraviolet rays of the sun; and by the many other physical and emotional stresses to which we subject our bodies. Wear and tear is not confined to our organs, however; it also takes place on the cellular level.

Of course, even if you've never touched a cigarette or had a glass of wine, stayed out of the sun and eaten only natural foods, simply using the organs with which nature endowed you is going to wear them out. Abuse will only wear them out more quickly. Likewise, as the body ages, our very cells feel the effect, no matter how healthy our lifestyle.

When we're young, the body's own maintenance and repair systems keep compensating for the effects of both normal and excessive wear and tear. (That's why young people can more easily get away with a night of heavy drinking or a binge of pizza or sweets.) With age, the body loses its abilty to repair damage—whether caused by diet, environmental toxins, bacteria, or a virus. Thus, many elderly people die of diseases that they could have resisted when they were younger.

By the same token, nutritional supplements and other treatments covered in this book can help reverse the aging process by stimulating the body's own ability to repair and maintain its organs and cells.

2. The Neuroendocrine Theory

This theory, developed by Vladimir Dilman, Ph.D., elaborates on the wear and tear theory by focusing on the neuroendocrine system, the complicated network of biochemicals that governs the release of our hormones and other vital bodily elements. When we're young, our hormones work together to regulate many bodily functions, including our responses to heat and cold, our experience and our sexual activity. Different organs release various hormones, all under the governance of the hypothalamus, a walnut-sized gland located within the brain.

The hypothalamus sets off various chain reactions, in which an organ releases a hormone which in turn stimulates the release of another hormone, which in turn stimulates yet another bodily response. The hypothalamus responds to the body's hormone levels as its guide for how to regulate hormonal activity.

When we're young, hormone levels tend to be high, accounting for, among other things, menstruation in women and high libido in both sexes. As we age, though, the body produces lower levels of hormones, which can have disastrous effects on our functioning. The growth hormones that help us form muscle mass, hGH, testosterone and thyroid, for example, drop dramatically as we age, so that even if an elderly person has not gained weight, he or she has undoubtedly increased the ratio of fat to muscle.

Hormones are vital for repairing and regulating our bodily functions, and when aging causes a drop in hormone production, it causes a decline in our body's ability to repair and regulate itself as well. Moreover, hormone production is highly interactive: the drop in production of any one hormone is likely to have a feedback effect on the whole mechanism, signaling other organs to release lower levels of other hormones which will cause other body parts to release lower levels of yet other hormones.

Thus, hormone replacement therapy—a frequent component of any anti-aging treatment—helps to reset the body's hormonal clock and so can reverse or delay the effects of aging. If our hormones are being produced at youthful levels, in a very real sense the cells of our bodies are stimulated to be metabolically active and thus, we stay young.

3. The Genetic Control Theory

This planned-obsolescence theory focuses on the genetic programming encoded within our DNA. We are born with a unique genetic code, a predetermined tendency to certain types of physical and mental functioning. And that genetic inheritance has a great deal to say about how quickly we age and how long we live. To use a macabre analogy, it's as though each of us comes into the world as a machine that is pre-programmed to self-destruct. Each of us has a biological clock ticking away, set to go off at a particular time, give or take a few years. And when that clock goes off, it signals our bodies first to age and then to die.

However, as with all aspects of our genetic inheritance, the timing on this genetic clock is subject to enormous variation, depending on what happens to us as we grow up and on how we actually live (the old "nature versus nurture" debate).

Anti-aging medicine addresses this issue by augmenting the basic building blocks of DNA within each of our cells, preventing damage to and increasing repair of DNA. In this way, we believe, anti-aging treatment can help us escape our genetic destinies, at least to some extent.

4) *The Free-Radical Theory*

This exciting development in anti-aging research was first introduced by R. Gerschman in 1954, but was developed by Dr. Denham Harman of the University of Nebraska College of Medicine. "Free radical" is a term used to describe any molecule that differs from conventional molecules in that it possesses a free electron, a property that makes it react with other molecules in highly volatile and destructive ways.

In a conventional molecule, the electrical charge is balanced. Electrons come in pairs, so that their electrical energies cancel

Denham Harman, father of the free radical theory of aging, receives the 1995 Infinity Award from Dr. Ronald Klatz at the Third International Conference on Anti-Aging Medicine and Biomedical Technology in Las Vegas, Nevada.

each other out. Atoms that are missing electrons combine with atoms that have extra electrons, creating a stable molecule with evenly paired electrons and a neutral electrical charge.

The free radical, on the other hand, has an extra electron, creating an extra negative charge. This unbalanced electrical energy makes the free radical tend to attach itself to other molecules, as it tries to steal a matching electron and attain electrical equilibrium. Some scientists speak of these free radicals as "promiscuous," breaking up the happy marriages of paired electrons in neighboring molecules in order to steal an electron "partner" for themselves. In doing so, they create new free radicals—and extensive bodily damage.

Of course, free radical activity within the body is not only or even primarily negative. Without free radical activity—that is, without biochemical electricity—we would not be able to produce energy, maintain immunity, transmit nerve impulses, synthesize hormones, or even contract our muscles. The body's electricity enables us to perform these functions, and that electricity comes from the unbalanced electron activity of free radicals.

But free radicals also attack the structure of our cell membranes, creating metabolic waste products, including substances known as lipofuscins. An excess of lipofuscins in the body is shown as a darkening of the skin in certain areas, so-called "aging spots" that indicate an excess of metabolic waste resulting from cellular destruction. Lipofuscins in turn interfere with our cells' ability to repair and reproduce themselves. They disturb DNA and RNA synthesis, interfere with synthesis of protein (thus lowering our energy levels and preventing the body from building muscle mass), and destroy cellular enzymes, which are needed for vital chemical processes.

This type of free radical damage begins when at birth and continues until we die. In our youth, its effects are relatively minor since the body has extensive repair and replacement mechanisms that in healthy young people function to keep cells and organs in working order. With age, however, the accumulated effects of free radical damage begin to take their toll. Free radical disruption of cell metabolism is part of what ages our cells. It may also create mutant cells, leading ultimately to cancer and death.

Moreover, free radicals attack collagen and elastin, the substances that keep our skin moist, smooth, flexible and elastic. These vital tissues fray and break under the assaults of free radicals, a process particularly noticeable in the face, where folds of skin and deep-cut wrinkles are testaments to the long-term effect of free radical attacks.

Another way of looking at free radical damage is to think of it as oxidation, the process of adding oxygen to a substance. Another word for oxidation, of course, is rust, and in a sense, our aging process is analogous to the rusting away of a once-intact piece of metal. Because forms of oxygen itself are free radicals, our very breathing, and our otherwise healthy aerobic exercise, generate free radicals that help along the aging process.

Hence, substances that prevent the harmful effects of oxidation are known as antioxidants. Natural antioxidants include vitamin C, vitamin E, and beta-carotene (the substance that our body uses to produce vitamin A). Specialists in anti-aging medicine prescribe a host of natural and manufactured antioxidants to help combat the effects of aging. (See Chapter 9.)

Another substance that combats free radical damage is known as a free radical scavenger. Free radical scavengers actually seek out free radicals and harmlessly bind them before they can attack themselves to other molecules and/or cause cross-linking. As we'll see in subsequent chapters, many vitamins, minerals, and other substances fight aging by acting as free radical scavengers.

Other theories of aging that have been proposed throughout the years are:

Waste Accumulation Theory

In the course of their life spans, cells produce more waste than they can properly dispose of. This waste can include various toxins which when accumulated to a certain level, can interfere with normal cell function, ultimately killing the cell.

Evidence supporting this theory is the presence of a waste product called lipofuscin or age pigment. The cells most commonly found to contain lipofuscin are nerve and heart muscle cells—both critical to life. Lipofuscin is formed by a complex reaction that binds fat in the cells to proteins. This waste accumulates in the cells as small granules and increases in size as a person ages. Because lipofuscin builds up over time, it has been described as "the ashes of our dwindling metabolic fires."

Limited Number of Cell Divisions Theory

The number of cell divisions is directly affected by the accumulation of the cell's waste products. The more waste we accumulate over time, the faster cells degenerate. Although an ordinary chicken does not live anywhere near 20 years, French surgeon Dr. Alexis Carrel was able to keep pieces of a chicken heart alive in a saline solution which contained minerals in the same proportion as chicken blood for 28 years. He believed that he had achieved this by disposing of the waste products daily. Although Carrel's theory was eventually overturned by Dr. Leonard Hayflick, when it was found that fresh cells had inadvertently been added to the cultures, making the chicken cells seem "immortal," the experiment helped explain why cells from older people with more waste divided fewer times than cells from embryos, which divided the most.

Hayflick Limit Theory

In 1961, two cell biologists, Dr. Hayflick and Dr. Moorehead, made one of the greatest contributions to the history of cellular biology, demonstrating the senescence of cultured human cells. Hayflick theorized that the aging process was controlled by a biological clock contained within each living cell. The 1961 studies concluded that human fibroblast cells (lung, skin, muscle, heart) have a limited life span. They divided approximately 50 times over a period of years and then suddenly stopped. Nutrition seemed to have an effect on the rate of cell division: overfed cells made up to 50 divisions in a year, while underfed cells took up to three times as long as normal cells to make the divisions. Alterations and degenerations occurred within some cells before they reached their growth limit; the most evident changes took place in the cell organelles, membranes, and genetic material.

This improper functioning of cells and loss of cells in organs and tissues may be responsible for the effects of aging.

> Aging is the only fatal affliction that all of us share.
> —Leonard Hayflick, Ph.D.

Death Hormone Theory (DECO)

Unlike other cells, brain cells or neurons do not replicate. We are born with roughly 12 billion of them and over a lifetime about 10 percent perish. Dr. Donner Denckla, an endocrinologist formerly at Harvard University was convinced that the "death hormone" or DECO (decreasing oxygen consumption hormone) released by the pituitary gland may contribute to the loss of neurons. When he removed the pituitary glands of rats, their immune systems revitalized, the rate of cross-linking in cells reduced, and cardiovascular function was restored to the levels of youth. Denckla speculated that as we age, the pituitary begins to release DECO which inhibits the ability of cells to use thyroxine, a hormone produced by the thyroid governing basal metabolism, the rate at which cells convert food to energy. The resulting changes in metabolic rate bring on and accelerate the process of aging.

Thymic-Stimulating Theory

"The thymus is the master gland of the immune system," says Dr. Alan Goldstein, chairman of the biochemistry department at George Washington University. The size of this gland reduces from 200 to 250 grams at birth and then shrinks to around three grams by age 60. Scientists are investigating whether the disappearance of the thymus contributes to the aging process by weakening the body's immune system.

Studies have shown that thymic factors are helpful in restoring the immune systems of children born without them as well as rejuvenating the poorly functioning immune systems of the elderly. Thymic hormones may also play a role in stimulating and controlling the production of neurotransmitters and brain and endocrine system hormones, which means they may be the pacemakers of aging itself as well as key regulators responsible for immunity.

Mitochondrial Theory

The free radical theory is supported by direct experimental observations of mitochondrial aging. Mitochondria are the energy-producing organelles in the cells that are responsible for producing ATP, our primary source of energy. They produce cell energy by a process that leads to the formation of potentially damaging free radicals. Mitochondria are also one of the easiest targets of free radical injury because they lack most of the defenses found in other parts of the cell. Evidence points to various kinds of accumulated DNA damage over time to be a contributing factor to disease, and new research in mitochondrial repair could play an important part in the fight against aging.

Errors and Repairs Theory

In 1963, Dr. Leslie Orgel of the Salk Institute suggested that because the "machinery for making protein in cells is so essential to life, an error in that machinery could be catastrophic." The production of proteins and the reproduction of DNA sometimes is not carried out with accuracy. The body's DNA is so vital that natural repair processes kick in when an error is made. But the system is incapable of making perfect repairs on these molecules every time, and therefore the accumulation of these flawed molecules can cause diseases and other age changes to occur. If DNA repair processes didn't exist, scientists estimate that enough damage would accumulate in cells in one year to make them nonfunctional.

Redundant DNA Theory

Like the errors and repairs theory, the redundant DNA theory blames errors accumulating in genes for age changes. But as these errors accumulate, this theory also blames reserve genetic sequences of identical DNA that take over until the system is worn out. Dr. Zhores Medvedev of the National Institute of Medical Research in London proposed that different species' life spans may be a function of the degree of these repeated gene sequences.

Cross-Linkage Theory

Developmental aging and cross-linking were first proposed in 1942 by Johan Bjorksten. He applied this theory to aging diseases such as sclerosis, a declining immune system and the most obvious example of cross-linking, loss of elasticity in the skin. One of the most common proteins found in the skin, tendons, ligaments, bone, and cartilage is collagen. The collagen protein can be compared to the legs of a ladder with very few rungs. Each protein is connected to its neighbors by other rungs, forming a cross-link. In young people, there are few cross-links and the ladders are free to move up and down. The collagen stays soft and pliable. With age, however, the number of cross-links increases, causing the skin to shrink and become less soft and pliable. It is thought that these cross-links begin to obstruct the passage of nutrients and waste between cells.

Cross-linking also appears to occur when older immune systems are incapable of cleaning out excess glucose molecules in the blood. These sugar molecules react with proteins, causing cross-links and the formation of destructive free radicals. Scientists once thought inflexibility of the body with age was due to cross-linking of tendon, bone, and muscle tissue. However, people who lead a more active lifestyle and follow a good diet seem to inhibit or delay the cross-linking process.

Autoimmune Theory

The immune system is the most important line of defense against foreign substances that enter the body. With age, the system's ability to produce necessary antibodies that fight disease declines, as does its ability to distinguish antibodies from proteins. In a sense, the immune system becomes self-destructive and reacts against itself. Examples of autoimmune diseases are lupus, scleroderma and adult-onset diabetes.

Calorie Restriction Theory

Calorie restriction, or energy restriction, is a theory proposed by respected gerontologist Dr. Roy Walford of the UCLA

Medical School. After years of animal experiments and research on longevity, Walford has developed a high-nutrient, low-calorie diet demonstrating that "undernutrition without malnutrition" can dramatically retard the functional if not the chronological aging process. An individual on this program would lose the necessary weight gradually until a point of metabolic efficiency was obtained for maximum health and lifespan. Walford stresses the importance of not only the high-low diet, but moderate vitamin and mineral supplements coupled with regular exercise.

Gene Mutation Theory

In the 1940s scientists investigated the role of mutations in aging. Mutations are changes that occur in the genes which are fundamental to life. Evidence supporting this idea came from experiments with radiation. It was observed that radiation not only increased animals' gene mutation rate but accelerated their aging process as well. However, later studies showed the radiation-induced changes were only mimicking age changes. This hypothesis further diminished in validity when experiments with moderate amounts of radiation actually increased the lifespan of rats!

The Rate of Living Theory

German physiologist Max Rubner, who discovered the relationship between metabolic rate, body size and longevity, first introduced this theory in 1908. It simply states that we are each born with a limited amount of energy. If we use this energy slowly, then our rate of aging is slowed. If the energy is consumed quickly, aging is hastened. Other rate of living theories focus on limiting factors such as amount of oxygen breathed or number of heartbeats spent.

Order to Disorder Theory

From the time of conception to sexual maturation, our bodies are undergoing a system of orderliness. We are, as Dr. Leonard Hayflick states, "directing most of our energies to fulfilling a genetically determined plan for the orderly production and arrangement of an enormous number and variety of molecules." After sexual maturation, however, these same energies start to diminish in efficiency. Disorder occurs in molecules, in turn causing other molecules to produce errors and so on. These chaotic changes in our cells, tissues, and organs is what causes aging. Disorderliness varies from individual to individual, and this may be the reason why our tissues and organs deteriorate at different rates.

The Telomerase Theory of Aging

A new theory of aging that holds many promising possibilities for the field of anti-aging medicine is the telomerase theory of aging. This theory was born from the surge of technological breakthroughs in genetics and genetic engineering. First discovered by a group of scientists at the Geron Corporation in Menlo Park, California, telomeres are sequences of nucleic acids extending from the ends of chromosomes. Telomeres act to maintain the integrity of our chromosomes. Every time our cells divide, telomeres are shortened, leading to cellular damage and cellular death associated with aging.

Scientists discovered that the key element in rebuilding our disappearing telomeres is the "immortalizing" enzyme telomerase—an enzyme found only in germ cells and cancer cells. Telomerase appears to repair and replace telomeres, manipulating the "clocking" mechanism that controls the lifespan of dividing cells. Future development of a telomerase inhibitor may be able to cease cancer cells from dividing and presumably convert them back into normal cells.

In spite of the monumental progress in aging research, there has yet to be a unanimous vote on one specific theory of aging. Most of these theories have been disputed by scientists over and over again and many of them, as Dr. Hans Kugler, editor of the *Journal of Longevity Research,* said, "are dying of old age." Age-related changes do not occur uniformly in individuals; rather, they are controlled jointly by genetic and environmental factors, which further heightens the difficulty of finding a universal theory. What *is* universal is that we are all involved in a global aging phenomenon—that, through theoretical gerontology and anti-aging medicine we may eventually discover that there is no limit to human lifespan.

Chapter 3

Melatonin

Imagine a "wonder drug" that extended your lifespan by 25 percent or more, allowing you to live to be 120 years old. Imagine, too, that this drug not only extended your life but maintained your youth, enabling you to enjoy work, sex, and social activities with the same zest and vigor that marked your life at 45. Imagine, finally, that this drug had no harmful side effects or known long-term dangers, because it was actually not a drug at all, but a substance that occurred naturally in your body.

The fact is, we don't have to imagine this "wonder drug" at all. It already exists, in every living substance from algae to humans, and its name is *melatonin*.

WHAT IS MELATONIN?

Melatonin is a hormone secreted by the pineal gland. Although research on this substance has been going on since its discovery in 1958, it is only recently that there has been such interest.

Why? Research breakthroughs over the past decade have revealed some startling properties of this amazing substance:

- Studies by Dr. Walter Pierpaoli and various colleagues have shown that melatonin treatments extended the life span of mice by as much as 25 percent. Moreover, mice who had been treated with melatonin not only lived longer—they appeared younger, healthier, more vigorous and sexually rejuvenated.
- Researchers at Tulane University School of Medicine in New Orleans have done studies suggesting that melatonin can stop or retard the growth of human breast cancer cells. Cancer specialists in Milan have added melatonin treatments to chemotherapy and immunotherapy in their treatment of cancer patients—and have found that such patients experienced tumor regression, besides living longer and suffering from fewer side effects than patients who received chemotherapy and immunotherapy alone.
- Studies suggest that melatonin may be a kind of "natural" sleeping pill, inducing sleep without suppressing REM (dream) sleep and producing side effects as sedatives and other artificial sleep aids do.
- Travelers have found that by using melatonin they can "reset their biological clocks" after flying across one or more time zones. Numerous studies have confirmed melatonin's efficacy in combating jet lag and restoring restful sleep patterns.
- Melatonin may help to prevent heart disease by lowering blood cholesterol in people with high cholesterol. (Interestingly, melatonin seems to have no such effect on those with normal cholesterol.)
- New research suggests that melatonin may be effective in combating, treating, or preventing AIDS, Alzheimer's and

Studies conducted by pioneering University of Texas melatonin researcher Dr. Russel Reiter, show melatonin to be the most potent scavenger of free radicals—these unstable molecules promote cancer and heart disease by damaging DNA, cells, and tissue.

Parkinson's diseases, asthma, cataracts, diabetes and Down's syndrome, and some scientists also believe that it may be the basis of a new estrogen-free birth control pill that combats breast cancer at the same time that it prevents conception.

HOW DOES MELATONIN WORK?

To understand more about how melatonin produces its extraordinary effects, we have to consider the aging process itself. Humans are born with the ability to grow, to develop, to mature sexually and to protect ourselves from disease. These functions are carried out via a complicated system whereby various glands secrete a number of different hormones, which in turn stimulate activity elsewhere in the body.

Previously, scientists had viewed the hormonal activity of different systems as relatively discrete. They understood that the endocrine system regulated growth and sexual develoment, while the immune system protected us from disease. What they didn't realize was that the two systems are interconnected—and that both operate under the direction of the pineal gland.

The pineal gland is a small organ behind the eyes that in reptiles is literally a "third eye"—a light-sensitive organ covered with a shield of clear cartilage. In humans, the pineal is hidden within the brain, although Hindu philosophy refers to a "third eye" that sees more deeply and truly than the other two. Indeed, the pineal does "see" in a way, for one of its jobs is to respond to changes in light and dark. Many creatures possess a pineal gland, which scientists now believe is a kind of natural clock, helping us to synchronize our activities with nature.

The pineal gland helps govern circadian rhythms, the biological rhythms that take place over a 24-hour day, such as the sleep-wake cycle. This may be one of the reasons why it feels "natural" to sleep at night.

The pineal gland also governs seasonal rhythms that extend over weeks or months. By registering changes in the length of each day, for example, the pineal gland helps creatures know

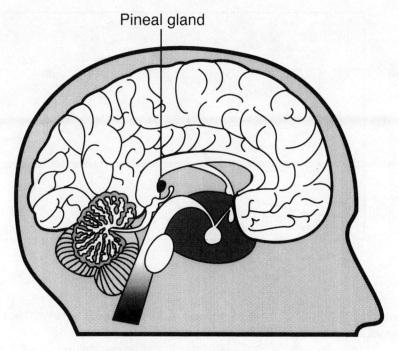

Pineal gland

The pineal gland.

how the seasons are changing. Animals who mate in the spring are responding to hormonal changes set off by the pineal gland, as are animals who migrate in the fall or hibernate in the winter.

Women who menstruate every 28 days or so are also following a kind of seasonal rhythm, keeping time to the pineal clock. Indeed, researchers have noticed that women's pineal glands are larger than men's, perhaps because women need more internal time cues than men do, to help regulate their menstrual patterns.

Immunologist Dr. Walter Pierpaoli of the Biancalana-Masera Foundation for the Aged in Ancona, Italy is the pioneer of much of the research into the function of the pineal gland. He sees this organ as a kind of orchestra conductor: just as an orchestra is composed of a lot of different instruments, so is the human body made up of many different systems. The orchestra conductor tells each group of instruments when to start playing, how loudly to play, when to stop and when to start once again. Likewise, the pineal gland "tells" our endocrine and immune

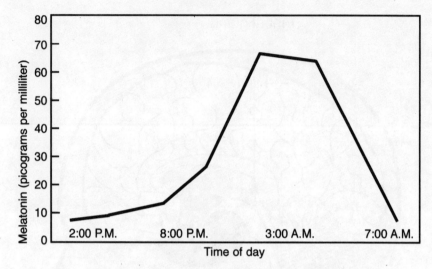

The 24-hour cycle of melatonin production.

systems when and how to release key substances: growth hormones, sexual hormones, and antibodies.

How does the pineal gland "tell" other systems what to do? Pierpaoli believes that the messenger is melatonin. Changes in our levels of melatonin tell the body to enter puberty and begin

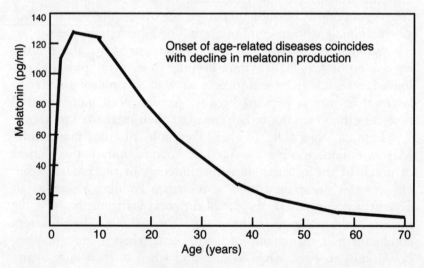

Melatonin levels through life.

sexual development. Melatonin may also be the trigger that sets the menstrual cycle in motion, that puts us to sleep and wakes us up, and that alerts our bodies to produce antibodies to combat disease. The complicated music of these processes is organized by that orchestra conductor, the pineal gland, using melatonin as a kind of baton.

HOW DOES MELATONIN PREVENT AGING?

As we've seen, nature isn't much interested in us after we've gotten too old to reproduce. One system after another starts to go, leaving us with lower levels of sexual functioning and a weakened immune system. This breakdown, too, is governed by the pineal gland, via its output of melatonin.

If we think of the pineal gland as our own internal clock, it "knows" how old we are—and it knows when we're past our reproductive prime. As soon as this gland senses that we're too old to reproduce effectively, sometime around age 45, it begins to produce far lower levels of melatonin. This in effect signals all of our other systems that it's time to break down, and the aging process begins. (Some scientists speculate that women's larger pineal gland is another reason why women age more slowly than men, and it may be why they live longer.)

But what if we could somehow raise our levels of melatonin after they start to fall? What if, at age 45, we could duplicate the levels of melatonin that we had in our youth? We would in effect be "tricking" our bodies into believing that they were still young. The pineal gland would continue to give orders appropriate to a young body, calling for higher levels of sex hormone, a well-functioning immune system, and so on. Chronologically, we'd be entering middle and old age; biologically, we'd still be young.

Researchers have found that doses of melatonin do, in fact, help the body to mimic a youthful state. Dr. Pierpaoli and Dr. Vladmir Lesnikov of the Institute of Experimental Medicine in St. Petersburg, Russia, cross-transplanted pineals between the brains of young and old mice. Tranplanting pineals from 18-

month-old mice into 4-month-old mice accelerated the animals' rate of aging. But the reverse procedure allowed the older mice to regain much of their youthfulness, and maintain excellent health throughout their maximum life span.

One of the key glands stimulated by melatonin is the thymus, a tiny entity that weighs only one-half ounce at birth, doubles in size by puberty, and then shrinks and all but disappears in adulthood, degenerating over 90 percent by age 65. The thymus plays a pivotal role in our immune system, for it is full of the white blood cells known as T lymphocytes or T cells that fight infection. T cells are originally manufactured in the bone marrow, but when we are still children, our T cells migrate to the thymus, which stores them as they mature and releases them when they're needed.

One of the reasons that we lose our ability to fight disease as we age is that the thymus degenerates and disappears—presumably in response to decreased levels of melatonin released by the pineal gland. When Pierpaoli and his associates put melatonin in the drinking water of older mice, the mice's ability to resist disease significantly improved. At the same time, the weight of their thymus glands increased, and their thymus cells became more active, suggesting that they were more actively producing T cells.

MELATONIN AND STRESS

One of the key causes for the breakdown of our immune systems is stress. Stress causes our adrenal glands to produce corticosterone or cortisol, the so-called "stress hormone," which helps our bodies key up for fight-or-flight. But corticosterone also suppresses our immune system, which is why we're so much more likely to get sick when we're under pressure or going through a grueling emotional time.

Melatonin seems to counter the immune-suppressing effects of corticosterone. That may be why younger people seem better able to handle high-pressure jobs or demanding schedules, as well as to bounce back more easily from emotional blows and life difficulties. Restoring melatonin levels may also restore our youthful ability to handle challenging situations with grace and resilience.

A 1995 study conducted by Italian researchers demonstrated that melatonin boosted the immune system of people under extreme stress. The subjects were 23 cancer patients who were undergoing traditional cancer therapy. Not only is the diagnosis of cancer in itself a stressful experience, but the psychological stress coupled with the negative side effects of chemotherapy and radiation severely weaken the immune system.

The patients were put on a program of 10 milligrams (mg) of melatonin taken at night. After a month of therapy, they found that melatonin strengthened their immune systems. The production of interferon-gamma and interleukin-2 (IL-2 is a hormone that aids in T-cell production) among other parts of the immune system essential in the body's fight against cancer had increased considerably. Melatonin acted as a stress buffer and also made the patients less likely to succumb to the cancer.

MELATONIN AND CANCER

A number of researchers have been exploring melatonin's potential role in combating cancer. It's been suggested for the treatment of colon, ovarian and prostate cancer, for melanoma, and for brain tumors. So far, though, the most exciting possibilities are emerging in the treatment of breast cancer.

According to Steven Hill, associate professor at Tulane University's School of Medicine's Cancer Center, more than half of all women with breast cancer have lower-than-normal levels of melatonin. This suggests that increasing levels of melatonin might help a woman prevent or treat breast cancer—a conclusion supported by several recent studies.

Breast cancer in women has been linked to their cumulative exposure to estrogen, the female hormone that is released every month during ovulation. Every time a woman becomes pregnant, she stops ovulating, giving her a "break" from estrogen exposure. That's why women who have few or no children are at an increased risk of cancer.

Moreover, according to Hill, more than half of all women with breast cancer have tumors marked by "estrogen receptors," chemical sites that help the tumor interact with estrogen. Thus, estrogen stimulates the growth of tumors with such receptors.

Melatonin seems to combat these effects of estrogen, stopping the tumors from growing and ultimately getting them to shrink. In a laboratory experiment, Hill exposed breast cancer cells with estrogen receptors to extremely high levels of melatonin. The number of estrogen receptors markedly decreased.

University of Arizona College of Medicine professor David Blask found that melatonin directly inhibited the growth of breast cancer tumors grown in lab dishes. Blask also administered melatonin to several hundred lab rats infected with breast cancer, and in half the cases tumors decreased by 50 to 70 percent. Blask found that melatonin was at least as effective as tamoxifen, a popular new estrogen-inhibiting anticancer drug, which had previously been used to combat estrogen-related breast cancer tumors, yet had far fewer negative side effects.

A study conducted in 1992 by Dr. Paolo Lissoni and his colleagues at San Gerardo Hospital in Monza, Italy, found that melatonin significantly increased the one-year survival rates of people with metastatic lung cancer. When patients were given 10 mg of a nightly melatonin supplement, growth of their tumor cells slowed. Lissoni and his lab also found that the melatonin enabled the IL-2 to work in smaller doses and seemed to amplify its activity.

Lissoni was involved in another study of 200 cancer patients with advanced solid tumors, for whom "no effective standard therapy was available." All patients had a predicted life expectancy of less than six months and among them, 90 had been previously treated with chemotherapy. IL-2 was injected subcutaneously at a dose of 3 million International Units a day for six days a week for four consecutive weeks. Melatonin was given orally at a dose of 40 mg/day every day, starting seven days before the first IL-2 injection. Complete response was achieved in two percent of the patients, partial response in 18 percent, and stability of the disease in 42 percent; progression of the disease occurred in 38 percent. Cancers located in the liver or the brain were less responsive to the treatment, as were cancers that had metastasized.

Prostate cancer and breast cancer have similiar properties, and this may be why melatonin has been shown to inhibit both of them. Both breast and prostate cancer are hormone-dependent in their initial stages of development and can be stopped if detected early. (Breast cancer is stimulated by estrogen and prolactin and prostate cancer is stimulated by testosterone.)

Studies done by Arizona's David Blask and a group of researchers showed that when prostate cancer cells were incubated with melatonin, the inhibition was 50 percent. Another similarity in people with breast cancer and prostate cancer is that they have very low levels of melatonin. It is not yet known if these low levels contribute to the disease.

Dr. Roman Rozencweig is a Montreal physician who has treated numerous patients with melatonin for more eight years. His then 71-year-old father had been diagnosed with prostate cancer through a routine PSA (prostate-specific antigen) test which was abnormally high. Rozencweig recommended melatonin (6 mg) each night. After six months of treatment, the results were better sleep and a lower PSA count, indicating that the tumor had become less active.

Melatonin, when used in conjunction with or substituted for the sex hormones estrogen, testosterone and progesterone, may also be used as prevention of certain cancers. Endocrinologist Dr. Michael Cohen of Applied Medical Research in Fairfax, Virginia is testing a drug that substitutes 75 mg of melatonin for the progesterone normally given to postmenopausal women on estrogen replacement threrapy. (In older women, progesterone can promote breast cancer and stimulate risk factors for heart disease; see Chapter 6.) In addition, Dr. Cohen already has a patent for a male contraceptive that combines melatonin with testosterone. The pill functions by stopping sperm production and reducing the risk of prostate cancer.

Clearly, we've just begun to explore the possibilities of using melatonin to fight cancer. Melatonin therapy for cancer is not clinically proven, and people diagnosed with cancer should not rely on melatonin alone. It may be used in conjunction with other treatments, but cancer is a serious disease that should be treated by a knowledgeable physician. The success of melatonin in this area is yet another reason scientists should pursue its research.

Melatonin Warning

Currently the immense popularity of melatonin has brought with it some unbalanced and potentially dangerous views on the hormone. The fact of the matter is that there are no conclusive human studies that guarantee any positive long-term results. We have found through personal experience and communication with multiple physicians who have treated patients with melatonin that its only proven safe use is as a short-term remedy for jet lag and sleep disorders. A note of caution should be raised, as the dosages recommended in many popular books and magazines, 3-10 mg, are many times more than the physiologic doses, and could have unforeseen long-term effects.

People under age 40 already manufacture adequate amounts of melatonin and supplementation should be avoided except for short-term use. Other people who should not take melatonin for *any* reason include pregnant or nursing mothers, women trying to conceive, people taking prescription steroid drugs, and anyone suffering from mental illness, severe allergies, autoimmune diseases such as multiple sclerosis, and immune system cancers such as lymphoma and leukemia.

MELATONIN AND SEXUAL FUNCTIONING

Just as lower levels of melatonin signal our immune systems to shut down, so do they signal our endocrine systems to produce fewer sex hormones. Lower levels of sex hormones in turn may lead to the atrophy of sexual organs in both men and women, as well as a decrease in sexual interest and ability to perform.

When the mice in Pierpaoli's experiments were given melatonin, they seemed to undergo a sexual transformation. Not only did they maintain a sexual interest and vigor characteristic of much younger mice, but the mice's sexual organs, male and female, actually underwent repair, regeneration and rejuvenation, making them comparable to those of younger animals.

MELATONIN AND FREE RADICALS

Much of the damage that we attribute to aging is the cumulative effect of bombardment by free radicals. One of the key ways that melatonin helps combat cancer is its ability to act as an intercellular antioxidant, preventing and reducing the damage done to the body by these free radicals. Melatonin is perhaps the only antioxidant that is capable of penetrating every cell of the body and is the most active and effective of all naturally-occurring antioxidant compounds.

In 1993, Dr. Russel Reiter of the University of Texas Health Science Center in San Antonio and his colleagues suggested that melatonin might be the most effective antioxidant or scavenger of free radicals. The team conducted a study in which rats were fed carcinogen-laced food designed to damage their DNA by producing oxygen-based free radicals. When melatonin was given to the rats before they ingested the carcinogenic food, they sustained 41 to 99 percent less genetic damage than rats that had not been treated with melatonin. And the more melatonin the rats had been given, the greater their protection from damage.

In several other tests, melatonin has continued to perform as well as or better than other antioxidants. For example, glutathione (GSH) is a valued scavenger for free radicals that travel between cells—yet melatonin proved to be five times more effective. Vitamin E is used to combat oxidants within cells—yet melatonin seems to be at least twice as effective.

Furthermore, most antioxidants work on only one part of the cell, either the lipid-rich membrane or the water-based cell itself. Melatonin is soluble in both fats and water, making it a wider-ranging antioxidant than its vitamin and mineral counterparts.

MELATONIN: NATURE'S SLEEP AID

According to a 1993 report by the National Commission on Sleep Disorders Research, frequent or chronic insomnia affects more than 60 million Americans—about one of every three adults, many of them elderly. Research on humans has shown that increasing melatonin levels may bring an end to those restless nights.

Melatonin production occurs almost entirely at night and is actually stimulated by darkness; bright light suppresses its secretion. The amount of melatonin that is produced is directly linked to how well we sleep, and its chemical structure is important in explaining our body's internal clock.

Melatonin, or N-acetyl-5-methoxytryptamine, is made from an amino acid called tryptophan. Tryptophan is an essential amino acid—we can only get it from foods that we ingest. The tryptophan we consume during the day is converted into serotonin, a brain chemical involved with mood. Serotonin, in turn, is converted into melatonin.

> A Gallup survey of more than 1,000 adults reported that 49 percent of American adults suffer sleep-related problems such as insomnia.

Recently, scientists discovered the enzyme that turns melatonin production on in the brain. According to David Klein of the National Institute of Child Health and Development, the enzyme's presence in the brain cells suggests that it regulates serotonin. This enzyme is turned on and off by the body's internal clock. In essence, serotonin and melatonin act as our day and night regulators. We get our high energy level from serotonin during the day and our restful state from melatonin at night. Daytime levels of melatonin are very low; nighttime levels may be 5 to10 times higher.

The National Institute of Mental Health found that subjects who spent 14 hours a day or more in darkness returned to what amounted to primordial sleep patterns, during which their brains produced high levels of melatonin. These levels decline with age, explaining the common occurrence of age-related insomnia.

A study conducted in Israel found that the quality of sleep

in the elderly was proportional to the amount of melatonin secreted by the pineal gland. Elderly people with insomina have half the amount of melatonin as young people. They may spend more time in bed but less time asleep.

New Findings on Melatonin

Recently it was found that the pineal gland is not the only site where melatonin is produced and secreted. Dr. Gerald Heuther of the Neurobiologisches Labor, Psychiatrische Universitatsklinik, Gottingen Germany, reported that melatonin has an extrapineal and gastorintestinal presence.

Melatonin was discovered in the gut when scientists were studying tryptophan metabolism in the body. It was found that administrating tryptophan to the body in turn increased circulating levels of melatonin. It is speculated that the concentration of melatonin present in the endocrine cells lining the gut, believed to act as a protectant for the stomach and intestines, may in fact be higher than in the pineal gland.

Small concentrations of melatonin were also found in the fibers of the retina, which act as a photoprotectant to light sensitivity in the eye. It is thought that the daytime trace levels of melatonin have their origin in the retina. However, the highest levels of melatonin in the plasma occur at night, which accords with pineal rhythms.

Dr. Steve Novil of the American Longevity Research Institute has been treating patients with melatonin for six years. One patient, an elderly woman in her eighties, had trouble falling back asleep after getting up to urinate frequently. She was put on a program of 3 mg of melatonin an hour before bedtime.

Within a week, the patient's sleep pattern had changed remarkably. Her need to urinate throughout the night lessened and when she did wake up to use the bathroom, she was able to fall back asleep without problem. In addition to a more restful night, the patient experienced pleasant, vivid dreams for the first time in many years, and woke up feeling refreshed. The melatonin allowed her to sleep more and sleep better.

Even very small doses of the hormone can shift the body's clock forward. Dr. Richard Wurtman, director of the Massachusetts Institute of Technology's Clinical Research Center, conducted a study in 1994 in which young adults took melatonin or a placebo before a midday nap. While the placebo group took an average of 25 minutes to fall asleep, those on melatonin fell asleep within six minutes. The sedative effect was noticeable on as little as 0.1 mg of melatonin.

Another study complementing the pilot study done at MIT was conducted in the United Kingdom by a team of researchers led by Dr. Phillip Cowen. The double-blind, placebo controlled cross-over study gave subjects two doses (.3 mg and 1.0 mg) of melatonin and a placebo on three different nights over several weeks. The subjects were then monitored as to how long it took them to fall asleep and the quality of their sleep. The researchers found that both doses of melatonin reduced the time it took to fall asleep, increased actual sleep time, increased quality of sleep as reflected in deep or "slow-wave" sleep, increased sleep efficiency as measured by the percentage of time in bed spent sleeping, and reduced the number of awakenings after the onset of sleep. The study supported the hypothesis that melatonin even at low doses has hypnotic effects, and unlike most currently available sleep aids, improves the quality of sleep as well.

MELATONIN: A CURE FOR JET-LAG

The dictionary definition of jet-lag is a "temporary disruption of bodily rhythm caused by high-speed travel across several time zones . . ." And as millions of long distance travellers know, it can feel more like a hangover with insomnia and symptoms of the flu. In addition, it can cause a lack of concentration and a feeling of disorientation. Disrupting the body's rhythm brings with it changes in blood pressure, blood sugar, mood, energy level, arousal, and hormonal levels.

Although conventional sleeping pills may help induce sleep, many times the other symptoms of jet lag are left hanging. Numerous human studies have shown that melatonin has become one of the most effective ways in combating jet lag or shift work because it resets the body's biological clock and restores balance. Melatonin is a hormone that is only released at night and giving it to people in the daytime can successfully trick the body into thinking it is in another time zone.

In Britain, an endocrinology professor at the University of Surrey tested the effects of melatonin on some 400 travelers and noted that those to whom melatonin was administered were able to reduce their jet lag by 50 percent.

Another study was conducted by French researchers, involving 30 volunteers who were scheduled to fly from the United States to France. All the volunteers had had difficulty with jet lag in the past. On the day of the flight and for three days thereafter, they took either a placebo or a tablet containing 8 mg of melatonin. The volunteers on melatonin were able to sleep and focus better and experienced fewer mood swings.

The Sleep Disorders Research Center reported that each year sleep disorders add about $15.9 billion to national health-care costs, contributing to problems such as heart disease. And this doesn't include accidents and lost productivity at work.

Melatonin functions on two levels—it helps you sleep better *and* it readjusts your body's clock faster. It may be nature's sleeping pill, but remember that "insomnia is a symptom and *not* a diagnosis," says Dr. David Zeiger. Zeiger was part of a sleep deprivation program at Stanford University, and now practices at Rhema Medical Associates in Chicago, where his patients with sleep disorders are treated with melatonin. He stresses that the causes of insomnia may be physical disorders, psychological difficulties, substance overuse/misuse, inadequate sleep habits, improper sleep environment or circadian-cycle abnormalities.

Scientists predict a rapidly expanding role for melatonin not only in treating sleep disorders and jet lag but for mental disorders as well. The newly discovered enzyme that turns on melatonin production may, some think, lead to the development of new therapies not only for improving sleep but also for improving alertness and wakefulness. In addition, the enzyme's regulation of the vital brain chemical serotonin, which has been linked to aggressive behavior, depression and psychosis, indicates that it might be a good candidate for treating mental disorders.

MELATONIN: WHAT TO CONSIDER

The first thing to remember is that sometimes less is more. Although melatonin plays an extremely important role in our bodies, it is present only in tiny amounts, even when we're at our youthful peak. Megadoses of melatonin won't necessarily help us maximize our energy or health. Rather, we should try to approximate the levels of melatonin that our youthful bodies once knew.

Nor should children be given melatonin. The highest levels of melatonin are found during childhood, and no additional help is needed.

People who have serious illnesses such as an autoimmune disorder, leukemia or lymphoma should consult a physician familiar with melatonin before usage. Immune-suppressing drugs such as cortisol and cyclosporine may react adversely with melatonin, as may antidepressants. People who are diabetic, experience major depression or have a hormonal imbalance should also take caution.

Finally, pregnant or nursing mothers should avoid melatonin supplements. They are already transmitting melatonin to the fetus or infant via the placenta or their milk. It is unknown if increasing melatonin levels might adversely affect the child.

On the other hand, women who are already taking hormone-replacement supplements may take melatonin without fear of any ill effects. Estrogen and melatonin coexist in young women's bodies, so there's no reason why hormones designed to replace estrogen should not coexist with melatonin in the bodies of older women.

WHEN SHOULD MELATONIN SUPPLEMENTS BEGIN?

We believe that melatonin levels drop most sharply at around age 45, so those taking melatonin to combat aging should probably begin then. People with a family history of cancer, cardiovascular disease, or heart disease might begin in their late 30s or early 40s, as melatonin might help combat their inherited predisposition to these diseases of aging.

Since the goal is to keep melatonin levels constant, starting earlier isn't going to head off aging later. The idea is to start taking melatonin when your levels drop, not before. On the other hand, if you are already past 45, you're not too late! You can begin reversing the effects of age no matter when your melatonin supplements start.

Remember, always take melatonin at bedtime. Because this substance helps regulate our sleep-wake cycles, it generally makes people very sleepy. If you work at night, take melatonin before your daytime bedtime. And in no case should anyone take melatonin before they need to drive, operate machinery, or otherwise be alert. Although melatonin will not make you feel drugged (e.g., you could still respond to an emergency call from a child) it will make you feel drowsy and relaxed.

HOW IS MELATONIN AVAILABLE?

Melatonin supplements are currently available in .75 mg, 2 mg, 3 mg, 5 mg, and 10 mg tablets or capsules. Lozenges are available in 2.5 mg and 5 mg. Melatonin is not patented, so a number of companies manufacture and distribute it. Also, since melatonin is not regulated by the FDA, its purity cannot be guaranteed. We recommend the synthetic form, rather than that which is made from animal melatonin, for standardization of strength and to eliminate risk of biological contamination.

If the tablets are too large for you, simply break them into smaller pieces. Capsules can be emptied into a small dish, mixing the amount you want into an ounce of liquid. The rest can be stored in a covered container in the refrigerator.

TAKING MELATONIN

Each person's physiology is unique and finding the right dosage of melatonin may be trial and error in the beginning. If you find that you're waking up tired and groggy, reduce your dose in increments of .5 mg until you find the amount that's right for you. It is wise to take melatonin every other day, as it is not yet known whether this supplementation can inhibit natural production.

Side effects of melatonin use have been minor. Grogginess in the morning is common. Some people find it more difficult to sleep when taking melatonin and experience nightmares. Others report mild headaches, upset stomach, lower sex drive and depressed feelings. Most side effects occur in people who take high doses of melatonin, are chronic users or are on medications. People taking 1 mg or less experience almost no side effects.

Melatonin in the range of .5 mg to 12 mg is usually effective in inducing and maintaining deep sleep. If you do not respond to a low dose, such as 1 or 2 mg, you are more likely to respond to higher doses, such as 5 to 10 mg. If there is no response to pills, lozenges can be tried. Lozenges seem to be more consistently effective than pills, since the melatonin goes directly into the bloodstream from absorption through the mouth.

Melatonin does not seem to be as consistently effective when taken on a full stomach; perhaps it is not absorbed as well, or it is absorbed too slowly. Taking it with a snack or on an empty stomach is more effective. There is a wide variation between people on the best time to take melatonin. But because of its drowsiness-producing effect (most people notice a yawn within 30 minutes of dosing), the best time is half an hour to two hours before going to bed; lozenges dissolved in the mouth should be taken 20 minutes to an hour before going to bed.

Withdrawal symptoms are not common, but for some people melatonin may cause rebound insomnia. Therefore, when deciding to stop taking melatonin (or any sleeping medicine), it is recommended to taper off over a period of 1 to 2 weeks. For example, if you have been using 4 mg of melatonin regularly and feel you don't need it any more, lower the dose to 3 mg for a few nights, then 2 mg for another few nights and so on. By tapering off melatonin, any sleep disturbances should be avoided.

Chapter 4

Human Growth Hormone (hGH)

A 60-year-old man becomes Mr. Physical Fitness USA.

A 50-year-old college instructor regains the face and figure of her modeling days.

A 43-year-old balding, enervated man finds both his hair and his energy restored.

A senior citizen recovers his interest in sex—and reports that his penis size has grown by 20 percent.

These are only some of the reports of the aging people who claim to have been helped by supplemental doses of human growth hormone (hGH). Human GH is another hormone that is naturally present in the human body when we're young but that tends to disappear as we age. People who have taken hGH have found it to produce striking improvements in their health, energy level, and sense of well-being. The list of benefits seems to grow with each new study. It now includes:

- younger, thicker skin
- stronger bones
- an average gain of 8.8 percent in muscle mass after six months, without exercise
- an average loss of 14.4 percent of body fat after six months, without dieting
- a stronger immune system
- tissue regeneration/healing of wounds and in recovery from surgery
- a higher energy level
- enhanced sexual performance, including growth of penis size in some users
- regrowth of heart, liver, spleen, kidneys, and other organs that shrink with age
- greater cardiac output
- better exercise performance
- improved kidney function
- lower blood pressure
- lower cholesterol
- fewer wrinkles
- elimination of cellulite
- sharper vision
- improved mood
- better retentive memory

WHAT IS HUMAN GROWTH HORMONE?

Human GH, or somatotropin, is a simple protein made up of a single chain of 191 amino acids. This substance is released by the pituitary gland, starting in childhood and continuing into old age. The hormone enters our bloodstream in pulses, generally in the early hours of sleep (another reason why sleep is so important to growing children!). The hormone then moves quickly from the bloodstream to the liver, where it is converted into substances called DGF 1 and 2. These are messenger molecules also known as "growth factors." They carry hGH's message of growth into other parts of the body.

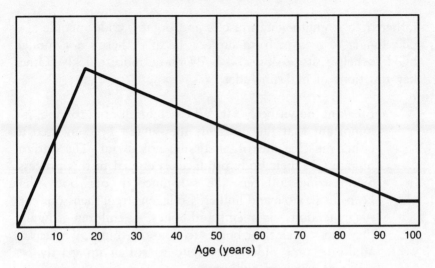

Growth hormone production peaks before 20, then declines steadily.

Like many hormones, hGH is released into the bloodstream in far greater quantities when we're young, peaking in our mid-twenties and then beginning a slow, gradual decline. By the time you're 60 or 70, your body has access to only 15 to 20 percent of the hGH that it used in your youth.

Human GH's primary function in childhood and young adults is to help bones lengthen and expand, so that from infancy until our mid-twenties, we are growing, becoming taller, longer-limbed, stronger-boned. Human GH also promotes growth by helping to transport amino acids between cells and by inducing cells to accept and synthesize amino acids. Amino acids are found in proteins and are used by the body to create muscles and to build and restore organs, including the heart and the skin. Thus hGH helps our bodies to use the protein we ingest for cellular repair and regeneration.

You can see how lower levels of hGH might affect us as we age. Without this vital hormone to help synthesize protein and keep nitrogen levels high, our muscle and organ tissue starts to break down. Even if we eat the same high-protein diet we followed when we were "growing boys and girls," our bodies no longer know how to use the protein as efficiently, producing fat rather than strengthening muscles and organs. Older people also take longer to recover from surgery, because there's not enough hGH to help restore skin and body tissue more quickly. Other key functions of hGH include:

- Breaking down body fat. When children are growing, it's important that the nutrients they ingest be converted to bone, muscle, and organ tissue, not to fat. The natural human GH their body produces is crucial to this process.
- Synthesizing collagen, the substance in our body that keeps us flexible and limber. Collagen strengthens our cartilage, tendons, ligaments and bones. As children grow up, they can stretch their bodies to do more things, whereas as adults become older, they tend to stiffen up, partly because of a loss of collagen.

SYNTHETIC hGH: A BOOST TO ADULTS AND ATHLETES

Until fairly recently, hGH supplements were difficult and expensive to synthesize. Supplemental hGH had to be harvested from the pituitary glands of human cadavers, and hGH treatments were extremely expensive. As a result, hGH supplements were used only in the medical treatment of children suffering from dwarfism (the failure to grow to normal height). And little research could be done on how any aspect of hGH might affect adults.

Then, in the mid-1980s, the drug firms Genentech Inc. and Eli Lilly and Co. found relatively inexpensive ways to synthesize hGH. Human GH was produced through recombinant DNA technology and sold under the names Protropin and Humatrope. Scientists began to explore how the newly available hormone might affect adults' health and growth.

In 1989, researchers at St. Thomas Hospital in London, led by Dr. Franco Salomon, began testing how hGH might affect 24 adults whose pituitary glands had been removed or were not producing sufficient hGH because of tumors. Salomon's experiment lasted six months, at the end of which patients who had received supplemental hGH had averaged a 12-pound gain in muscle and a 12-pound loss in fat. Their serum cholesterol levels had also gone down.

Salomon and colleagues were working with adults who had pituitary problems. Researchers wondered how supplemental hGH might affect healthy adults. Some work on this question had already been done by exercise physiologist Douglas Crist and his colleagues at the University of New Mexico School of Medicine in Albuquerque in 1987. Crist and his associates worked with eight healthy, athletic young people, five men and three women, all between the ages of 22 and 33. After six weeks of getting hGH injections three times a week, these young adults—already in good shape—had nevertheless gained an average of close to three pounds of muscle while losing an average 1.5 percent of their body fat. Their overall ratio of muscle to fat—a key sign of being well conditioned—improved by an average of close to 25 percent.

Even before Crist, Dr. Robert Kerr had been administering hGH to healthy adult athletes. Kerr, a family physician in San Gabriel, California, had treated some 8,000 athletes in the course of his practice, prescribing first anabolic steroids and later hGH.

Human GH replacement therapy was anecdotally successful with some authors claiming it provided the beneficial effects of anabolic steroids without the harmful side effects. Typically, Kerr said, his patients took hGH for only three to six weeks. In that short time, bodybuilders claimed they got results that lasted up to 12 months. Some athletes claimed to have gained up to 40 pounds in six weeks while reducing their body fat. Others claimed to have gained appreciably in height: of his first 150 patients to take hGH, aged 29 to 52, one in six gained from three-quarters to one inch, while many others said they gained from one-eighth to one-fourth. Subsequent patients in their twenties claimed to have gained even more. Although some of these height gains were later erased by the aging process—gravity tends to pull us down as we age, compressing our vertebrae and lowering the arches in our feet—Kerr pointed out that many patients experienced relief from chronic lower back pain when they grew taller. Although they did not always retain the height, neither did their pain return. Human GH seems to allow the body to grow closer to the level of potential programmed into the individual's genes. However, it should be noted that a number of athletes took well in excess of body physiological doses of hGH, as well as anabolic steroids. Due to these extensive dose regimens, some individuals experienced serious health problems. Normal, healthy, hormonally balanced young people below the age of 40 should not be taking hGH.

HUMAN GROWTH HORMONE AND AGING

Researchers and doctors had shown that hGH supplements could indeed benefit adults. But how might this powerful hormone affect the elderly and the aging process?

Transforming a person's muscle-to-fat ratio and rebuilding muscle is hGH's most dramatic result. Elderly people may be said to lose 20 years from their biological age, at least as far as bones and muscles are concerned.

The first landmark study to show the effects of hGH on elderly humans was reported in 1990 by Dr. Daniel Rudman, professor of medicine at the Medical College of Wisconsin and associate chief of staff for extended care at the Milwaukee Veterans Affairs Medical Center. Rudman and his colleagues conducted the study to determine whether hGH would produce physiological changes in men who were deficient in the hormone.

Twenty-one men between the ages of 60 and 80 were injected with supplemental hGH three times a week for six months. Another nine men in the same age range served as a control group. All 27 men were given the same diet: 15 percent protein, 50 percent carbohydrates, 35 percent fat. Yet the men receiving hGH showed marked improvement in health and appearance: a 14.4 percent decrease in fatty tissue, an 8.8 percent increase in muscle and lean tissue, a 7.1 percent increase in skin thickness, and a 1.6 percent increase in average density of the vertebrae in the lower back. In effect, a decade or two of aging had actually been reversed.

Because the study was done at the VA Center, it was restricted to men. However, Rudman said, basic findings should apply to women as well.

To fully appreciate the results of Rudman's experiment, it helps to recall the way our muscle-fat ratio tends to change as we age. Some 80 percent of a young adult's body is lean body mass: muscles, organs, and bone. Only 20 percent is fatty (adipose) tissue. For most people after age 30, muscles tend to atrophy, partly from genetic programming, partly from underuse. Every decade thereafter an average of 5 percent of lean body mass is replaced by fatty tissue, so that by the time most of us reach age 70, we've gone from an 80-20 lean-fat ratio to a ratio that is closer to 50-50.

The increase in fatty tissue is related to a variety of cardiovascular problems, whereas the loss of lean body mass is part of what causes the elderly to lose energy, strength, and mobility. Anything that can slow or reverse the trend towards more fatty tissue in effect slows or reverses the aging process itself.

Another symptom of aging is thinner, less flexible skin, partly due to loss of collagen. If hGH helps the body to synthesize collagen at youthful levels, it can prevent or even reverse an aging person's tendency to have fragile, wrinkled skin.

Dr. Julian Whitaker of the Whitaker Health and Wellness Institute in Newport Beach, California, has been prescribing hGH to his elderly patients as well as taking it himself. He states, "In the 20 years I have practiced nutritional and rejuvenative medicine, I have not seen anything that even comes close to the restorative power of hGH supplementation."

One of Dr. Whitaker's patients, a 75-year-old woman named Elaine, had been supplementing with hGH for four months. She stated that she became much stronger, and was able to lift things that she previously depended on her husband to lift. The chronic back pain she used to have in the evenings was completely gone, and her overall energy level had increased substantially. She also reported that she was having sex with her husband more frequently, and enjoying it more now at 75 than she ever had.

Dr. Whitaker took hGH for five months, and although he noted no major changes in energy level or activities, he no longer needed the reading glasses he had used for 10 years. Other patients reported similar effects.

Contrary to Dr. Whitaker's experience, most researchers

have not found hGH to have an appreciable impact on the eyes, ears, elastic tissue (ligament and tendons) or brain. However, Whitaker believes that hGH-inspired increases in the level of cellular water in the eyes makes lenses more flexible and so able to focus better. And others speculate that hGH strengthens eye muscle fibers, which contributes to focus and lessens eyestrain.

In addition to the quantifiable effects of hGH treatment, many who have taken this supplement report an emotional response similar to that of Dr. Whitaker's patient Elaine: they feel better and more energetic, are better able to care for themselves and to get around, and experience a renewed interest and pleasure in sex. In Whitaker's opinion, hGH is most effective in combating the effects of chronic diseases that involve muscle wasting: stroke, chronic obstructive pulmonary disease, and AIDS. He thinks it can also be useful in treating severe burns and in helping patients recover from surgery—both instances in which skin and other organs must be regenerated and restored.

Dr. Bengt-Ake Bengtsson of Gothenburg, Sweden, who has studied the effect of hGH on both normal and hGH-deficient adults, has observed results much like Whitaker's patients. He found that "Patients did not want to stop treatment. Moreover, nine out of ten commented on improved fatigue and physical performance, and five out of ten also reported improved mood." In Dr. Bengtsson's opinion, the effects of six months of human growth hormone therapy on lean body mass and fatty tissue was equivalent to reversing the aging process by ten to twenty years.

Dr. Rudman doesn't believe that hGH therapy will make people live longer, but that it will improve the quality of life. Stronger muscles and healthier skin should result in improved mobility and independence, fewer falls and faster healing from wounds. This may prove beneficial, for example, to frail bodies of elderly people about to undergo surgery. Obviously, more research into the possible benefits and hazards of hGH are necessary before such therapy becomes common.

hGH: LIMITS AND SIDE EFFECTS

Although hGH is a drug that can only be prescribed by a physician, it is important to remember that like many hormonal treatments, the long-term effects are unknown. Proponents of hGH stress that negative effects can occur, but only when the patient is taking over the physiologic dose for a long period of time. Some of these effects have included carpal tunnel syndrome, arthritis, high blood pressure, vocal cord thickening, excess fluid in the legs, the growth of small breasts in men (gynecomastia), osteoporosis, heat intolerance, impotence, acromegaly—the enlargement of the bones in the head, hands and feet, and diabetes-like symptoms.

Researchers also have expressed concern over the hormone's ability to spur cell growth and how this may promote malignancies. However, no studies have shown a statistically significant increase in cancer incidence in humans.

Dr. Mary Lee Vance, a University of Virginia endocrinologist, believes that Rudman's study "does demonstrate clear-cut effects of growth hormone, but to say it reverses the effects of aging is an overstatement. It's just one part of the equation." She cautions users of hGH that, because there are so many unanswered questions about the use of the hormone in the elderly and in adults with growth hormone deficiency, its general use now or in the immediate future is not justified. Furthermore, there is potential for widespread abuse in healthy adolescents and adults.

Dr. Richard Cutler, a gerontologist at the National Institute on Aging in Bethesda, Maryland, is even more specific, suggesting that the age-related decrease of growth hormone may be a positive phenomenon that doctors shouldn't tamper with. "We really don't know why growth hormone secretion decreases with age," Cutler says. "It could be that older people need more fat to keep warm. A lean, muscled 80-year-old may be more prone to pneumonia."

The concern over negative side effects of hGH increased when many of the men in a new study by Dr. Rudman had to drop out due to incidence of carpal tunnel syndrome, diabetes, and gynecomastia. Rudman's later study followed 42 healthy elderly men who were given hGH supplements for twelve months. Those taking the highest doses had to stop taking the supplement, due to adverse side effects.

However, the other hGH users in Dr. Rudman's study increased their lean body mass by 6 percent, decreased their body fat by 16 percent, and generally experienced an improved level of physical fitness. An untreated control group, monitored over the same period, actually lost an average of 3 percent of their lean body mass. Supporters of hGH say it's just a matter of finding the correct dosage for each individual.

Despite these concerns, recent studies have indicated that most if not all undesirable side effects are reversed when the patient stops taking hGH or the dose is titrated downward. Of course, the positive benefits also disappear at about the same time.

Critics of hGH point out how expensive it is to use. A year's treatment could cost as much as $30,000, but recent cost cutting, thanks to several new brands being made available by other pharmaceutical companies, has lowered the price of hGH for anti-aging therapeutics to $13,000 a year and as low as $8,000 a year.

Researchers are also turning to testosterone replacement therapy in elderly men as an alternative to hGH (see Chapter 7). At $32 for a year's worth of treatment, it is far less expensive than growth hormone. But synthetic hGH costs as little to make as insulin, and because the seven-year monopoly held by Eli Lilly and Genentech on this drug has expired, we expect that competition within the industry may eventually drive prices down to even more affordable levels.

NATURAL hGH RELEASERS

People who are concerned about cost and side effects, yet want the innumerable benefits of hGH, may consider another option: producing the hormone themselves! Aging means that your body releases less hGH into your bloodstream. No matter how old you are, though, your production of hGH remains virtually constant. As scientists have come to understand more about this remarkable substance, they have also come to find ways that we can get our own bodies to begin producing more of it again, at levels comparable to those of our youth—a process that is safe, inexpensive, and often quite satisfying. And this method of raising hGH levels avoids virtually all of the side effects associated with taking hGH supplements themselves.

The amino acid arginine, in adequate quantities, has been shown to stimulate the pituitary gland to release hGH. In cases of severe burn victims, arginine-induced hGH has been effective in speeding the healing process of already weakened immune systems. In fact, hGH is so essential to the immune system that it actually increased resistance to injections of cancer cells in animals. A 1988 article in *Science* magazine reported that hGH activates macrophages, immune system cells that seek out and kill disease-causing microbes and cancer cells, by increasing the production of superoxide radicals. These radicals are made by the macrophages to kill the bacteria. Antioxidants such as vitamins C, E, the mineral selenium, and the amino acid cysteine (see chapters 8 and 9), protect uninfected tissues from damage by superoxide radicals.

Another amino acid that can trigger the release of hGH is ornithine. According to Durk Pearson and Sandy Shaw of the *Life Extension Newsletter,* arginine and ornithine both cause hGH release via the brain's cholinergic nervous system, "the system that uses acetylcholine—made in the brain from the nutrient choline with the help of the cofactor vitamin B5—to transmit information between nerve cells." Acetylcholine is a necessary ingredient for the hGH releasers to be effective. Therefore, Pearson and Shaw recommend taking choline and B5 supplements in conjunction with arginine and ornithine.

Other nutrients that have been shown to increase hGH release include niacin, tyrosine, glutathione, and methionine. Some people have also had good results taking hGH-releasing hormone (somatomedin C), which costs only a fraction of hGH itself. As always, it is important to consult with a knowledgeable physician when supplementing with any pharmacotherapy.

Although the relationship between hGH and melatonin is still questionable, the majority of studies indicate that it can stimulate the production of hGH. In a recent study, eight adult men were given 10 mg of melatonin during the day and showed a slight increase in hGH levels. But when melatonin was given prior to administration of GHRH (growth hormone-releasing hormone), the levels of hGH in the men doubled.

Exercise is an excellent way to increase your body's access to hGH. High-intensity exercise, such as free-weight, multi-joint training two to three times per week, will raise your hGH levels. Be sure you are doing only the most strenuous lifting—loads you can only lift six times, rather than the lighter loads that can be hefted fifteen times or more. (Check with a doctor before undertaking any strenuous new exercise program, of course.) Lower-body workouts seem to be most effective with regard to hGH, so allot at least half your workout time to leg lifts.

Other people have found that sprinting, squash, or handball two or more times a week also tends to raise hGH levels. Long-distance running doesn't seem as effective; hGH seems to be released in response to particularly intense and strenuous activity. (Again, check with your doctor before you begin.)

Of course, the most powerful combination of all is exercise plus hGH supplements (or vitamin supplements that help produce hGH). Likewise, taking hGH supplements (or their equivalents) is no substitute for watching what you eat and reducing fat, and perhaps calories, in your daily diet.

"Anti-aging has long been equated with trying to live longer, but if we can move the emphasis away from death prevention and towards quality of life, then I don't see anything wrong with that," says George Annas, a Boston University bioethicist. "We all have to age, but the aged should be allowed to age gracefully." Human GH alone is not the antidote to aging, but it may contribute to living more productively for many of the elderly. Used wisely, under a knowledgeable physician's care, this hormone may add more than a few drops from the fountain of youth.

Chapter 5

DHEA

Hormones and aging have long enjoyed a kind of chicken-and-egg relationship. Does aging result in falling levels of key hormones, or does a drop in the levels of key hormones bring on the aging process?

Either way, researchers have been impressed that restoring levels of the body's hormones seems not only to halt aging but also to combat a number of debilitating diseases and possibly even reverse the process of aging for some of the body's organs. DHEA—dehydroepiandrosterone—is the most abundant naturally-occurring steroid hormone, and one that seems capable of producing potentially dramatic results. Proponents of DHEA believe that it may be able to:

- enhance the immune system to protect against infection
- reduce the incidence of cancer, atherosclerosis (coronary artery disease), and osteoporosis—diseases generally associated with aging
- lower blood cholesterol while improving liver function
- stabilize blood sugar levels and help prevent the onset of diabetes in adults

- assist in weight loss and convert fat to lean muscle mass
- control Alzheimer's disease, lupus, AIDS, Epstein-Barr and chronic fatigue syndrome
- treat herpes, menopause, depression, memory and learning problems
- prolong life expectancy

Much research on DHEA remains to be done. But a few doctors are already prescribing this key hormone to otherwise healthy elderly patients. In their view, DHEA may be the key to a longer, healthier, and happier life.

WHAT IS DHEA?

DHEA is produced by the adrenal glands. It's been dubbed "the mother of all hormones" because the body uses it to produce the male and female sex hormones testosterone, estrogen, and progesterone, as well as using it to make corticosterone. Production of DHEA is high even when the fetus is still developing. Our body's DHEA levels continue to rise up to about age 25, when production drops off sharply, so that by age 75, we're producing only 10 to 20 percent of the DHEA that our bodies manufactured at age 20.

As with melatonin and human growth hormone, falling levels of DHEA are closely associated with a number of age-related diseases and disabilities. Scientists speculate that if aging men and women can restore their DHEA to youthful levels, their youthful health and vigor will also be restored.

> By age 75, DHEA levels are only 10 to 20 percent of what they were at age 20.

According to Dr. Samuel Yen, reproductive endocrinologist and principal investigator of a DHEA study at the University of California at San Diego, DHEA is "a drug that may help people

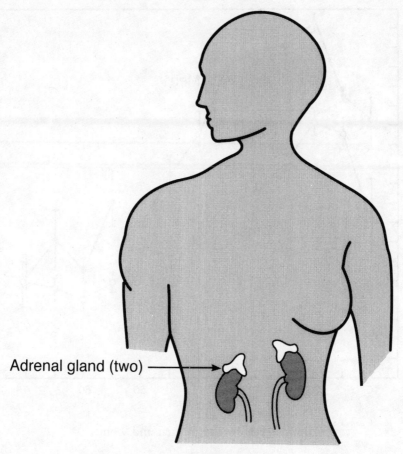

Adrenal gland (two)

The adrenal glands.

age more gracefully." When taking DHEA, 82 percent of women and 67 percent of men scored higher tests rating their ability to cope with stress, their quality of sleep, and their basic well-being. Only 10 percent of the group not receiving the hormone reported feeling any better.

If DHEA decreases with age, then increasing our levels later in life may just be the answer. Dr. William Regelson, a medical oncologist at Virginia Commonwealth University's medical college, agrees. "If you want to maintain a youthful level of health, then you have to be youthful physiologically and that means maintaining youthful levels of these hormones [DHEA]."

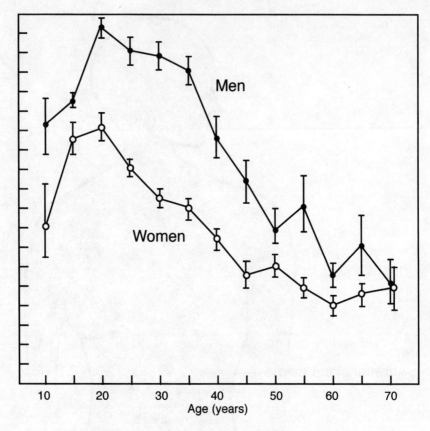

DHEA levels by age in men and women.

DHEA AND IMMUNITY

One of DHEA's key jobs is to help our bodies fight bacterial and viral infection. Our immune system is based on the cooperation of several different types of cells, which learn to recognize and then attack infectious viruses and bacteria. Vaccines work on the principle that if our body is "introduced" to a relatively harmless form of an infectious bacteria, it will form antibodies to combat the intruder—antibodies that will then move quickly to attack similar germs when next exposed to them.

In the elderly, however, this process often breaks down. It's not that antibodies can't destroy infectious bacteria, it's that

Small amounts of DHEA were found to lessen amnesia and enhance long-term memory in mice. Even very low levels of DHEA supplementation may increase the number of neurons in the brain as well as prevent neuronal loss and/or damage.

somehow the immune system fails to recognize them. According to Dr. Peter Hornsby of the Huffington Center on Aging in Houston, Texas, the adrenal gland, where DHEA is produced, atrophies significantly as we get older, possibly putting elderly people at an even greater risk for lower immunity. The body doesn't mobilize to fight the disease until the person has already gotten sick.

The Journal of Clinical Endocrinology and Metabolism reported that "an enzyme essential for synthesis of DHEA is functionally reduced with aging," resulting possibly in the loss of DHEA as we age. However, whatever the cause of this hormonal decrease, Dr. John Nestler of the New York Academy of Sciences has found that the loss may be at least partially reversible. According to Nestler, "DHEA is one of the most abundant hormones in humans, so it stands to reason that it has some biological effect on us, [and] if I had to guess which of those effects were the strongest, I would say protection against heart disease and boosting immunity."

DHEA seems to wake up elderly immune systems to youthful levels of efficiency. Dr. Raymond Daynes, associate chair of pathology and head of the division of cell biology and immunology at the University of Utah at Salt Lake City, has been experimenting with ways that DHEA might enhance the effectiveness of vaccines given to the elderly and to others whose immune systems have been weakened. He combined DHEA with a vaccine that he gave to elderly mice—and found that their bodies then manufactured antibodies with the same speed and efficiency shown by younger mice. Dr. Daynes observed this improved immune reaction to vaccines against hepatitis B, influenza, diphtheria, and tetanus.

He also reported that DHEA may stimulate T-cell proliferation and IL-2 cytokine production by mitogen (invader)-activated

T cells. Therefore, DHEA may very well be responsible for decreasing age-related suceptibility to immune system "invaders" that can make us ill.

Other studies seem to support Daynes's sense that DHEA enhances the body's ability to combat infection. A 1991 study of mice with viral encephalitis found that DHEA eased some symptoms, reduced the death rate, and significantly delayed the onset of both disease and death. According to Daynes, the animals he placed on DHEA replacement therapy looked "far, far healthier in their later months" than animals not receiving the hormone. Although DHEA doesn't seem to affect the virus itself, it apparently does equip our systems to better resist infection.

Not only the elderly suffer from weakened immune systems. People who have been severely burned are also in a debilitated condition, because the burns tend to suppress the immune function. Immunologist Dr. Barbara Araneo, an associate professor of pathology at the University of Utah Medical School, administered DHEA to anesthetized lab mice whose burns covered 50 to 60 percent of their skin. She found that if DHEA was administered within three hours of the burn, the mice healed quickly and well. The DHEA also appeared to preserve their immune systems.

Dr. Araneo also found that DHEA given with a hepatitis-B antigen restored immune vaccine responsiveness in aging mice. This study suggests that DHEA may be able to reverse the impaired, degenerated immune responsiveness typically associated with aging in humans as well.

The thymus gland regulates T cells, the cells that our immune systems use to search for and destroy infectious agents. As we age, our thymus glands shrink, which scientists have linked with the reduced immunity that seems typical of the elderly. One way that DHEA may enhance immunity is by protecting the thymus gland. Studies with animals have shown that DHEA treatments have prevented thymic atrophy and improved the thymus's ability to control T cells. Many researchers believe that DHEA supplements might also stave off thymic decline in people.

However, the immune-enhancing effects of DHEA still need to be researched further; aging, infection and stress are all crucial factors that may affect its production.

DHEA AND CANCER: A CONTRADICTORY SITUATION

Scientists now believe that a person's risk of cancer may be correlated with the levels of DHEA or DHEA-S to be found in his or
her blood or urine. (DHEA-sulfate or DHEA-S is the form in
which DHEA appears in the bloodstream.) Dr. Daynes has conducted a study linking DHEA with enhanced immunity to cancer
in particular. Daynes implanted elderly mice with cancerous tumors that would normally have killed them; when the mice were
treated with DHEA, however, they were able to fend off the
cancer.

Other animal studies have shown that DHEA can block the
growth of mammary tumors, thus suggesting that it may be an
inhibitor of breast cancer in women. Likewise, patients who suffer from ovarian cancer have extremely low levels of DHEA,
suggesting that the hormone helps to prevent this type of cancer.

Another study, conducted by Dr. Regelson and Dr. Moham-
mad Kalimi, examined the action of DHEA on spontaneous mas-
tosarcomas in dogs and cats. In six of seven animals, there was
a regression at 10 mg of DHEA per day. Later, a human clinical
study of 129 advanced cancer patients on 40 mg of DHEA per
day found that while there wasn't significant regression of the
cancer, two patients with renal cancer stabilized their conditions
and tolerated the DHEA therapy without side effects for two
and a half years. And according to Regelson and Kalimi, DHEA
may be our best agent for blocking stress-mediated support of
tumor growth.

In other cases, though, DHEA has been reported to stimulate the growth of breast tumors, making its use in cancer uncer-
tain. And in one mouse study, DHEA appeared to induce ovarian
tumors. Clearly, more research needs to be done.

At one time, doctors were concerned about reports that
DHEA might lead to prostate enlargement, but these fears appear
to be unfounded. However, DHEA encourages the production of
testosterone, which can theoretically exacerbate a prostate condition; therefore, doctors don't recommend its use in men with
enlarged prostates or in cases where prostate cancer is feared.

Other studies have explored the role of DHEA in preventing
urinary, colon, and lung cancer. Researchers are hopeful that

once we better understand the relationship of DHEA to aging itself, we'll know more about how to treat age-related diseases like cancer.

DHEA AND CARDIOVASCULAR CONDITIONS

Another typically age-related disease is atherosclerosis, in which the arteries' inner walls are lined with fat, or "plaque," posing a potential risk of coronary heart disease. One study that extended nearly 20 years found that the DHEA-S levels were far lower in men who died of coronary heart disease than in healthier men. DHEA was also found effective in reducing the levels of plaque in rabbits suffering from atherosclerosis: animals with high levels of DHEA were able to reduce plaque by almost 50 percent over those with lower levels. Some scientists believe that DHEA's preventive effect on diseases such as atherosclerosis may relate to its ability to decrease platelet adhesiveness.

> Clinical studies on DHEA show that supplemental oral DHEA intake can lower total serum cholesterol, particularly LDL cholesterol by an average of 18 percent without modification of lifestyle.

DHEA certainly seems to be a predictor of coronary heart disease. In one study of 32 men suffering from myocardial infarction, ages 26 to 40, DHEA levels were found to be abnormally low. A 1986 study published in the *New England Journal of Medicine* measured the DHEA levels in 242 men, ages 59-79. (The typical blood level of DHEA in a 20-year-old ranges from 300-500 mcg per deciliter of blood.) It was found that men whose DHEA levels were 140 mcg or higher were less than half as likely to die of heart disease—even when allowing for smoking and high cholesterol levels. This doesn't necessarily indicate that raising DHEA levels would cure or even reduce the men's heart conditions. In fact, there is a sex difference in regard to coronary disease; testosterone appears to protect men against heart dis-

DHEA levels are an accurate indicator of arterial blockage, LDL cholesterol levels, hypertension and other risk factors associated with heart disease.

eases, while estrogen appears to protect women. How DHEA plays a role in this gender difference is yet to be discovered.

DHEA AND ALZHEIMER'S DISEASE

One of DHEA's key jobs is to maintain the function of our brain cells. It seems that brain tissue contains five to six times more DHEA than any other tissue in the human body. In studies of people with Alzheimer's disease—another condition strongly associated with aging—DHEA levels were found to be abnormally low. Studies have shown that people with Alzheimer's disease have an overwhelming 48 percent less DHEA in their blood than do matched controls of the same age group! When small amounts of DHEA were added to nerve cell tissue cultures, not only was the number of neurons increased, but the neurons' ability to establish contacts and connections also improved. Therefore, many scientists believe that DHEA may play a key role in improving the functioning of human brain tissue cells, and reducing the debilitating symptoms of Alzheimer's disease.

A study conducted on 61 men confined to nursing homes, ages 57-104, found that plasma DHEA-S levels were inversely related to the degree of dependence the men had in performing daily activities. In fact, the men confined to the nursing home had 40 percent subnormal DHEA-S levels, as compared to men studied outside of the nursing home who had only 6 percent subnormal levels.

According to Dr. Majewska of the Maryland National Institute on Drug Abuse, DHEA-S could play a role in the GABA theory of aging (gamma-aminobutyric acid is a naturally-occurring brain neurotransmitter chemical that acts similarly to Valium), which is linked to Alzheimer's disease. According to this theory, the brain enzyme that manufactures GABA rises as we age and stimulates effects that slow the brain and promote neurodegeneration. DHEA-S would be expected to act as an antagonist to this GABA function.

Furthermore, the excessive GABA we manufacture as we age has been found to lower nerve growth factor in the brain. DHEA, therefore, could logically block GABA's neurodestructive effects and help promote neuron activity in the aging brain. Majewska also believes that DHEA-S may have fewer side effects than the anti-GABA drugs on the market today. Such results give scientists hope that eventually DHEA will be beneficial in treatment or prevention of Alzheimer's disease. In laboratory tests on rodents, DHEA also seemed to improve short-term and long-term memory and lessen amnesia.

> Women with higher DHEA levels tend to have greater bone mass than those with lower DHEA levels.

DHEA AND OSTEOPOROSIS

Most of us are familiar with the term menopause—the condition in women in which the ovary stops making estrogen, progesterone and testosterone, menstruation stops, and conception is no longer possible. What researchers are now discovering is that menopause is also associated with low levels of DHEA, and subsequent reduced bone mass in women. When ovarian production of DHEA slows down during menopause, the adrenal glands cannot adequately take over, and the resulting DHEA deficiency may be why osteoporosis afflicts so many older women. One study showed the average plasma level (ng/100 ml) of DHEA in premenopausal women to be 542, 197 in postmenopausal women, and only 126 in women who had their ovaries surgically removed! The lower a woman's DHEA level, the lower her bone density, and the higher her risk for developing osteoporosis.

DHEA can improve osteoporosis by increasing resorption and formation of bone, and by increasing estrogen, progesterone and testosterone levels.

DHEA AND LUPUS

Systemic lupus erythematosus is a chronic inflammatory disease in which a defective immune system causes abnormalities in the blood vessels and connective tissues, as well as damaging the kidneys, nervous system, joints, and skin. The usual treatment for lupus—steroids and the kind of chemotherapy used to treat cancer—is often more painful and debilitating than the disease itself.

Now scientists are wondering whether DHEA might be a safer and more effective treatment for lupus. Dr. James McGuire, chief of staff at Stanford University Hospital, and Dr. Ronald van Vollenhoven, assistant professor of immunology and rheumatology at Stanford, administered 50 to 200 mg of oral DHEA to 57 women afflicted with lupus. Over the three to 12 months that the study lasted, some two-thirds of the patients reported that their symptoms had been relieved, at least to some extent: their skin rashes were less severe and less frequent, they suffered less from joint pain, headaches, and fatigue. Many also reported a higher tolerance for exercise and better concentration.

DHEA AND DIABETES

Another disease frequently associated with aging is mature-onset diabetes. Here, too, DHEA may be an effective preventive treatment. Dr. Nestler, of the Medical College of Virginia at Richmond, hypothesized that the age-related decrease in DHEA and DHEA-S levels may be attributed to the typical age-related rise in insulin levels in the human body. This rise in insulin is a significant phenomenon on its own, as it can lead to obesity, hypertension and most commonly, diabetes. Nestler observed that certain drugs can reverse the high amount of insulin produced as we age, and therefore restore levels of DHEA in elderly people to what they were in mid-life.

One way of understanding diabetes is to think of it as a problem metabolizing carbohydrates. Although a person with a normal metabolism can absorb these nutrients, a diabetic needs extra insulin to help the process along.

While some 10 percent of diabetics suffer from an insufficient production of insulin, the other 90 percent suffer from a condition known as insulin resistance. That is, their bodies manufacture a normal, or even a high, amount of insulin—but they have difficulty making use of it.

As a result, diabetics with high amounts of (unused) insulin in their bodies tend to have relatively low levels of DHEA. These low levels in turn may contribute to the cardiovascular problems and tendency to be overweight that are typical of diabetics, particularly of those who acquire the condition late in life.

In laboratory experiments, Nestler noted that not only did increased levels of insulin drive DHEA levels down, but insulin also interfered with the adrenal activity responsible for DHEA synthesis. Insulin actually stimulated the enzyme that destroys DHEA! In studies of rats genetically predisposed to diabetes, injections of DHEA appeared to reduce their need for insulin and inhibit the onset of the disease.

In studies on both insulin-resistant mice and normal aging mice, DHEA seemed to increase the sensitivity to insulin. It also ameliorated the effects of diabetes in disease-prone mice. Although no full-scale studies have yet been done on the effect of this hormone on human diabetics, some physicians report that DHEA treatment reduces the need for insulin in humans.

DHEA, WEIGHT LOSS, AND MUSCLE MASS

As we have seen, aging usually brings with it a shift in the body's composition. The older we get, the greater the proportion of fat in our bodies. Many older people tend to gain weight; others lose muscle mass and gain fat, even if their aggregate weights remain the same.

Many hormones have the effect of restoring muscle mass and reducing fat, and DHEA is no exception. It seems to behave similarly to thyroid hormone in regard to weight loss, by indirectly enhancing thermogenesis and declining mitochondrial metabolic efficacy.

Various studies have shown low levels of DHEA to be associated with obesity. For example, a 1964 study found that DHEA was completely absent from urine samples of 32 elderly, obese diabetics. Obese people were also found to excrete less DHEA than people of normal weight.

Many researchers believe that DHEA's antiobesity effects are due to its ability to block a specific enzyme called glucose-6-phosphate-dehydrogenase (G6PD). Scientists believe that DHEA, by inhibiting G6PD, actually blocks the body's ability to store and produce fat.

In a year-long study of 15 people conducted at the University of California at San Diego, Dr. Yen discovered that DHEA increased muscle mass in men and women, and that men gained strength and lost fat.

> Studies have shown DHEA to work against obesity by encouraging weight loss by raising metabolism and decreasing appetite and fat storage.

Dr. Edmund Chein is a strong supporter of DHEA supplementation and is the founder of the Palm Springs Life Extension Institute. He reported that his patients respond with comments such as "I've never felt this good," and "I can't believe how much weight I've lost." Dr. Chein believes that this weight loss and increase in muscle strength can lead to greater personal independence and freedom as we age.

In a human study conducted in 1988, DHEA was given to five male normal-weight subjects at a dose of 1,600 mg per day. After 28 days of treatment, four out of the five subjects reported an average body fat decrease of 31 percent with no overall weight change; their fat loss had been balanced by a gain in muscle mass! Simultaneously, LDL cholesterol levels dropped by 7.5 percent, therefore protecting against cardiovascular disease as well. Some researchers hypothesize that DHEA's effect on weight loss and muscle mass increase may be due in part to its ability to help expend energy, rather than store it for further use.

In the 1980s, Dr. Arthur Schwartz of the Fells Institute for Cancer Research and Molecular Biology at Temple University found that administering DHEA to lab animals caused them to lose weight no matter what they ate. DHEA appeared to stimulate the production of cholecytokinin, or CCK, the substance that signals us to feel "full."

When Dr. Schwartz gave DHEA to five normal-weight male rats over a period of 28 days, controlling their diet and activity, he found that four of them lost an average of 31 percent of their body fat. These animals did not lose weight; rather, their metabolisms had shifted from producing fat to creating muscle and energy. Scientists are now doing research into the possibility of treating obese humans with DHEA.

STRESS REDUCTION AND DHEA

Reducing stress, some scientists say, may also help increase our depleting levels of DHEA. In a study conducted by the Institute of Heartmath in Boulder Creek, California, it was found that people can raise their levels of DHEA by practicing emotional stress management techniques and listening to relaxing music. In fact, out of the 14 men and 14 women, ages 24 to 52, who participated in the study, results showed a 100 percent increase in DHEA levels and a 23 percent decrease in the hormone cortisol—also known as the "stress hormone." The results of this study were recorded after only one month of practicing the relaxation techniques, and scientists believe that even greater results may be achieved if the techniques are continued over a longer period of time.

DHEA, CONTRACEPTION AND CAFFEINE

One finding concerning DHEA has specific importance to women. According to DHEA studies conducted in Australia, oral contraceptives have been found to lower DHEA levels, but not DHEA-S levels. However, it has been suggested that women taking oral contraceptives consider possible DHEA replacement therapy to negate the depleting effects of the pill.

DHEA may also be linked to that cup of coffee we have in the morning. Dr. Ian Mason and his team of researchers at the University of Texas Southwestern Medical Center in Dallas believe DHEA may be produced in response to agents such as caffeine, which is known for its ability to increase intracellular cyclic AMP concentrations (energy chemicals in our body's cells important in producing ATP, a high-octane energy molecule).

DHEA AND THE AGING PROCESS

Consider the biological results of growing old: a greater susceptibility to the "aging" diseases of cancer, heart disease, diabetes, and Alzheimer's; a tendency to gain weight and a gradually increasing proportion of body fat; a general weakening of the immune system. DHEA appears to respond to each of these conditions, yet levels of this vital hormone begin falling drastically after the age of 25. It would seem logical that restoring DHEA levels would help to restore a biological condition of youth.

Moreover, studies have shown that DHEA prolongs life expectancy up to 50 percent in laboratory animals. Although much remains to be learned about the side effects and the limits of DHEA, we're justified in feeling optimistic about this "mother" of all hormones.

TAKING DHEA

In comparison to human growth hormone, DHEA replacement therapy is a much less expensive alternative. A one-month supply of 100 mg capsules may cost as little as $30. However, the anti-aging benefits of DHEA are not yet proven in long-term human studies and the FDA has approved it by prescription only.

Medical supervision should always be sought when using DHEA. Common dosages usually range from 25-150 mg/day, but it is best to start at the lower end of the spectrum and up the dosage later if needed. For best results, it is recommended to divide DHEA dosages into three or four smaller doses. You should also have your DHEA levels measured every two to three months and supplement your diet with additional antioxidants during therapy.

> Human studies on DHEA and its ability to inhibit or reverse diseases such as diabetes, certain cancers, cardiovascular disease and memory disorders are still inadequate and no conclusive evidence exists on the long-term use of DHEA.

Take note that too much DHEA supplementation could suppress the body's natural ability to synthesize it. Therefore, it might be wise to take DHEA every other day, alternating with a DHEA precursor such as wild yam capsules. Scientifically referred to as *Dioscorea,* the wild yam is a plant that grows mainly in China, Japan and Central America. It's been reported to improve overall health, boost the immune system, increase energy and help balance the hormonal system.

Men with prostate cancer or women with ovarian cancer should avoid DHEA replacement therapy, as the hormone stimulation associated with DHEA may aggravate these conditions. And everyone involved in hormonal replacement therapies should monitor their biomarkers for early cancer detection at least once a year.

Chapter 6

The Female Sex Hormones: Estrogen and Progesterone

The number one prescription drug in America is estrogen, the female sex hormone. Some 10 million American women—about 20 percent of those in or past menopause—regularly opt for estrogen replacement therapy (ERT). As the baby boom generation approaches menopause, these numbers are going to skyrocket.

The multibillion-dollar business in female hormones has generated enormous controversy. Proponents claim that estrogen, usually given with the hormone progesterone, can help curb menopausal symptoms such as hot flashes, night sweats, vaginal dryness and aging skin, while also lessening a woman's chances of heart disease, osteoporosis, colon cancer and mental deterioration.

Skeptics reply that hormone replacement therapy puts women at a higher risk of breast, uterine, and ovarian cancer;

Men have more heart attacks than women until women pass the age of menopause. Researchers think the high level of estrogen in premenopausal women helps protect them from heart disease.

73

that it frequently induces a sense of lethargy or sluggishness; and that diet, exercise, and vitamin and mineral supplements can combat most of the dangers of aging and menopause. If necessary, say some doctors, women can treat certain symptoms with estrogen creams and/or with natural sources of progesterone, rather than undergoing expensive and potentially dangerous synthetic hormone therapy.

However, more and more research is providing strong evidence that taking estrogen replacement therapy significantly reduces the rate of death from *all* causes for postmenopausal women, and offers even greater protection against heart attack and stroke.

A study evaluated the medical history of 454 healthy women born between 1900 and 1915 and compared the health outcomes of those who started estrogen supplementation and those who did not. About half the group used estrogen for at least a year starting in 1969. Among those women who did not use ERT, there were 87 deaths from all causes compared to 53 deaths among the estrogen users—a 46 percent lower overall mortality rate. More specifically, the estrogen group had a 60 percent reduction in mortality for coronary heart disease and a 75 percent reduction for other cardiovascular problems such as stroke. Although there was a slightly higher rate of breast cancer death among estrogen users, this was statistically offset by a slightly lower rate of death from lung cancer.

> On average, women are 10 times likelier to die from heart disease than from breast cancer, suggesting that estrogen's benefit in reducing heart disease risk outweighs a possibly greater risk of breast cancer.

WHAT IS ESTROGEN?

Estrogen is one of the female hormones that help regulate a woman's passage through menstruation, fertility, and menopause. Estrogen is one of the most powerful hormones in the human body. Some 300 different tissues are equipped with estrogen receptors—chemical sites that make them responsive to estrogen. That means that estrogen levels in the body can affect a wide range of tissues and organs, from the brain to the liver and to the bones themselves. The uterus, urinary tract, breasts, skin, and blood vessels depend on estrogen to stay toned and flexible.

Although we are used to thinking of menarche (the onset of menstruation and fertility) and menopause (the cessation of menstruation and fertility) as single points in life's journey, they are actually more like peaks and valleys. Estrogen levels start to rise well before menarche, as early as age 8 in some girls. The hypothalamus is the prime mover in this process, signaling the pituitary to release hormones, which in turn signals the ovaries to produce more estrogen.

For three or four years, estrogen levels continue to rise, and by age 11 or 12, they are sufficiently high enough (along with other key hormones) to start the menstruation process. Estrogen also sets off the development of the breasts and the growth of hair under the arms and in the pubic region. The body often responds to this new hormonal activity with confusion: oily hair, acne, sexual interest, mood swings, and sometimes severe menstrual cramps.

MENSTRUATION AND PERIMENOPAUSE

Under normal circumstances, the healthy body will continue to menstruate for many years, from about age 12 until sometimes the early fifties. However, just as hormone levels began to rise well before the onset of menstruation, they begin to fall well before the onset of menopause. By the early thirties, most women are experiencing decreased levels of estrogen and progesterone, with a consequent drop in fertility.

Then, sometime in their early forties, most women enter the climacteric, a period in which falling hormones begin to have more obvious symptoms. This is known as perimenopause—the period just before menopause. Skin tends to become dryer, hair grows more brittle, pubic and underarm hair becomes more sparse. Some women experience a loss in libido; others suffer "adolescent" mood swings.

In addition, although women are still menstruating, hormonal fluctuations often play havoc with their systems, especially before and during their periods. Endocrinologist Dr. Lila Nachtigall of New York University explains that falling estrogen levels cause the hypothalamus to send out ever more signals to incite the ovaries to produce more estrogen. The ovaries contain aging eggs which respond rather erratically to the frantic signals from the hypothalamus. These erratic responses result in fluctuating hormone levels that may rise and fall within a single day, "and that can drive you crazy."

According to Dr. Williams, this craziness is not only the result of fluctuating estrogen; it's also the result of insufficient progesterone. Williams cites the work of British physician Katharina Dalton, who in the early 1950s identified premenstrual syndrome (PMS), the bundle of symptoms that plague many women three to ten days before their periods. Dr. Dalton found that progesterone supplements helped alleviate her own menstrual migraines, and went on to develop progesterone-based treatments that helped thousands of women with PMS.

Ideally, both estrogen and progesterone levels will rise from the time of ovulation until just before the menstrual flow begins. But if estrogen levels alone are rising, the hormonal imbalance may lead to a host of symptoms: salt and fluid retention; low blood sugar levels; blood clotting; fibroid and tumor development; interference with thyroid hormone function (leading to weight gain and/or feelings of exhaustion); increased cholesterol and triglyceride levels; allergic reaction; increased production of body fat; reduced oxygen levels in the cells (creating a sluggish, low-energy feeling); and a number of adverse mineral reactions, such as retention of copper and loss of zinc.

These symptoms may occur even in relatively young women. However, they tend to intensify—or to appear, intensely, for the first time—in perimemopausal women. Still-menstruating women in their forties and fifties note painful menstrual migraines, hot flashes and night sweats, extreme irritability, and difficulty with bladder control (resulting from loss of uterine tone). They also describe unusually heavy, gushing periods, and periods that last from ten days to six weeks.

MENOPAUSE

An estimated 40 million American women are in or past menopause, with another 20 million due to reach menopause within the next decade. With the increase in life expectancy, many women will be spending one-third or more of their lives in post-menopausal years. Menopause by definition begins after the last spontaneous menstrual period.

Once a woman has gone from six to twelve months without a period, she is considered to have reached menopause. In the United States, the average age for menopause is 50, although considerable variation certainly exists.

Many people tend to associate menopause with a host of psychological problems, particularly depression, loss of energy, and crying episodes. It isn't clear what amount of these reactions stems from hormonal changes and what may be due to negative images of older women. In any case, many women experience renewed zest and vigor after menopause. Anthropologist Margaret Mead called this period "postmenopausal zest," while author Gail Sheehy commented that postmenopausal women feel "a greater sense of well-being than any other stage of their lives."

> Studies show that women who predict that menopause will be miserable do, in fact, suffer more negative emotional and physical symptoms than women who expect it to be easier.

Hot Flashes   Some 85 percent of all women do experience hot flushes, either during perimenopause or in menopause itself. The physiology of the hot flash is still not understood, but it appears to start in the hypothalamus, "the body's thermostat," in response to a drop in estrogen. During a flash, a woman experiences a severe feeling of heat, especially in the head and neck, often in the entire upper half of the body. Sometimes the face is blotched and ruddy as a result of the dilation of blood vessels on the surface of the skin. In some cases, flashes are accompanied by disruptions in sleep patterns and night sweats.

In the Massachusetts Women's Health Study, the incidence of hot flashes rose from about 10 percent during the perimenopausal period to about 50 percent just after cessation of menses, and dropped back to about 20 percent four years after menopause.

Flashes usually last for only a few minutes, but may continue for up to an hour. The body will attempt to cool down by beading with perspiration. Hot weather, hot food or drink, stress, and other sources of heat can trigger flashes without warning. Although most women experience them, few—only one in four—find them uncomfortable enough to seek treatment.

> Some studies have shown that as little as 15 to 30 IU of vitamin E daily helps ease hot flashes, vaginal dryness, prevents hysterectomy and in some cases eliminates the need for estrogen shots.

Many women who seek estrogen treatment for their hot flashes do find relief. Yet in all cases, whether treated or not, they will eventually stop as soon as the body adjusts to postmenopausal levels of estrogen.

Lower Sex Drive Another key symptom of menopause is the atrophy of the reproductive tract. Estrogen produced by the ovaries keep the uterus, vagina, and base of the bladder moist and supple. When estrogen levels start to fall, these organs start to shrink, and the vaginal walls thin. Generally, blood flow to the area decreases, as does lubrication. Women may have difficulty controlling their bladders under stress and they're more likely to suffer from vaginal itching, dryness, and sometimes, pain during or after intercourse. As a result, some women become less interested in sex. Other women may experience a loss in libido even without these symptoms.

Osteoporosis This bone disease is another common response to menopause. Up until the mid-thirties, bone mass continues to grow; that is, our bodies use minerals, especially calcium, to strengthen, widen and perhaps lengthen our bones. By age 40, however, minerals begin to be leached out of the bones, making them more brittle. The extreme version of this condition is known as osteoporosis, a disease that affects 10 to 15 million Americans and causes some 1.3 million fractures a year. Of these, some 120,000 are elderly women who break their hips—accidents whose complications result in close to 20,000 annual deaths.

ESTROGEN: HOW IT CAN EASE MENOPAUSE

Proponents of estrogen cite both scientific studies and the experience of numerous women to show that this female hormone can ease or eliminate menopausal woes. Estrogen supplements, which are available as transdermal patches, topical creams and long-lasting injections, appear to relieve hot flashes, night sweats and other discomforts, as well as vaginal dryness and atrophy. Some women find that the hormone helps keep their skins thicker, moister, and more youthful-looking. Collagen is the main protein in the dermis, and is stimulated by estrogen. A loss of collagen results in increased wrinkling, bruisability and thinning of the skin. Administering estrogen not only prevents collagen loss but increased collagen synthesis, which can relieve symptoms of diminished urinary control sometimes experienced by menopausal women. Dr. Nachtigall also believes that estrogen improves an older woman's sex drive and warns, "Without it, you may soon have no sex life at all." Estrogen moistens the vaginal mucous membranes, which increases lubrication and also helps maintain flexibility of the connective tissues.

Estrogen and progesterone supplements have also been proven to reduce the bone loss associated with osteoporosis. Women's bones slowly begin to lose minerals and become less dense even before menopause. After menopause, however, the pace accelerates rapidly for five to ten years. Estrogen inhibits

Investigators found fewer than three percent of women on estrogen replacement therapy continued to lose bone density from the spine.

bone resorption and progesterone stimulates bone formation. Unless a woman is taking these hormones, she has about a one-in-four chance of developing serious osteoporosis.

Osteoporosis increases the risk of bone fractures and all their ensuring complications. One study found that older women who took estrogen were subject to only half the bone fractures of those women who avoided the hormone supplement.

A recent analysis by the Postmenopausal Estrogen and Progestin Intervention trial revealed that estrogen alone and in various combinations with progesterone is equally effective in increasing bone mass in postmenopausal women. Data found that fewer than three percent of women on therapy continued to lose a clinically relevant and measurable fraction of bone density at the spine.

By age 70, almost 50 percent of women have had at least one osteoporotic fracture, at an estimated cost of $7 to $10 billion annually in the United States. A menopause symposium sponsored by the Oregon Health Sciences University School of Medicine concluded that estrogen is the therapy of choice for prevention and treatment of osteoporosis. Although supplemental calcium, diet, and exercise are also beneficial, they don't seem to be as effective as estrogen.

The most important benefit of estrogen replacement is the reported reduction in coronary artery disease—the leading cause of death in postmenopausal women. Some 500,000 women a year die from coronary artery disease—that's twice as many women as die each year from cancer. Apparently, the high premenopausal levels of estrogen tend to protect women from heart disease, partly by keeping levels of HDL cholesterol high and LDL cholesterol low.

Without estrogen replacement, a woman's risk of heart attack becomes equal to a man's within 15 years after menopause. Simply being postmenopausal puts a woman at a higher risk for heart disease, and having just one additional risk factor—smoking, high blood pressure, HDL cholesterol bellow 35, diabetes, or a family history of heart disease—is an even higher risk. With estrogen, however, the blood vessels dilate slightly, cholesterol balance is maintained, and the risk of heart disease vastly decreases. This can be seen in a report from a 10-year study of some 48,470 nurses—one of the largest studies to date—which found that estrogen use reduced the risk of major coronary disease and fatal cardiovascular disease in half.

Dr. Lawrence Brass of Yale University School of Medicine

Botanical Nutrients That May Ease Menopause

Several botanical therapies that are commonly used to alleviate symptoms at the onset of menopause and that may provide comfort include:

- **Black cohosh** and **blue cohosh** are used extensively for hot flashes and in regulating the menstrual cycle and bringing on uterine bleeding. Both contain phytosterols, which have estrogen-like activities.
- **Dong quai** is a Chinese herb otherwise known as angelica with anticoagulant properties. It is used to relieve menstrual cramping associated with PMS and to regulate hormonal imbalances in menopausal women. Dong quai has vital estrogen compounds mimicking the body's natural estrogen.
- **Motherwort** is one of the most popular herbs used to combat menopausal symptoms. It has been shown to decrease the frequency, duration, and severity of hot flashes; thickens the vaginal wall; relieves anxiety; and lessens menstrual cramping and stress-related palpitations. May cause a rash in high doses.
- **Licorice root** contains flavonoids which have an estrogen-like activity, and saponin, which has progestational-like activity. The root also has anti-inflammatory properties. Note that licorice root promotes potassium loss and sodium retention, can cause hypertension and is dangerous in those taking antihypertensives or diuretics, and can be addictive.
- **Red raspberry** is a uterine wall relaxant and an antispasmodic, used to decrease uterine bleeding.

predicts that estrogen replacement therapy may soon emerge as one of the most effective therapies for stroke prevention, cutting the risk of stroke in post menopausal women in half. He believes that because estrogen prevents heart disease by 50 to 70 percent, it may also "plausibly" prevent stroke.

In a Leisure World prospective cohort study, estrogen therapy was associated with a 46 percent overall reduction in the risk of death from stroke, with a 70 percent reduction in recent users. This protection was present in women both with and without hypertension and in both smokers and nonsmokers. In addition, a population-based cohort study in Uppsala, Sweden, documented a 30 percent reduced incidence of stroke in postmenopausal users of estrogen, as well as in women given an estrogen-progestin combination.

However, a large cohort from the Nurses' Health Study (National Health and Nutrition Examination Survey-NHANES) produced results in striking contrast, failing to show a protective effect of estrogen against stroke. But critics have pointed to the fact that the women in the study were too young, where there was little protective effect against stroke.

In addition to reducing the risk of cardiovascular disease and osteoporosis, postmenopausal hormone replacement therapy may allow more women to retain their teeth as they age. By preventing osteoporosis, estrogen may add the benefit of preventing tooth loss and the need for dentures in older women. A new study of 3,921 women found that those on hormone replacement were 19 percent less likely to wear dentures and 36 percent less likely to have no teeth than women who had never taken hormones. Researchers also suggest that because tooth loss provides a measure of skeletal bone health, it may be the first clinical sign of osteoporosis.

Estrogen also seems to reduce the risk of colon cancer—and the longer a woman takes estrogen, the lower her risk. New research has found that estrogen users had a 29 percent lower risk of dying from colon cancer than nonusers; users of 10 years or more enjoyed a risk that was 55 percent lower.

The North American Menopause Society suggests that the addition of a low-dose testosterone to oral estrogen therapy may be more effective than estrogen alone in ameliorating psychologic and psychiatric symptoms of menopause in older women. Hot flashes and vaginal dryness seem to improve, and most significantly, fatigue, insomnia, irritability and nervousness are relieved.

> Tooth decay and rates of tooth loss were significantly lower in estrogen users than in nonusers.

In order to get the positive benefits of estrogen, doctors believe you have to take it for at least seven years, although a full 95 percent of the women engaged in hormone replacement therapy continue only for three years or less. And according to Dr. John Gallagher, an endocrinologist at Creighton University in Omaha, Nebraska, three years is "not long enough to get any positive effects on their bones."

ESTROGEN AND ALZHEIMER'S DISEASE

Mounting evidence suggests that estrogen supplements help ease the mental fogginess and memory lapses that many women experience after menopause. Studies have shown that women are three times more likely than men to suffer from Alzheimer's disease. Women produce estrogen until menopause, while men's bodies continue converting testosterone to estrogen into later life. Researchers believe this could give men a natural protection against Alzheimer's. Estrogen replacement therapy has has been shown to reduce or eliminate some of the symptoms of this disease by supporting the production of acetylcholine, a chemical that helps transmit nerve signals across synapses, which is abnormally low in Alzheimer's patients, and may explain their impaired abilities to learn and remember.

Estrogen plays a large role in the development and maintenance of our brain cells. Scientists now understand that estrogen helps shape the brain during the fetus's earliest stages of development, as both male and female fetuses are exposed to the estrogen in their mother's system. By the twelfth week of gestation, male fetuses are also producing testosterone in their testes, so that some male-female differences in learning and memory may be "hard-wired" very early on. Thus, boys tend to have greater facility with math, while girls have greater facility with language, have slightly superior hearing, and have more talent at interpreting facial expressions.

As children mature, they continue to rely on estrogen to keep their brains functioning at peak level. (Boys convert some testosterone to estrogen in the brain.) Apparently, estrogen increases the number of synapses, or connections, among nerve cells in the hippocampus, the region in the brain where new memories are formed. Research by Catherine Woolley of the University of Washington and Bruce McEwen of Rockefeller University found that removing the ovaries from rats caused the number of synapses in their hippocampuses to decline rapidly—although when the rats were given estrogen supplements, their synapses remained relatively intact.

> Although estrogen is primarily a female hormone, men also produce it. In fact, estrogen levels in men can be higher than in post menopausal women.

In a related process, estrogen appears to protect nerve cells that produce acetylcholine. Meharvan Singh and James Simpkins of the University of Florida found that giving estrogen supplements to rats increased the rats' production of an enzyme needed for the production of acetylcholine. Rats that had access to estrogen, either from their own ovaries or from supplements, were twice as successful at learning to avoid an electric shock than were rats that had no ovaries and therefore no estrogen.

Apparently, estrogen helped the rats synthesize a protein known as the nerve-growth factor. Nerve-growth factor, created within the brain itself, promotes the health of cholinergic neurons, the cells that make and use acetycholine. When rats had their ovaries removed and stopped producing estrogen, nerve-growth factor declined by nearly 45 percent over a period of only three months.

The part of our brain that governs new memory is helped by estrogen in two ways: estrogen creates more connections among nerve cells, and it helps information travel more easily along those connections. Conversely, a loss of estrogen leads to the following scenario: less estrogen means that we're manufacturing less nerve-growth factor; less nerve-growth factor means that our brains have access to fewer cholinergic neurons; fewer cholinergic neurons means that we have less acetyocholine in the brain; and less acetycholine means that we'll have a harder time learning and remembering new things.

Tests of 158 postmenopausal women with either Alzheimer's or ischemic vascular dementia found that these women were only half as likely as 148 cognitively normal women of the same age to have been on ERT. A lack of estrogen actually doubled the risk of these dementias.

In a Massachusetts research protocol, women who had undergone surgical menopause (removal of ovaries), were more likely to become depressed than those who went through natural menopause. Researchers speculate that the sudden termination of estrogen supply from the body instead of diminishing gradually may explain the psychological impact as well as the decline in libido and orgasmic capacity.

Psychologist Barbara Sherwin of Montreal's McGill University administered estrogen supplements to women who had had their ovaries removed and so produced very little natural estrogen. Women who had the supplements, she found, could more easily learn and recall pairs of words than those who were only given a placebo. Interestingly, the estrogen seemed only to affect their verbal skills, having no effect on their visual memory.

Moreover, Sherwin found, young women with intact ovaries did better on word-pair memory tests during the phase of their menstrual cycle when estrogen levels were highest, while they did less well during menstruation itself, when estrogen levels had dropped. Sherwin says that the changes are too minor "to have any effect in the real world." Nevertheless, her results suggest the relationship between estrogen and mental functioning, a relationship that has powerful implications for women with Alzheimer's disease.

Dr. Howard Fillit, a geriatrician at Mount Sinai Medical Center in New York City, has given estrogen supplements to women with mild to moderate Alzheimer's. After only three weeks of daily hormone treatment, patients who could not remember the month or year were suddenly able to recall them. The women also seemed more alert, showed improved social behavior, and ate and slept better. (Fillit suspects that male patients will benefit from testosterone supplements in similar ways.)

A larger-scale study at the University of Southern California found that estrogen supplements also helped in preventing Alzheimer's. Researchers examined the medical histories of some 2,418 women who had lived at a retirement home over a period of 11 years. Many of the women had been taking estrogen supplements for reasons unrelated to Alzheimer's. Statistics showed that women who had taken estrogen were 40 percent less likely to have developed the disease than those who hadn't. And the longer they had taken estrogen, the more their risk was reduced.

THE ROLE OF PROGESTERONE

When estrogen treatments were first discovered, this female hormone was generally prescribed alone. Doctors later discovered that it was more effective and often safer in combination with progesterone.

Progesterone is the gestational hormone which prepares the lining of the uterus for the fertilized ovum and maintains pregnancy. It is derived primarily from the corpus luteum that is formed in the ovary from the ruptured follicle. It is also produced in the placenta during pregnancy and in small amounts by the adrenal cortex. Progesterone is a "precursor" hormone, which can be converted by the body into other steroid hormones.

Artifically produced progesterone or progestins are synthetic hormones which closely resemble biosynthesized progesterone, but differ in important ways. Both natural and synthetic hormones share the ability to sustain human secretory endometrium, but progestins do not have the full range of biological activity of natural progesterone. Progestin has actually been shown to inhibit biosynthesis of progesterone.

Some doctors now believe that progestin is responsible for a long list of side effects. And since many women engaged in hormone replacement therapy are filling their prescriptions with synthetic progesterone, they are exposing themselves to unnecessary risks.

According to Dr. David G. Williams, progestin can cause abnormal menstrual flow or cessation, fluid retention, nausea, insomnia, jaundice, depression, fever, weight fluctuations, allergic reactions, and the development of male characteristics. Natural progesterone, on the other hand, has few side effects: occasionally it may cause a feeling of euphoria, and for some women, it may alter the timing of their menstrual cycles.

Dr. Williams recommends that women begin by taking vitamin supplements to increase their own production of progesterone. Animal studies suggest that beta-carotene can stimulate the production of this vital hormone. Likewise, a daily dose of 150 IU of vitamin E can raise progesterone levels, although dosages of 300 to 600 IU of vitamin E can actually lower levels of the hormone.

San Francisco nutritionist Linda Ojeda advocates dietary sources of estrogen and progesterone: soybean products such as tofu, miso and soy milk. These products contain phytoestrogens which have differet levels of estrogenic activity. Women who are reluctant to take synthetic estrogens may consider phytoestrogens as an alternative therapeutic agent. Ojeda points out that Japanese women experience a very low rate of menopausal complaints, which she attributes to their high consumption of soybeans.

For women who want more, Dr. Williams recommends natural progesterone. Unfortunately, natural hormone supplements are hard to come by, since drug companies cannot patent them and therefore are not interested in selling them commercially. Cream extracted from the Mexican wild yam (Dioscorea mexicana), has long been recognized as a natural source of estrogen and progesterone. Dioscorea is not a hormone. It is the food for hormone production in the body, and because of its effect on

DHEA, it affects the production of all hormones, not only estrogen and progesterone. Products made from cows' ovaries, may help a woman who still has her ovaries raise her own progesterone levels. Other alternatives are creams containing plant-derived estrogens and progesterones.

Dr. Julian Whitaker, medical director of the Wellness Institute in Newport Beach, California, also points to the importance of progesterone in treating menopause:

> Estrogen slows down the leaching of calcium from the bone, but does not facilitate deposition of calcium in the bone to strengthen it. Progesterone does that, and given by itself, will not only prevent osteoporosis, but will even reverse it.

Like Dr. Williams, Dr. Whitaker recommends natural, 'topical hormone creams for both progesterone and estrogen supplements. He cites the work of Dr. John Lee, who treated a group of 100 patients over six years with transdermal ("through the skin") natural progesterone only. Lee's patients experienced no significant side effects while enjoying increased bone density and strength.

HORMONE REPLACEMENT THERAPY: LIMITS AND POSSIBLE DANGERS

Unfortunately, as breast-cancer specialist Dr. Susan Love points out, "there's no free lunch." In addition to its unquestioned benefits, estrogen also poses a number of proven and suspected dangers, drawbacks that may make it an undesirable treatment for many women.

Estrogen therapy has come under controversy in light of recent studies on its possible link to various cancers, most notably breast cancer. One study demostrated that patients receiving estrogen (with and without progestin) had a 30 to 40 percent increased risk of breast cancer. Another study, however, reported no increased risk of breast cancer in women who had ever taken combined estrogen-progestin hormone replacement therapy. These conflicting results underscore the continued uncertainty over estrogen's possible role in breast cancer risk.

Some researchers estimate that a woman's risk of endometrial cancer is four times greater if she is taking estrogen supplements. A study of 240,000 women sponsored by the American Cancer Society found that women who took estrogen for at least six years had a 40 percent increased risk of contracting ovarian cancer; women who had taken estrogen for 11 or more years faced an increased risk of 70 percent. Again, this risk can be greatly eliminated by the coadministration of progestin.

Other proven risks of estrogen replacement include the possible return of menstrual bleeding when taken with progesterone. Women sometimes experience premenstrual symptoms such as fluid retention, tender breasts, irritability and a possible increase in the growth of benign fibroid tumors in the uterus. Many women also risk abnormal blood clots, weight gain, an increased likelihood of gallstones, and migraine headaches.

For these reasons, estrogen treatments are usually not recommended for women at high risk for breast cancer. People who suffer from high blood pressure are also advised not to take estrogen, as the supplement tends to raise levels.

Estrogen/progesterone combined should be avoided in women with any of the following conditions or circumstances: known or suspected pregnancy; known or suspected cancer of the breast; known or suspected estrogen-dependent neoplasia; undiagnosed abnormal genital bleeding; active or past history of thrombophlebitis, thromboembolic disorders, or stroke; liver dysfunction or disease. *Always consult with your physician before embarking on estrogen/progesterone or any hormone replacement therapy.*

HORMONE REPLACMENT THERAPY AND BREAST CANCER: WEIGHING THE BENEFITS AND RISKS

The relationship between the estrogens and the risk of breast cancer has been studied intensively. At the present time there is no conclusive evidence that the estrogen doses known to protect against osteoporosis and cardiovascular disease increase the risk of breast cancer. However, various studies have suggested that the two hormones increase a woman's risk of breast cancer by as much as 30 percent. And studies have found that women whose ovaries were removed early in life have markedly reduced rates of breast cancer, presumably because they lack ovarian estrogen and progesterone. Early menarche and late menopause—an extended period of estrogen production—have also been shown to increase the risk of breast cancer.

In The Nurses' Health Study, Harvard researchers looked at 70,000 healthy women who had reached menopause. Roughly one-third used ERT, and a third of those used a formulation that included synthetic progesterone. Using estrogen for more than five years gave women 1.3 to 1.4 times the risk of developing breast cancer. Therefore, taking hormones continuously from age 55 onward gave a woman a three percent chance of the disease between the ages of 60 and 65, whereas a woman who chose not to receive ERT would have less than a two percent chance. And the use of synthetic progesterone neither increased or decreased the risks found with estrogen alone. The risk rapidly diminished when women stopped taking the hormones altogether.

Industrial pollutants having potent estrogenic effects called xeno-estrogens, are recognized as a pervasive environmental threat, and a contributing factor in the incidence of breast cancer.

An extended follow-up of participants in the Nurses' Health Study showed that current estrogen users were 32 percent more likely to develop breast cancer, and current users of estrogen and progestin were 41 percent more likely to develop breast cancer than women who had never taken hormones. Women who were currently on estrogen, and had been for more than five years, were 46 percent more likely to develop breast cancer than nonusers. The risk was even greater for older women. A 60- to 64-year-old woman who had been on estrogen therapy for more than five years was 71 percent more likely to develop breast cancer than a nonuser of the same age.

Breast Cancer and Early Detection

Early detection is crucial in the battle against breast cancer which will strike one out of eight women, nearly 78 percent of cases occurring in women over age 50. Despite strong evidence that yearly mammograms could cut the number of breast cancer deaths by one-third, a National Cancer Institute study found that in 1990 only 39 percent of women in their fifties, and 36 percent of those 60 and older had a mammogram in the past year. And forty percent of women over 50 have never had a mammogram!

- This year there will be more than 175,000 new cases of breast cancer in the United States, 42,000 of these cases will be fatal.
- If a malignancy is present in a woman over 50, mammography has a 90 percent chance of finding it.
- Women who undergo regular mammography are more likely to be diagnosed early, when the chances of being cured are higher and less radical treatment options are available.

In a study of over 1,000 women with operable breast cancer, those whose cancers were diagnosed by mammography had tumors that were significantly smaller and more often lymph node-negative (both a result of early diagnosis), compared to women whose malignances were not detected by mammography. If you are over 40, it is important for a physician to examine your breasts every one to three years. After age 40, the American Cancer Society recommends a screening mammography every one to two years. And if you are 50 or older, its a good idea to have a mammogram every year.

It is important to realize that breast cancer should not be categorized by age. It does strike women under the age of 40, some cases even occurring in women in their twenties. Therefore, if you have a history of breast cancer in your family or have any suspicious lumps, do not rule out mammography as a protective measure. The dose of radiation needed to get a clear image of the breast today is one-fourth as high as it was 10 years ago. Facilities accredited by the American College of Radiology use equipment that exposes the breast to 0.3 rad (radiation-absorbed dose) which is comparable to the exposure in a dental X-ray.

Doctors are at odds about how seriously to take these reports. "The benefits of [hormone replacement therapy] will outweigh the risks for most people," says Dr. William Andrews, former president of the American College of Obstetrics and Gynecology. "Eight times as many women die of heart attacks as die of breast cancer." On the other hand, Dr. Isaac Schiff, chief of obstetrics and gynecology at Massachusetts General Hospital, comments, "Basically, you're presenting women with the possibility of increasing the risk of getting breast cancer at 60 in order to prevent a heart attack at 70 and a hip fracture at age 80. How can you make that decision for a patient?"

It is important to realize that not all estrogens are equivalent in their actions on breast tissue. Natural estrogen actually takes three forms: estrone, estradiol, and estriol. Estrone is the most stimulating to breast tissue, estradiol is second, and estriol is by far the least. Estradiol has actually been shown to decrease the risk of breast cancer. Synthetic estrogen supplements are composed primarily of estrone and estradiol. On the other hand, natural estrogen is high in estriol.

> Breast cancer is more likely to occur in premenopausal women with normal or high estrogen levels and low progesterone levels. This situation may occur in early adult life in a few women but is quite common after age 35. It also occurs after menopause when women are given estrogen supplements without progesterone.

Over 30 years ago, it was reported that women with breast cancer excreted 30-60 percent less estriol than non-cancer controls and that remission of cancer in patients receiving occurred mainly in those whose estriol levels rose. Therefore, low levels of natural estrogen relative to estradiol and estrone correlate with an increased risk of breast cancer.

Women should realize that estrogen alone does not contribute to breast cancer. Many other hormone-related risk factors seem to appear as a woman approaches menopause. For example, postmenopausal obese women have a greater chance of suffering breast cancer because fatty tissue produces a form of estrogen. But, interestingly enough, premenopausal obese women enjoy significantly less risk of early breast cancer than leaner women. A woman who gives birth in her late teens or early twenties increases her risk of early breast cancer, as do women who have children after age 30. Over time the risk falls, becoming much smaller after menopause.

These are but a few examples that illustrate how complicated the biology of breast cancer really is. Will estrogen therapy increase a woman's chances of developing breast cancer? Conflicting evidence has kept this controversy alive, but the risk appears to be small, weighed against the long-term benefits for heart and bone.

> In addition to having an anticancer effect on cells, soybeans manipulate estrogen by blocking its ability to stimulate malignant changes in breast tissue. Thus, soybeans should help thwart both the occurrence and spread of breast cancer in both premenopausal and postmenopausal women.

COMING TO TERMS WITH MENOPAUSE

Although many women take estrogen supplements, many also report feeling worried, skeptical, or discouraged about the effects. A 1987 national poll showed that one-fifth of the women given a prescription for estrogen never even fill it. Of those who do, one-third stop within nine months, and more than half stop within a year. Still others stop their hormone supplements and then start them again, shuttling between the discomforts of being on estrogen and the frustrations of being off it.

Natural supplements like those mentioned in this chapter may be the solution for some of these women. However, these therapies are not nearly as powerful as hormonal supplementation. Women may also benefit from a healthy regimen: not smoking, moderate alcohol intake, regular aerobic exercise (20 to 30 minutes, three to five times a week), a low-fat, high-fiber diet, and vitamin and mineral supplements. Indeed, many women have

New Estrogen Delivery System

Estrogen replacement therapy has taken another step forward with the release of Vivelle Estradiol Transdermal System which is a translucent, thin patch placed twice per week for hormonal replacement therapy. This newly released Ciba Pharmaceuticals product is a patch without the multiple membranes of old reservoir patches. The medication is actually embedded in the adhesive itself in a multipolymer, thinner, clear, flexible patch. This gives the skin direct contact with the medication and allows the skin itself to control the rate of transmission.

reported that their menopausal symptoms eased or disappeared as they paid more attention to diet and exercise.

Making a decision about hormone replacement therapy can be difficult—but it's a decision that virtually all women over 40 have to face sooner or later. Knowing the facts can help. So, too, can coming to terms with your own responses to aging. Women approaching, entering, or living with menopause can derive huge benefits from a holistic approach to their condition, considering hormone therapy, diet and lifestyle, and emotional support as they seek the treatment that is right for them.

Chapter 7

The Male Sex Hormone: Testosterone

Just as estrogen and progesterone are the female sex hormones, testosterone is the male sex hormone (although women have testosterone levels one-tenth to one-twelfth those of men). Testosterone is the main hormone produced in the testicles and secreted by the testes.

Major effects of testosterone are:

- promotes libido, aggressiveness, and sexual desire
- stimulates the growth of certain organs
- promotes protein anabolism, that is, the use of protein to build muscle, skin and bone, and militates against protein catabolism, or breakdown
- stimulates sperm production
- nourishes all the tissues of the male urinary and reproductive systems
- regulates the production of prostaglandin, which seems to keep prostate growth under control

The effects of testosterone are most pronounced during puberty. It brings on the enlarged larynx, thicker vocal cords, new

95

body hair, increased muscle mass, and increased oil-gland secretion by the skin commonly associated with puberty. After puberty, levels of testosterone drop gradually in men, with profound effects on physical health and well-being and particularly on mood and libido.

Some males suffer from a condition in which the body produces insufficient levels of testosterone, resulting in a condition called hypogonadism. Hypogonadism can be caused by conditions of the testes such as testicular injury or infection. Klinefelter's syndrome (a chromosomal abnormality), and from disorders of the pituitary and hypothalamus.

Dr. Anthony Karpas, director of the Institute for Endocrinology and Reproductive Medicine in Atlanta, believes that the condition is underdiagnosed: "As many as 20 percent of men over age 50 may be hypogonadal."

Some telltale signs of hypogonadism are:

- Loss of sex drive/inability to maintain an erection
- Fatigue
- Irritability
- Depressed mood
- Aches and pains in the joints
- Dry skin
- Osteoporosis
- Loss of weight
- The absence or regression of secondary sexual characteristics, such as muscle development, deep voice, and hair distribution on the chest and face

Testosterone production is affected by a number of external factors, such as illness, medications, psychological state, obesity, exercise, and lifestyle (smoking and excessive alcohol intake). Factors such as reduced activity, nutritional deficiency, diabetes, and growth hormone deficiency can also contribute to lower levels.

It is estimated that testosterone levels in 20 percent of men after age 50 will drop to abnormally low levels.

"ANDROPAUSE": THE MALE MENOPAUSE

The phenomenon termed "andropause," (known in England as "viropause") involves the progressive decline of free testosterone levels with age, coupled with an increase in production of a protein called sex hormone-binding globulin. Testosterone links with the protein, reducing its availability to the tissues. As a result of these hormonal changes, men as early as age forty can develop impotency or libido problems.

A large-scale epidermiological study of male sexual behavior called The Massachusetts Male Aging Study of 1984–89 looked at a cross-sectional random sample of 1709 men between the ages of 40 and 70 years. It was found that mean testosterone levels decline annually by about one percent. And 51 percent of normal, healthy males in this age group reported experiencing some degree of impotence. However, Dr. Irwin Goldstein, an organizer of the study, points out that organic factors contribute to impotence in up to 80 percent of men affected. She cites diabetes, hypertension (medications used), smoking, chronic alcohol use and high cholesterol as major factors in male potency loss.

Andropause is not universal and the phenomenon is still relatively new. But scientists do know that it is not analogous to menopause. As we learned in Chapter 6, the profound reduc-

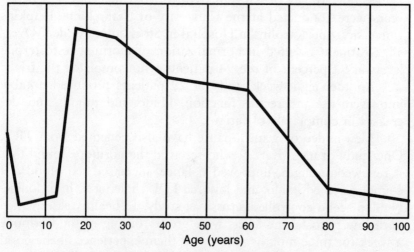

Testosterone levels by age.

After age 60, hip fracture rates in men increase dramatically, doubling each decade.

tion in ovarian function at the time of menopause for women has substantial physiologic consequences, including an accelerated loss of bone mass, sleep and behavioral changes, vaginal atrophy and the loss of fertility. Andropause can also have profound effects on physical health and well-being in men, particularly on mood and libido and some even experience sweating and hot flashes at night. But the difference is that men experience a more gradual and *incomplete* loss of testicular function with increasing age (many men can sire children well into older age), resulting in reduced testosterone and sperm production.

TESTOSTERONE REPLACEMENT THERAPY

Men diagnosed with hypogonadism are good candidates for testosterone replacement therapy. However, only about five percent of the estimated four to five million American men with hypogonadism currently receive TRT.

Major studies of TRT in hypogonadal men ages 15 to 65 years were conducted at the University of Utah, Johns Hopkins University, and Karolinska Hospital in Stockholm Sweden. Overall, treatment resulted in normalization of morning testosterone levels in 92 percent of the 94 patients who completed the trials.

Another eight-week study of 29 patients produced notable improvements in erectile function, libido and mood, and decreases in complaints of fatigue.

Men undergoing menopause have also benefited from TRT. One study of men over 50 who received the hormone found that it renewed strength, improved balance, increased red blood cell count, increased libido, and lowered LDL cholesterol. In a double-blind, placebo-controlled, crossover study, 13 healthy elderly men with low testosterone levels were given 100 mg of the hormone a week for three months. Twelve of them experienced behavioral changes such as increased libido and feelings of well-being.

Another study of men aged 57 to 75 found that testosterone supplements likewise increased red blood cell count and lowered LDL cholesterol as well as overall cholesterol levels. Of the 13 men in the study who were receiving testosterone (as compared to a control group who were receiving a placebo), 12 could predict that they were, in fact, getting the actual supplement, because they felt more aggressive and energetic at work. In addition, the men reported better sexual performance, initiation of sexual intercourse, and increased ability to maintain an erection.

Dr. Michael Perring, medical director of the Optimal Health Clinic in London, which specializes in hormone replacement therapies, has seen over 800 patients with symptoms of andropause. Perring believes that the benefits of testosterone replacement therapy in conjunction with other hormone precursors such as DHEA, are beneficial to men who have demonstrably low testosterone levels for their age. But he stresses the importance of a *full* patient assessment, including a careful history, clinical examination, and endocrine, biochemical and hematological profiles before embarking on therapeutic interventions.

In addition, Perring points out that an individual's lifestyle, including physical, emotional and sexual factors, can put strain on the prostate. "The lifestyles of men attending the clinic suggest a high prevalence of stress either in the workplace or at home, with poor communication within the primary relationship. There may be excessive alcohol intake, high cigarette consumption, and a sedentary job with inadequate or inappropriate exercise. The total and HDL cholesterol levels may be elevated with a diet that is erratic, and imbalanced by too much saturated fat and insufficient fresh fruit, vegetables and fibre."

Numerous studies have found correlations between low testosterone levels and higher risks of cardiovascular disease. Men who have had heart attacks tend to have low testosterone levels, according to Dr. Gerald Phillips of Columbia University Medical School. Phillips studied 55 men undergoing X-ray exams of their arteries and found that those with low testosterone levels had higher degrees of heart disease. He also found that men with higher testosterone levels also had higher protective HDL cholesterol levels.

Another study demonstrating the positive effects of testosterone on heart disease was conducted by Dr. Maurice Lesser. He studied the effect of testosterone injections in 100 individuals with angina pectoris—caused by a spasm or blockage of arteries in the heart. Ninety-one of the 100 showed "moderate to marked" improvement in chest pain, with both the frequency and severity of heart attacks reduced. Only nine showed no improvement at all.

Advocates of human growth hormone in elderly men are also focusing on testosterone replacement therapy because of its comparative inexpensiveness and bone-strengthening qualities. After age 60, hip fracture rates in men increase dramatically. Short-term studies with testosterone on mildly deficient elderly males have reported beneficial effects on lean body mass and muscle. According to Dr. Fran Kaiser, associate director of geriatric medicine at St. Louis University School of Medicine, hypogonadal males are more than six times as likely to break a hip during a fall as those with normal testosterone levels.

Administration of Testosterone

Most physicians today prefer to use pure natural testosterone, which may be administered by intramuscular injections, suppositories, a patch attached to the scrotum, a cream applied to the scrotum, oral micronized capsules or sublingual lozenges. There are also experimental forms which include pellets that are implanted under the skin. Administration of testosterone in the form of a percutaneous gel (absorbed by skin into the bloodstream) is currently used in Europe and has been shown to be very effective in mimicking the natural mode. The least effective method seems to be via the oral route, in that studies have shown the testosterone to inactivate. Synthetic testosterones such as methyl testosterone are not recommended because of their link to liver damage.

Testosterone for Women

Women's ovaries and adrenal glands do provide a modest amount of testosterone—one-tenth to one-twelfth in the blood.

Androderm

There have been significant advances in testosterone replacement delivery systems. A new product recently released by SmithKline Beecham Pharmaceuticals called Androderm, is a testosterone transdermal system that is used to restore male hormonal balance at physiologic levels mimicking the natural diural testosterone, DHT and estradiol cycles. The patch can be worn on upper arms, thighs, back or abdomen, and this convenient once-a-day application replaces the peaks and valleys associated with intramuscular injections, as well as the previous generation of patches that had to be placed on the testes, with the need for frequent replacement after bathing and so on. The common applications for this type of therapy are to improve libido, erectile function, energy and mood.

When the ovaries shut down during menopause, the quantity is cut in half. Women who opt for estrogen replacement therapy (ERT) usually notice a lessening of hot flashes and other symptoms. However, a small number of women do not. Researchers believe that these women may be more sensitive to the accompanying loss of testosterone. Dr. John Moran of the Optimal Health Clinic in London has pioneered hormone replacement therapy over the past few years, prescribing testosterone to men and women as well. He has noticed that many women respond positively when a dash of testosterone is added to their ERT program. Notably, libido and energy seem to be replenished.

However, more research is needed to determine if the benefits outweigh the risks. Possible side effects can range from masculinization, including unnatural body hair growth and deep voice to acne, oily skin, an increase in blood pressure, and an increase in risk of heart disease.

A WORD ABOUT TESTICULAR CANCER

While prostate cancer usually hits men after the age of 50, testicular cancer is the most common malignancy diagnosed in men between ages 20 and 35. However, this type of cancer is not common, accounting for one percent of cancers in men.

Unlike prostrate cancer, testicular cancer is virtually symptomless. Some men experience a dull ache or a sensation of heaviness in the lower abdomen or groin area. But even if no pain exists, it is important to do a monthly self-exam.

- Perform the exam after a warm bath or when the scrotal skin is relaxed.
- Massage the surface of the testicle lightly, using both hands. Remember to check both testicles.
- If you experience any pain, feel any lumps or hardness, or notice that one testicle is larger than the other, consult your physician. He may administer blood tests and/or an ultrasound to find the problem.

Diet and exercise don't play much of a role in prevention of testicular cancer. The most important measure a man can take to detect any cancers early is self-examination.

THE PROSTATE AND PROSTATE CANCER

The prostate gland, otherwise known as the "male breast" because of some of its parallels to the mammary gland in women, is about the size of a chestnut, contains about 70 percent glandular tissue and 30 percent fibromuscular tissue, weighs less than an ounce, and plays a significant role in the male reproductive system. Responsible for the production of semen, the prostate adds fluid to the sperm to power it during ejaculation and increase its mobility. It also provides a potassium- and enzyme-rich fluid that bathes and nourishes the sperm for good health, and serves as its storage area.

The prostate sits just below the urinary bladder in the bottom of the pelvis, surrounding the urethra. All during a man's life, the prostate continues to grow. At puberty it reaches adult size; around the age of 25 it goes through a second stage of growth; and it enlarges again between the ages of 40 and 50. It is in the last stage that the prostate gland may cause problems.

> Of men aged 70, over 50 percent will have an enlarged prostate gland. And by the age 80, the number goes up to 80 percent.

These problems have become so prevalent that cancer of the prostate has become the second most diagnosed malignancy in men. Nearly 200,000 men were diagnosed with prostate cancer in 1995, and close to 50,000 men will die as a result of it. It is the second leading killer of men after heart disease. However, very few of these cases occur in men under the age of 50. And the risk for African-American men, overall, is substantially higher, perhaps due to a diet higher in saturated fat.

The best way to detect prostate enlargement early is to have a routine physical exam of the prostate after age 40 and a PSA blood test (discussed later in this chapter). However, because first symptoms of prostrate cancer are so vague, 90 percent of these cancers go undetected. Therefore, it is important to familiarize yourself with the prostate and signs of abnormality in order to spot cancers before they spread beyond the easily treated stage.

Some symptoms of prostate enlargement include:

- frequent daytime and nighttime urination
- slight pain or a burning sensation during urination
- dribbling and difficulty starting or stopping urine flow
- standing a long time before urination
- leakage of urine
- straining to empty your bladder
- blood in the urine
- inflammation or swelling
- decreased sexual activity/painful intercourse
- back pain

Three of the most common problems associated with the prostate are infection, enlargement and cancer. The condition known as benign prostate hyperplasia (BPH), the medical term for a non-cancerous enlarged prostate, involves an infection that usually starts in some other part of the body and travels to the prostrate. BPH can be also be caused by an inflammation (prostatitis), a benign tumor, or even a dietary or nutritional imbalance. The prostate swells and pinches off urine flow to the urethra, and if not treated immediately can completely block the flow of urine. This squeezing of the urethra causes painful constriction and an excess of urine in the bladder. The bladder then becomes infected, passing the infection on to the kidneys. Some researchers believe this enlargement may be caused by a reduced production of testosterone with age, coupled with increased production of testosterone in the form of DHT (dihydrotestosterone). DHT is what causes baldness in men and overproduction of cells in the prostate.

The PSA Blood Test: Lifesaving Information

In addition to the digital rectal exam (DRE), where a physician feels the back of the prostate with his fingers, the Prostate Specific Antigen (PSA) blood test significantly increases the ability to detect cancers and identify any abnormalities early, even before they can be felt on the exam. A recent study published in the *Journal of the American Medical Association* suggests that "a combination of PSA testing and DRE may nearly double the detection rate for localized prostate cancer . . ."

The PSA is a test of an enzyme produced by normal and cancerous prostate cells. Normally, a small amount of PSA is constantly released into the bloodstream. When the prostate is irritated or damaged, larger amounts of PSA can be detected by the blood test, suggesting an increased possibility of having cancer.

The normal range of a healthy PSA level is 0.0 to 4.0. Some PSA tests have the upper limit of normal as 2.5, depending on the type of test administered. Men with prostate cancer usually have PSA levels in the 10s or 20s, and sometimes as high as the hundreds or thousands, indicating that the cancer may have spread to the bones or lymph nodes. However, an elevated PSA level doesn't always indicate cancer. Causes can include inflammation or infection of the prostate, simple enlargement or BPH, prostate stones, a recent urinary procedure, a recent prostate biopsy or prostate or bladder surgery. Also, because the test is organ-specific, non-urinary infections such as the flu will not affect PSA level.

Most physicians recommend both the prostate exam and the PSA test once a year after the age of 50. Perring recommends three yearly ultrasounds in addition to a PSA test every six months.

Treatments for Prostate Disorders

The standard treatment for prostate cancers are radical prostectomy (total removal of the prostate gland) and radiation therapy. But both treatments can cause serious side effects such as impotence and urinary incontinence. According to a review conducted by the Patient Outcomes Research Team (PORT), 25 percent of men after surgery and six percent of men after radiation suffer from incontinence. And about 85 percent of men after surgery and 40 percent after radiation reported changes in sexual function.

Although radiation and surgery may be the only alternative for advanced prostate disorders, drugs such as Finasteride and Terazosin are available to treat prostate enlargement without an operation.

Finasteride has been shown to shrink the prostate by blocking the activity of an enzyme that converts testosterone into DHT, which is responsible for overproduction of prostate cells and enlargement. However, the results which can take anywhere from three to six months, have been mixed. A study of 895 men conducted at 25 medical centers across the U.S. found that 50 percent of men tested experienced an overall reduction in BPH. Other studies have shown a less than 50 percent reduction rate or no effect—positive or negative—on prostate cancer.

Note that a problem with Finasteride is that it reduces PSA level, which can complicate an accurate reading on the blood test. According to Dr. Jerome Richie, professor of surgery at Harvard and chief of urology at Brigham and Women's Hospital, if PSA levels have not dropped by one-third to one-half after taking Finasteride for several months, it is possible that cancer may be present.

The other drug often prescribed for BPH is Terazosin, an alpha-blocker drug—it works by alleviating some of the most troublesome symptoms of BPH by relaxing muscle tissue and deconstricting urine flow. Studies have shown that Terazosin can produce results in a few weeks and doesn't affect PSA levels. Something common to both drugs is that once you stop taking them prostate symptoms return.

Preventing Prostate Problems

Diet and lifestyle play a critical role in the health of the prostate. Research points to a sedentary lifestyle, a diet high in fat and low in fiber with an abundance of sugar and processed foods, and excessive intake of alcohol and caffeine as the main cause of many prostate disorders. Dr. James Balch reported in *The Journal of Longevity Research* that "the evidence that diet and lifestyle are important comes from the observation of health patterns in many underdeveloped countries, where unrefined, high-fiber diets and physical activity typify daily life—and where prostate ailments are extremely rare."

It is imperative that men take a preventative approach towards prostate care. Of course, not smoking and drinking little or no alcohol are obvious initiatives for maintaining overall health. Here are some of the other dietary and lifestyle changes that we recommend:

Lower cholesterol. The American Heart Association recommends lowering total blood cholesterol levels to no more than 200 mg/deciliter of blood. Enlarged prostate tissue is high in cholesterol, and lowering levels seems to improve symptoms.

Eat less fat. Some researchers believe that fat actually triggers prostate disease and can speed its growth. In particular, red meat, dairy products and fried foods are red light areas. Countries with low-fat diets, such as Japan, have a notably lower prostate cancer rate than those of western countries, with their much higher-fat diets. Another major reason for Japan's lower rate may be a high soybean intake, which researchers strongly believe inhibits prostate growth and cancers in general.

As with breast cancer, high fat intake increases the risk of prostate cancer. However, high-fat diets appear to be associated only with aggressive, rapidly developing prostate cancer, and not with the much more common localized, slow-growing form that often remains dormant for years.

Avoid red meat and dairy foods.   Some studies have indicated that the fatty alpha-linolenic acid might be a strong link in stimulating tumor growth. Red meat and dairy foods are high in alpha-linolenic acid and low in linolenic acid, a polysaturated fat abundant in corn, safflower, soybean and sunflower oils. Researchers believe the imbalance of these two fats that may contribute to tumor growth.

Eat more vegetables.   Cruciferous vegetables such as broccoli, cabbage, cauliflower, brussel sprouts, Swiss chard, kale, spinach, beets, carrots, sweet potatoes and yams, all contain powerful anticancer nutrients. These foods are high in beta-carotene, which has been shown to reduce and/or slow rapid cell growth in cancers. In order to reduce your risk of cancer, it is important to eat five to ten servings of fresh fruit and vegetables a day, every day, not just once in a while.

Get enough zinc.   Studies show that men with genitourinary problems tend to be zinc deficient and should be supplementing or eating foods rich in the mineral. In fact, a healthy prostate gland normally contains about 10 times more zinc than any other organ in the body! *The Journal of Steroid Biochemistry* reported that zinc prevents the hormonal action that causes prostate enlargement. Furthermore, it has an antibacterial factor that kills organisms causing urinary infections, and, aside from being critical to testosterone synthesis and sperm formation, zinc is essential to healthy prostate functioning. When zinc is administered orally, Dr. Gary Evans and Dr. E. C. Johnson recommend, in an article in the *Journal of Nutrition*, taking the nutrient pyridoxine in conjunction, because it is essential in converting zinc to a form readily used by the prostate.

Vitamin A and E   are known as "protector nutrients" that have an exceptional ability to aid in recovery from prostate ailments. Both vitamins also play a significant role in sustaining and enhancing the immune system.

Vitamin B6   enhances zinc absorption and helps combat the adverse effects of too much prolactin. Increased prolactin levels in men over 40 can contribute to the development of tumors in the prostate.

Selenium   Early research points to a relationship between increased selenium intake and a reduced risk for developing prostate cancer. Selenium also fights the noxious effects of cadmium, found in cigarettes and beverages and foods such as coffee, tea, soft drinks, seafood—and in the atmosphere (car batteries), which have been shown to cause prostate enlargement in males.

Magnesium   is helpful for benign prostate problems and prostatitis. It improves muscle function, muscle relaxation and contraction, and aids the immune system in fighting off infection. However, it is important to balance high doses of magnesium with vitamin B6.

Lycopene is the natural substance that gives tomatoes their red color. It is a very powerful anticancer chemical that has been shown to prevent and slow down the growth of cancer cells. Specifically, a study indicated that lycopene intake reduced the risk of prostate cancer considerably, the benefit increasing with the number of servings consumed per week. Also, the study found that in addition to tomatoes with the skin on, strawberries also lowered prostate-cancer risk.

Saw palmetto extract   (Serenoa repens) The saw palmetto berry can be found in health food stores and has been used in France under the name Permixon since 1982. Studies have shown it to be a valuable nutritional supplement for BPH and prostatitis with no significant side effects. Its effectiveness is in limiting the conversion of testosterone to DHT. *The British Journal of Clinical Pharmacology* reported that Saw palmetto contains sterol-like compounds that inhibit the formation of DHT, which contributes to an enlarged prostate. Instead of being used by the body, DHT is broken down and excreted. Saw palmetto is also known as a mild aphrodisiac, which can help restore reduced libidos.

Evergreen tree extract (Pygeum africanum) The evergreen tree is indigenous to Africa, and the bark which contains anti-inflammatory and antibacterial substances, has long been used to treat urinary tract disorders. It is sold in health food stores and has shown to be extremely effective when taken in combination with Saw palmetto extract or stinging nettles. It can reduce prostate inflammation and pain and throbbing, increase sperm count, improve urinary flow, help in achieving and sustaining of erections and improve sexual vigor.

Exercise, exercise Men who exercise for at least an hour a day are at significantly less risk for prostate cancer than men who don't (see Chapter 11). Drink a lot of steam-distilled water. Two to three quarts of water a day stimulates urine flow and helps prevent retention, cystitis and kidney infection. Also, vigorous exercise on a routine basis, has proven to maintain free circulating testosterone in the body.

Other helpful nutrients which can prevent and aid in relieving many of the symptoms of an enlarged and inflamed prostate are the three amino acids glycine, alanine and glutamic acid; nettle root extract; and essential fatty acids such as linseed (flax) oil and omega-3 oils found mainly in fish, Panax ginseng, Equisetum arvense (horsetail) and bee pollen.

Although many men experience the positive impact of testosterone on the prostate and genitourinary problems, some men have reported adverse side effects: atrophying of the testicles with prolonged use, a high red blood cell count, depression, fluid retention, reduced sperm count and volume of semen, and a reduction in HDL cholesterol levels. Testosterone supplementation can indeed produce dangerous side effects if administered to men with normal levels. In fact, extra doses will inhibit natural production and may contribute to prostate growth.

The major concern about testosterone is its potential to stimulate and/or accelerate the growth of benign or malignant prostate tumors. The popular hypothesis is that the buildup of testosterone in the form of DHT within the prostate is potentially dangerous. But scientists have not yet concluded if it is DHT that causes prostate disorders. In fact, eliminating or drastically reducing DHT production can be harmful. Some studies have indicated an increase in DHT in the prostate cells of men with BPH, compared to normal prostates of men the same age. But generally, both testosterone and DHT levels decrease with age. Is it the decreasing testosterone and DHT that occurs in aging men with an increase in other hormones—estradiol (a female sex hormone), and prolactin, LH and FSH from the pituitary gland that contributes to the risk of prostate disease? Scientists do not have any definite answers yet.

TESTOSTERONE: LIMITS AND POSSIBLE DANGERS

When contemplating the use of testosterone replacement, the possible risks as well as the benefits must be considered. Of course, the largest concern is the potential to stimulate benign or malignant prostate tumor growth—and to reduce HDL cholesterol levels, which increases the risk of coronary artery disease.

Testosterone supplementation can produce dangerous side effects if administered to men with normal levels. In fact, extra doses will inhibit your own natural production and many contribute to stimulating the growth of preexisting prostrate tumors.

Dr. Adrian Dobs, associate professor of medicine and director of the Endocrinology and Metabolism Clinical Studies Unit at Johns Hopkins University in Baltimore, warns, "You're just going to have the same level. But you're going to be dependent on this medication to get it, as opposed to your own body making it." An easy way for men with normal levels of the hormone to ensure proper testosterone levels in the body is to exercise.

Meanwhile, additional studies have found correlations between low testosterone levels and higher risks of cardiovascular disease, suggesting another reason for aging hypogonadal men to consider testosterone supplements as an anti-aging treatment.

Chapter 8

The Miracle Minerals: Chromium, Selenium, and Magnesium

Rats treated with chromium supplements lived an average of two and a half years, one-third longer than their normal life span. In humans, that would be the equivalent of extending life from age 75 to age 102.

Selenium supplements can help protect you from cancer, heart disease, infectious viruses, and other signs of rapid aging.

Without enough magnesium, you're running higher than necessary risks of heart failure, heart attack, chronic high blood pressure, osteoporosis, and unstable blood sugar.

Even if you're eating a balanced diet, you may not be getting enough vital minerals. Today we are bombarded with over-processed, low-nutrient foods and polluted environments, all of which make it difficult to get the proper amount of vitamins and minerals we need from diet alone. USDA scientists have estimated that in order to get just 200 micrograms of chromium (the amount that most anti-aging specialists recommend) you'd have to consume over 12,000 calories a day of the typical American diet.

Yet it's not enough simply to start taking supplements. Some forms of mineral supplements are harder for your body to digest or absorb. And, like most substances in the body, minerals don't act alone. They engage in a complicated series of transactions with other minerals, vitamins, and hormones. In order to choose your supplements wisely, you need to know how each one works and how it interacts with the other nutrients you consume.

A study recently published in *The Lancet* reported that elderly people taking multivitamins with minerals had improved immune function and had 50 percent fewer sick days.

CHROMIUM: THE MINERAL THAT BALANCES BLOOD SUGAR

Perhaps the most compelling reason to take chromium supplements is this miracle mineral's effect on your blood sugar. Up to the age of 35, most people's bodies are relatively efficient at processing blood sugar. When you eat something, your digestive process breaks down the food into its component parts: carbohydrates (a combination of carbon and water found in every living thing), protein, vitamins, minerals, fat, and waste.

All of the nutrients pass into your bloodstream, so that your blood can carry them to all of your different body tissues. Anything that can't be used right away is stored, partly as body fat (which is how you gain weight), partly as glycogen, a substance that can be converted into glucose, or blood sugar.

Your body is always striving to keep your blood sugar at a constant level. Whenever the level falls too low—say, if you burn up glucose in vigorous exercise, emotional stress, or heavy thinking—the body draws on glycogen to make up the difference. The substance that the body uses to break down and store blood sugar is insulin, a hormone produced by the pancreas.

In diabetics, this process hits a few roadblocks. Some 10 percent of all diabetics find that their pancreases simply don't produce enough insulin to break down all their blood sugar. They have to take insulin supplements to be able to absorb the nutrients they consume.

However, the other 90 percent of diabetics produce enough insulin—but their bodies resist it. In other words, although the insulin-resistant diabetic's blood is full of insulin, blood-sugar levels continue to remain high. The body's cells are simply not able to use insulin efficiently to process the blood sugar.

There is another category of people who tend to be insulin-resistant—people over the age of 35. The older you get, the less efficient your cells become at using insulin. As a result, your bloodstream has extremely high levels of both blood sugar and insulin—and both substances are extremely bad for your heart, arteries, and metabolism.

> The odds of developing diabetes are about one in nine. Type I or insulin-dependent diabetes typically strikes during puberty. Type II or non-insulin-dependent diabetes typically strikes after age 40.

This condition sets off a vicious cycle. The higher the levels of glucose in your blood, the more insulin your pancreas is stimulated to release. Yet the more insulin that bombards your cells, the less sensitive to it they become. You start needing more and more insulin to get your cells to do their job—resulting in both insulin and blood sugar levels climbing ever higher as you get older.

Scientists estimate that one-quarter of all Americans past middle age have some kind of serious insulin disorder. And one in four Americans may be suffering from mild to severe blood glucose intolerance, also known as carbohydrate insensitivity (trouble digesting carbohydrates). Researchers believe that some 40 million—four out of five—could benefit by including chromium and other insulin-regulating cofactors in their diets.

Chromium picolinate, in particular, was found to be an effective glucose-lowering agent. Some researchers believe that this specific form of chromium works best because of its ability to transport chromium into cells more efficiently.

In a 1992 study done by Dr. Gary Evans of the American Aging Association in San Francisco, Evans fed three groups of rats purified diets supplemented with a different form of chromium. One group received chromium picolinate, one received chromium dinicotinate, and the third received chromic chloride. The results? The group receiving the chromium picolinate achieved an average life span of 45 months—one full year longer than the other two groups, showing a dramatic 36 percent increase in average life span.

In addition, Evans measured the levels of blood sugar in these rats, and it was found to be consistently lower in those receiving the chromium picolinate. Many of the results of this study bear a resemblance to the effects of underfeeding, or administering highly restrictive diets to laboratory animals. However, for humans, underfeeding is hardly a feasible lifestyle option. Taking a chromium supplement, therefore, may produce these same glucose-lowering effects, without the hardship of restrictive caloric intake.

Another important role chromium plays is synthesizing proteins. Insulin eases digested proteins (amino acids) into muscle cells, aiding the development of muscle proteins. Therefore, the more efficient your insulin metabolism, the more muscle you can build.

Other dangers posed by excess insulin and blood sugar in your bloodstream include:

- mature-onset diabetes
- the buildup of arterial "plaque," or atherosclerosis
- an increase in LDL cholesterol
- a consequent greater risk of heart attack and stroke
- falling levels of DHEA (see Chapter 5).

HOW CHROMIUM FIGHTS THE AGING PROCESS

One of the key ways that chromium helps combat aging is by stabilizing your blood sugar levels and improving your insulin's efficiency, so that you need less insulin to process the same amount of blood sugar. In fact, chromium is vital for producing glucose tolerance factor (GTF), the substance on which your insulin depends to do its job. It is this glucose tolerance factor that aids us in turning carbohydrates into glucose. In a recent study, eight people with glucose intolerances were administered 200 micrograms (mcg) of chromium a day for five weeks. Out of those eight, seven showed dramatic improvements in blood sugar levels. Even diabetics may benefit from chromium, but they should consult their physician before taking any supplements.

Ironically, sugar helps destroy chromium at the same time that it calls forth huge surges of insulin. So people whose diet has been high in sugar are even more likely to suffer from insulin resistance—and to be deficient in chromium. (When we say "sugar," we include both processed sugar and high-fructose corn syrup, sweeteners that are added to a wide range of processed foods and beverages.) Moreover, the person who consumes one-third of his or her calories in sugar will suffer three times as great a loss of chromium as the person whose sugar intake makes up only one-tenth of his or her diet. People who have been consuming high amounts of sugar would benefit both by changing their diets and by taking chromium supplements to reverse the damage already done. Even basic everyday stress adds to our body's loss of chromium.

Chromium doesn't just help people who suffer from high blood sugar. It also helps normalize blood-sugar levels of people with a tendency to have low blood sugar. And if your blood sugar is normal, taking chromium will have no effect on it. Chromium's role is not to raise or lower insulin amounts per se, but rather to improve insulin's efficiency, which automatically stabilizes blood-sugar levels.

Efficient insulin also means a more efficient immune system. That's because insulin is the hormone that directs interferon and T lymphocytes (white blood cells, or T cells), substances the body produces to fight disease. Thus chromium also boosts your body's ability to resist infection.

Also, lowering the level of insulin in your blood helps prevent insulin from attacking your artery walls. This in turn prevents atherosclerosis, a condition in which your artery walls are lined with plaque. Animals studies have shown that animals deprived of chromium experience plaque buildup, whereas injections of chromium cause plaque to shrink, so that atherosclerosis is actually reversed.

Chromium apparently works to lower triglycerides and LDL cholesterol while raising HDL cholesterol. A study done in North Carolina showed that in a group of 63 men, two months of supplementation with 600 mcg of chromium per day raised HDL cholesterol levels significantly.

Another study of 23 men who were given 200 mcg of chromium found that their artery-cleansing HDL cholesterol rose by 11 percent. An Israeli study revealed that doses of 250 mcg of chromium per day sent the HDL levels of elderly heart disease patients rising by about 20 percent. And an eight-week study at Auburn University in Alabama found that men with low cholesterol who received 200 daily mcg of niacin-bound chromium experienced a 14 percent drop in their total cholesterol.

Finally, chromium seems to play a key role in preventing heart disease. For three decades, researchers have known that people who died of heart disease had abnormally low levels of chromium in their aortas. A recent study found that people who suffered from heart disease might have up to 40 percent less chromium in their blood than healthy people.

TAKING CHROMIUM SUPPLEMENTS

In determining whether you are chromium deficient, some specific telltale signs to look for or ask your doctor about are:

- blood tests that show high insulin levels
- low HDL cholesterol levels

- high triglyceride levels
- fatigue
- frequent urination
- gaining weight

When taking chromium supplements, look for an organic rather than an inorganic supplement. Your body will have a far easier time absorbing the organic chromium and will make more efficient use of it. Another good idea is to supplement your diet with a team of nutrients including chromium, rather than just taking chromium on its own, since certain groups of nutrients work better together than alone.

Our grandmothers and grandfathers probably got more chromium from their diets than we do, just from cooking in those old cast-iron kettles; however, even today, in the age of Tupperware and TV dinners, we have a variety of wholesome foods and herbs to choose from which will help us increase our daily chromium intakes.

Brewer's yeast is one good source of chromium. Other food sources to check out and add to your daily menu should include whole grains, meats, grape juice, orange juice, broccoli, black pepper, thyme, and even that summertime favorite, barbecue sauce! Niacin-bound chromium is also an easily digestible form (brands include ChromeMate and Solgar GTF). However, chromium chloride, the inorganic form in which most multivitamins contain chromium, is not a particularly effective way to take your supplement.

Many anti-aging scientists generally recommend about 200 mcg for adults and teenagers. Diabetics, however, should not alter their intake of chromium without consulting their physicians; the supplement might affect their need for insulin.

Within a few days or weeks, you may notice the supplement's effect on your blood sugar. Within a few weeks or months, you'll be getting the benefits of chromium on your cholesterol levels and triglycerides.

It's unlikely that you could overdose on chromium, since there's no record of anyone ever experiencing a toxic or even an uncomfortable dose. Conceivably, you could take 300 times the recommended dose without ill effect. However, the mineral is

Chromium

Benefits	Helps to balance blood sugar levels, lowers triglyceride and "bad" cholesterol levels, prevents heart disease
Cautions	No known toxicity
Food sources	Brewer's yeast, whole grains, meat, orange and grape juice, broccoli, thyme

being stored in your liver and kidneys, so you might want to exercise reasonable caution and check your doctor's recommendations.

It's ironic that many of the symptoms of chromium deficiency—insulin resistance, mature-onset diabetes, rising cholesterol and triglyceride levels—are often mistaken for the symptoms of "normal" aging.

SELENIUM: THE ANTIVIRUS SUPPLEMENT

Selenium offers a number of benefits. The most striking may be that it helps keep our immune systems functioning at youthful levels of effectiveness.

Orville Levander and Melinda Beck of the University of North Carolina found a particularly dramatic example of selenium's antivirus action. They experimented on mice infected with a normally harmless virus, artificially lowering the mice's selenium levels. Suddenly, the "harmless" virus turned virulent, breaking out of the cells where it had been contained and aggressively attacking the muscles of the heart. Meanwhile, mice who maintained high levels of selenium and vitamin E continued to coexist peacefully with the virus.

Will Taylor of the University of Georgia College of Pharmacy suggests that selenium may be a powerful weapon in the fight against AIDS. He points out that the HIV virus that causes AIDS depletes selenium. When a cell's selenium supply is still high, the HIV virus creates a protein to repress itself. But when selenium levels have been depleted, the virus replicates itself and breaks out of its cells to search for more selenium.

Dr. Gerhard Schrauzer, professor of biochemistry at the University of California, San Diego, has noticed a similar phenomenon. "As long as there is enough selenium around in the cells, the virus behaves itself," he comments. "When the selenium is depleted, then the virus can switch into a high rate of replication and cause full-blown AIDS."

This news about selenium's pro-immune properties is significant for the elderly as well as for people with AIDS. As we've seen, declining immunity is one of the hallmarks of aging, leaving older people vulnerable to cancer, heart disease, and other illnesses. But a University of Brussels team of researchers found that giving elderly patients 100 daily mcg of selenium for six months caused the lymphocyte response to mitogens (invaders) to increase by some 79 percent, reaching levels typically found in the young.

Other studies have also found selenium to strengthen the immune system. The mineral not only stimulates lymphocytes to produce more antibodies, but it also encourages the production of phagocytes—Pac-Man-like entities that literally gobble up cancer cells, bacteria, and viruses.

How Selenium Fights Aging

After age 60, our selenium levels drop by 7 percent; after age 75, they drop by 24 percent. Yet high selenium levels can help keep us healthy in a variety of ways.

Selenium helps block cancer. One recent study looked at mice that were likely to develop cancer. Out of all the mice receiving selenium supplements, only 10 percent developed the cancer—compared to the mice not receiving the mineral, an overwhelming 82 percent did develop the disease. In animals, selenium has been shown to block up to 100 percent of some types of tumors.

In worldwide studies, the lowest rates of cancer are found in those countries with the highest concentrations of selenium in food, water, and soil. In fact, it was found that there were fewer instances of cancer of the lung, rectum, bladder, esophagus, cervix, and uterus in areas that were geologically rich in selenium. Likewise, in national studies, those parts of the United States high in selenium—like South Dakota—are extremely low in cancer, whereas low-selenium areas—like Ohio—are among the most cancer-prone regions of the country.

Looking in other parts of the globe, it was found that in the Keshan region of China, a large selenium depleted area, many women and children suffer from intense selenium deficiencies that make them much more susceptible to diseases that damage heart muscles and can result in sudden heart failure.

Specific studies on selenium and cancer bear out the finding that the mineral helps prevent the disease. A study of 1700 elderly people conducted by the University of Arizona found that those with the lowest levels of selenium in their blood were most likely to have polyps, small growths that may lead to colon cancer; one-third of those with polyps had the lowest levels of selenium in the group, while only nine percent of those with the highest levels of selenium had polyps. And a Dutch study of 3,000 older people found that those with higher levels of selenium had only half as great a chance of getting cancer as their low-selenium counterparts.

Selenium reduces heart disease. Apparently, selenium prevents blood platelets from sticking together, reducing the risk of blood clots, heart attack, and stroke. It's also a powerful antioxidant, blocking the oxidation of LDL cholesterol. Scientists have long suspected that low levels of selenium make you more vulnerable to heart disease of various types. Now a large-scale Finnish study has borne this out. According to the Finnish researchers, people with the lowest levels of selenium were three times more likely to die of heart disease than those with the highest levels of the mineral. Another study found that the lower a person's levels of selenium, the greater the degree of blockage in the arteries he or she was likely to have.

Blocked arteries can threaten your health in two ways. Both

involve vasospasms, in which arteries suddenly contract, as a result of alcohol consumption, smoking, stress, or the consumption of a fatty substance. (Because fatty foods take several hours to digest, the vasospasm is likely to come some time after the meal or snack.) A spasm in a blocked artery might result either in partial shutoff of blood flow and oxygen supply to a part of the body, or in total shutoff. Partial shutoff results in stroke; total shutoff generally produces cardiac arrest—a heart attack.

Thus, by preventing platelets from clumping together, selenium helps keep your arteries unclogged, preventing vasospasms and their dire effects. Of course, vitamins E and C and niacin are also vital in this process, and all four substances work together to eliminate atherosclerotic plaque.

Another interesting use of regional studies found a correlation between the so-called "Stroke Belt"—Georgia and the Carolinas, where the stroke rate is by far the highest in the U.S.—and low levels of selenium in the soil and water. (Low-selenium areas in the United States include New England, western Oregon, and parts of the mid-west, while high-selenium areas include Colorado, Kansas, Nebraska, North and South Dakota, and Wyoming.)

Selenium is a powerful antioxidant that helps detoxify your body. Along with the antioxidant glutathione, selenium works to bind the toxic heavy metals mercury, lead, and cadmium in a process called chelation, picking them up and carrying them into the urine, where they can be flushed out of the system. Selenium also helps detoxify peroxidized fats, alcohol, tobacco smoke, and drugs. The anti-cancer medication Adriamycin is often administered with selenium, which helps to modify its toxic side effects without diminishing its ability to fight cancer.

Selenium helps to relieve anxiety. A double-blind study conducted by psychologists David Benton and Richard Cook of University College, Swansea, Wales, found that of the 50 healthy men and women who got 100 mcg of selenium a day, most felt less anxious, depressed, and tired after only five weeks. The subjects who had been most deficient in selenium enjoyed the most dramatic improvements, suggesting that restoring their selenium

Selenium

Benefits	Reduces heart disease, blocks cancer, acts as a powerful antioxidant, enhances immune function.
Cautions	High dosages (1000 mg a day or more) may result in raised serum cholesterol level, an increase in malignant tumors, or premature death
Food sources	Brazil nuts, grains, meat, garlic, seafood

levels had eased their mental states and increased their energy. Other studies have found that when the elderly are given selenium plus vitamin E or another antioxidant, they notice an improvement in mood and mental ability, as well as receiving better blood flow to the brain.

Taking Selenium Supplements

You can get natural selenium in grains, sunflower seeds, meat, garlic, and seafood, particularly tuna, swordfish, and oysters. The best natural source of selenium, however, is Brazil nuts in the shell. (The nuts that are sold already shelled come from a different part of Brazil, one with less selenium in the soil.) Just one unshelled nut contains about 100 mcg of selenium.

If you're not going to eat Brazil nuts every day, then you do need a supplement of 100-200 mcg a day, to protect against cancer as well as for general anti-aging benefits. High doses of selenium can be toxic—there have been cases where doses over 1,000 mcg per day have resulted in complications ranging from elevated serum cholesterol levels to an increase in malignant tumors, to premature death.

Still, Japanese fishers, who get a high quantity of selenium in their seafood diets, consume a relatively high dosage of 500 mcg of selenium a day without apparent harm. Again, check with your doctor. Many anti-aging experts are themselves supplementing with 100-200 mcg a day.

MAGNESIUM: THE CALCIUM-LOVER'S FRIEND

"Animals starved of magnesium are nearly perfect specimens of accelerated aging," say French researchers, and the symptoms of a magnesium deficiency do indeed read like a catalog of the woes of old age: clogged arteries, irregular heartbeat, vulnerability to heart attack, high blood pressure, osteoporosis, resistance to insulin and the concomitant threat of diabetes. Researchers point out that only one American in four gets the USDA's Recommended Daily Allowance of this key mineral, an amount that most nutritionists believe is already too low. Some two-thirds of the elderly, who need magnesium the most, consume less than 75 percent of the RDA. But not only the elderly need to be concerned about a magnesium deficiency; also, diabetics, people on low-calorie diets, alcoholics, people with fat malabsorption problems, those who perform strenuous exercise and those who are taking prescribed heart medications need to be aware of their magnesium intakes and make sure that they are supplementing if they are deficient.

Animal studies suggest that the lower the levels of magnesium, the more rapidly the animal ages and the sooner it is likely to die. Young animals who are deprived of magnesium develop vascular changes and neuromuscular abnormalities that resemble the health problems of aging animals—yet when these younger animals are given magnesium supplements their aging symptoms disappear.

Clearly, magnesium protects the cells against aging in a variety of ways. Not only does it protect against heart disease, fight chronic fatigue syndrome. lower blood pressure, prevent recurring kidney stones, ward off diabetes and strengthen muscles, but central to its importance is its ability to work with calcium to keep bones strong and prevent osteoporosis.

Although many Americans are now familiar with the need to take calcium supplements, particularly with increasing age, far fewer know about the importance of magnesium as a mineral that works with calcium (and with vitamin D) to keep bones strong. According to Dr. Mildred Seelig, adjunct professor of nutrition at the University of North Carolina, long-term deficiencies in magnesium as well as in calcium can trigger osteoporosis, particularly in women.

Without magnesium, the elderly person taking calcium supplements is at risk of blood clots, heart attack, and stroke. Ideally, you should take half as much magnesium as calcium, but many older people are getting only one-fourth as much, especially if they're taking calcium supplements. Thus, a person taking 1,200 mg of calcium daily needs 600 mg of magnesium—perhaps more if the diet is high in fat and sugar.

While calcium supplements help ease the symptoms of women suffering from premenstrual syndrome (PMS), magnesium would both help the calcium work better and make its own contribution to their relief. Refined sugar and dairy products—which many women crave during the premenstrual time—actually interfere with the absorption of magnesium, creating a deficiency that can exacerbate PMS symptoms. The anxiety, irritability, and mood swings common to this time may perhaps be attributed to insufficient magnesium, for it is needed to manufacture dopamine, a key neurotransmitter that helps the brain function. Dopamine is the chemical on which all other brain chemicals depend, and increasing dopamine levels in the brain may act like a natural tranquilizer and mood elevator. Magnesium's general antioxidant properties might also help to bring relief to the premenstrual time.

How Magnesium Fights Aging

Magnesium is a powerful antioxidant that curbs free radical activity. Without magnesium, cell membranes become rigid and more vulnerable to free radicals, destroying the integrity of the cell and disrupting proper calcium flow. Long-term magnesium deficiency also leads to falling levels of vitamin E, perhaps because the E is used up in fending off the free radicals "invited in" by the magnesium deficiency. Animals deprived of magnesium also seem to produce cytokines, inflammatory substances that in turn create more free radicals and further cell damage.

Perhaps the most important antioxidant role of magnesium is played at the level of the mitochondria, the "energy factories" of the cell. Mitochondria are particularly vital to the heart, as that organ requires such a great deal of energy to function properly. Apparently, a shortage of magnesium leads directly to damage in the mitochondria, which some scientists believe is a significant mechanism of aging.

It's not surprising, then, that elderly people with low magnesium are far more likely to have heart disease, according to "about 20 worldwide population studies" cited by National Institute of Health researcher Dr. Ronald Elin. Also, a survey of seven studies involving 1,301 heart attack patients found that 8.2 percent of those who did not receive magnesium supplementation died, while the mortality rate of those who received the mineral intravenously while recuperating was only 3.8 percent. Magnesium protects the heart in a number of ways:

- *Magnesium acts as a gatekeeper*, regulating the amount of calcium needed to maintain a steady heartbeat. Thus a deficiency in magnesium can produce heartbeat abnormalities that may lead to death.
- *Magnesium prevents spasm of the coronary artery.* As we saw when we looked at selenium, arterial spasms can be set off by tobacco smoke, alcohol, fatty foods, and stress; such spasms can lead to stroke and heart attack.
- *Magnesium inhibits the formation of blood clots.* According to Dr. Jerry Nadler of the City of Hope Medical Center in Duarte, California, magnesium inhibits the release of thromboxane, a substance that makes blood platelets "stickier" and more likely to clot.

In one study of a cardiac care unit, some 53 percent of the heart patients there were found to have low magnesium levels. Another study found that a person's magnesium level could be used to predict whether he or she would live or die in the event of a heart attack. A 10-year study of 2,812 men in Wales found that those with low-magnesium diets had a one-and-one-half times greater risk of sudden death from heart attacks than those who consumed only 33 percent more magnesium. And those on a high-magnesium diet were only half as likely to have cardiovascular problems of any kind, including nonfatal heart attacks, stroke, angina (chest pain), or heart surgery. The vital difference in magnesium intake was strikingly low: 30 mg, or about the amount found in half an ounce of almonds. Magnesium also appears to help lower blood pressure. A four-year study of 58,000 women found that those who consumed 800 mg of calcium in conjunction with 300 mg of magnesium reduced their chances of developing high blood pressure by one third! Research has also shown that people with already high blood pressure have much more success controlling their conditions when taking additional magnesium.

A Harvard University study found that people with low magnesium levels were more apt to have high blood pressure, while a Swedish study found that administering 360 mg of daily magnesium to patients produced dramatic drops in blood pressure: from an average of 154 to 146 for systolic (the upper number) and from an average of 100 to 82 for diastolic (the lower number).

A new test reported in *Modern Medicine* may help better predict which healthy patients may develop heart disease or stroke later in life. According to Dr. Lewis Kuller, professor and chairman of the department of epidemiology at the University of Pittsburgh, the ankle-brachial (A-B) test can measure the difference in systolic blood pressure between the legs and arms.

It seems that people with low A-B blood pressure, according to Dr. Kuller, were found to have a greater risk of heart attack, stroke, and peripheral vascular disease within the succeeding few years. As vascular disease develops in the lower body, it begins to develop in the cerebral system and coronary arteries as well.

While the A-B test is still in its early stages, Dr. Kuller believes that physicians will soon be able to predict whether a person is at risk for a heart attack or stroke within the following two to three years.

Like selenium, magnesium is also a key mineral in the prevention and possibly the reversal of diabetes. Italian researchers found that supplements of 4,500 mg of magnesium per day for four weeks dramatically improved glucose tolerance in elderly people. Diabetics often have low magnesium levels in their cells and blood, and some researchers believe that they might even have a defect in the metabolism of magnesium that exacerbates the disease. Even if you're not a diabetic, you're likely to suffer from insulin resistance if you're low in magnesium: one recent study found that normal, healthy adults developed a 25 percent greater insulin resistance on a magnesium-deficient diet. Presumably, magnesium supplements would correspondingly lower insulin resistance.

Another benefit of taking magnesium is the relief it can bring to chronic fatigue syndrome (CFS). In a study of 32 people afflicted with CFS, one group received magnesium supplements for two weeks, while the other received a placebo. In the group receiving the additional mineral in their diet, 12 out of the 15 people reported feeling better, while only 3 out of the 17 in the placebo group reported feeling any better.

Recent studies have pointed towards evidence that magnesium even helps build stronger muscles. In a study done at the Exercise and Sport Science lab in Seattle, Washington, scientists put 26 formerly inactive people on a weight-lifting program for two weeks. One group was administered 507 mg of magnesium per day, while the other group only received 246 mg. The group receiving the higher dosage reported an average 26 percent increase in strength, while the group receiving the lesser amount only reported an average increase of 11 percent. One reason researchers believe magnesium to be such a muscle builder lies in its unique ability to help synthesize proteins.

Magnesium has also been found to prevent the recurrence of painful kidney stones. The pain and discomfort associated with the long, drawn out passing of one of these stones is an experience most of us would hope to avoid. A Swedish study found that daily magnesium supplementation reduced stone recurrence by an overwhelming 90 percent! It is thought that magnesium alleviates this problem by binding with oxylate, an ingredient found in most kidney stones.

Magnesium

Benefits	Prevents osteoporosis, eases PMS symptoms, acts as an antioxidant, protects against heart disease, lowers blood pressure, prevents diabetes
Cautions	600–700 mg daily may cause diarrhea. People with kidney problems, heart failure or history of heart attacks should consult a physician before considering magnesium supplements.
Food sources	Whole grains, nuts, seeds, legumes

Taking Magnesium Supplements

You can in fact get a great deal of magnesium from food sources: whole grains, nuts, seeds, and legumes. A serving of bran cereal plus some nuts would probably insure you a 300 mg daily dose of magnesium—just the amount recommended by the USDA. If you don't eat magnesium-rich foods, though, you should probably take a 200 to 300 mg supplement each day. A typical multivitamin generally includes only 100 mg of magnesium, so you may need an additional supplement.

Magnesium oxide is the only type of supplement not recommended; most people just don't tolerate it well. You can choose among magnesium chloride, magnesium aspartate, magnesium gluconate, and magnesium lactate.

Note that more than 600 or 700 mg daily of magnesium can cause diarrhea—that's why they use this mineral in milk of magnesia! Most people can tolerate up to 500 mg daily, if they have normal kidney function. People with kidney problems, severe heart failure, or a history of heart attack should definitely consult a physician before considering magnesium supplements.

WORKING WITH THE "MIRACLE MINERALS"

No one yet knows all the possible anti-aging benefits the miracle minerals have to offer. And, as we've seen, they'll affect you differently depending on your current state of health and energy. It's best if you can work with a physician or nutritionist to develop a mineral supplement program that's right for you. Remember to use caution, keep within the recommended doses, and stay aware of how you feel. Learning how to listen to your body and its responses can be one of the most important side effects of your anti-aging campaign!

Chapter 9

The Vital Antioxidants: Vitamins C, E, and A (Beta-Carotene), and CoQ-10

According to the late two-time Nobel Prize-winning scientist Linus Pauling, who lived to the age of 93, we could add 12 to 18 more years onto our lives, by taking 3,200 to 12,000 milligrams of vitamin C a day.

Dr. Eric Rimm, one of the authors of a Harvard study on the role of vitamin E in heart disease found that "The risk for not taking vitamin E was equivalent to the risk of smoking."

Over a hundred studies have shown that people with a high level of beta-carotene in their diet and blood are only about half as likely to develop cancer in the lung, mouth, throat, esophagus, larynx, stomach, breast, or bladder.

Harvard researchers studying some 87,000 female nurses found that a high intake of C cut the risk of heart disease by 20 percent; high doses of E caused the risk to drop by 34 percent; and high levels of beta-carotene reduced heart disease risk by 22 percent. Moreover, high doses of all three vitamins slashed the risk of heart disease by nearly 50 percent.

Coenzyme Q-10 (CoQ-10) helps prevent atherosclerosis, angina, and heart attacks.

Just as supplements of minerals found in your daily diet can improve health and vigor while reducing the risks of aging, megadoses of vitamins can also help stop the aging clock. The most important antioxidant vitamins are vitamin C, vitamin E and vitamin A, or beta-carotene. They are called antioxidants because of their unique ability to deactivate harmful free radicals that accumulate in our bodies, in addition to their ability to maintain the structure and function of our cells.

In essence, oxygen creates these free radicals, be it through our immune system battling foreign substances, or even through

How Antioxidants Work

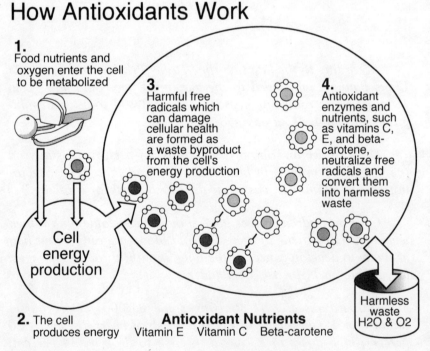

1.
Food nutrients and oxygen enter the cell to be metabolized

3.
Harmful free radicals which can damage cellular health are formed as a waste byproduct from the cell's energy production

4.
Antioxidant enzymes and nutrients, such as vitamins C, E, and beta-carotene, neutralize free radicals and convert them into harmless waste

Cell energy production

2. The cell produces energy

Antioxidant Nutrients
Vitamin E   Vitamin C   Beta-carotene

Harmless waste
H2O & O2

How antioxidants work.

strenuous exercise when we are consuming massive amounts of oxygen into our bodies. It is these antioxidant vitamins that quench the destructive path of free radicals, and stabilize them back into the state of normal, healthy molecules. While the key antioxidant vitamins are C, E, and A, most doctors now recommend supplements of beta-carotene rather than vitamin A itself. Vitamin A is essential to prevent night blindness and the formation of cataracts. It is also important in the development, maintenance, and repair of healthy bones, skin, hair and mucous membranes. Beta-carotene is a substance that your body can use to make its own A, so that it poses none of A's risk of toxicity. However, it's a good idea to consult with a knowledgeable doctor before taking any kind of supplement.

Warning: Vitamin A Associated with Birth Defects

The results of a study published in the *New England Journal of Medicine* indicate that women who take large amounts of preformed vitamin A either prior to pregnancy or in the first few months of pregnancy, are more likely to bear children with birth defects. The study tracked 22,748 pregnant women from three and one-half to five months' gestation until after the baby was born. Babies born to women who consumed more than 10,000 IU (200 percent of the Recommended Daily Value) of preformed vitamin A daily in supplements were 2.4 times more likely to have birth defects than babies born to women who consumed 5,000 IU or less. Of the 339 reported cases of birth defects, 121 were of cranial neural crest origin—defects of the cranium, face, central nervous system, thymus or heart.

Vitamin A's toxicity is something to take quite seriously, however. According to Dr. Robert Russell, professor of medicine and nutrition at Tufts University, too much vitamin A may overwhelm the liver's ability to store it, resulting in symptoms as minor as headaches to the possibility of an enlarged liver. Other toxic side effects of large doses of A include a condition known as hypervitaminosis A, which occurs when too much A accumulates in your body. These toxic effects usually occur through

RDAs and Optimal Doses for Antioxidant Vitamins.

Vitamin	RDA	Optimal Dosage
Vitamin C	60 mg	500–1500 mg
Vitamin E	30 IU (♂ 10 mg/♀ 8mg)	100–400 IU
Beta-carotene	50 IU	10,000 IU
Vitamin A	♂ 1000 mcg ♀ 800 mcg	5,000 IU (Recent research has produced considerable confusion about optimal doses of some of these nutrients.)

consuming an excess amount of vitamin A supplements—not through eating a lot of vitamin A-rich foods. The only food reported to cause ill effects in humans is polar bear liver, which contains 13,000-18,000 IU per gram. The elderly, in particular, are at a higher risk of vitamin A toxicity, due to a decreased clearance of vitamin A from their blood. Therefore, most physicians would recommend beta-carotene as a preferred supplement, but a safe amount of straight vitamin A is believed to be about 5,000 IU—the amount found in most multivitamin supplements.

RECOMMENDED DAILY ALLOWANCES VS. OPTIMUM DAILY ALLOWANCES

Now, it's certainly possible to get enough C, E, and A in your daily diet—if you are measuring "enough" by the U.S. Department of Agriculture's Recommended Daily Allowance (RDA).

Calculated by government officials, RDA standards are just enough to avoid common vitamin deficiency diseases, such as scurvy, rickets, or beri-beri. They do not, however, account for what's needed to maintain maximum health. RDAs are not only too low to reach optimum health, but they can't even be easily obtained from today's foods. What people should be striving for is an optimum daily allowance (ODA), which translates into doses 5 to 100 times higher than RDA requirements.

According to Linus Pauling, the amounts "recommended" to the general public are hardly enough to reap any anti-aging benefits:

> They're quite straightforward about saying that the RDA of vitamin C is the amount that keeps you from dying of scurvy, that the RDA of vitamin B1 is the amount that keeps you from dying of beriberi. These quantities keep people in ordinary poor health. . . . The purpose of RDAs is to keep prisoners in institutions, people in old folks' homes, and children in boarding schools and such from being seriously maltreated through poor nutrition.

And despite RDA standards being so low, a disturbing reality is that many people ages 65 to 75 do not even meet these skimpy requirements.

If, however, "ordinary poor health" is not good enough for you, and you want to benefit from the remarkable anti-aging properties of these antioxidant nutrients, then it behooves you to know more. The right supplemental doses of E, C, beta-carotene and CoQ-10 could literally save your life—while helping to make life more worth living.

VITAMIN C: PROLONGING LIFE AND FIGHTING VIRUSES

Dr. Pauling had maintained for years that megadoses of vitamin C offered innumerable benefits, from overcoming the common cold to stopping the onslaught of cancer, but it is only recently that the full range of this vitamin's advantages have become widely accepted in the scientific community.

The many benefits of vitamin C include:

- It's an antioxidant that fights the aging effects of air pollution, radiation, and chemotherapy.

- As an anti-inflammatory agent, vitamin C reduces the chronic degenerative symptoms typical of arthritis.
- It stimulates the creation of connective tissue, or collagen, used both to keep skin looking youthful and to keep tendons and ligaments supple and flexible.
- Vitamin C supports chemical entities known as mucopolysaccharides, which help protect our arteries from atherosclerosis, or hardening of the arteries.
- It increases our blood levels of HDL cholesterol, helping to protect us from cardiovascular disease.
- Vitamin C facilitates the absorption of iron, which we need for healthy blood as well as for energy and for optimal brain functioning.
- It helps in the synthesis of carnitine, a fat-burning nutrient.
- Vitamin C can act as an antihistamine, helping us to overcome allergies and their symptoms.
- It activates folic acid, which we need to protect the linings of our stomach and colon and to help prevent the formation of polyps and other precancerous conditions.
- Vitamin C further prevents cancer by boosting our immune response, increasing the ability of our white blood "scavenger" cells to resist diseases of all types.
- Vitamin C is a powerful stimulant to the adrenal glands, improving mental alertness by raising levels of noradrenaline in the brain (noradrenaline also seems to help fight depression); at the same time, C stimulates the adrenals to release cortisol, which protects us against stress.

We know that most mammals produce their own vitamin C; only humans and guinea pigs and a few other creatures seem to have lost this capacity in the course of the evolutionary process. Apparently, some 250,000 years ago, we "traded" our liver's capacity to produce C for the ability to synthesize greater quantities of glucose, or blood sugar. This trade-off may have made evolutionary sense, for having access to sudden bursts of blood sugar may have allowed early humans to create huge, sudden spurts of energy that were needed for "fight or flight." And humans' early diets—relying heavily on fresh fruits and vegetables gathered from the wild—were rich in natural C.

Since civilization has changed our diets, our needs for C are not being met as well as they used to be. Consider that a 150-pound mammal manufactures 10,000 mg of vitamin C a day—that's the amount of C you'd find in 100 glasses of orange juice! And under stress, both human and animal bodies need extra C to counter the aging effects of the free radicals that stress creates. A goat that weighs what a human does will produce 13,000 mg of C under only mild stress.

As a result, according to University of Alabama professor Dr. Emanuel Cheraskin, "virtually nobody gets enough vitamin C." One-fourth of all Americans don't even get the 60 mg needed for the body's basic functions. Yet, according to UCLA researcher Dr. James Enstrom, you can expect even greater health benefits from taking vitamin C supplements than you can from lowering cholesterol and cutting the fat in your diet. He believes that people who take vitamin C can expect to live longer, even if they smoke, eat high-fat diets, are overweight, and fail to exercise!

As with other supplements, vitamin C fights aging both by supporting the body's general health and by combating the diseases associated with aging.

Vitamin C and Heart Disease

A 20-year study by Dr. Anthony Verlangieri, director of the Atherosclerosis Research Laboratories at the University of Mississippi, found that low levels of vitamins C and E are to blame for many cardiovascular problems. C and E help to form substances known as glycosaminoglycans, which help maintain the linings of the arteries. Glycosaminoglycans inhibit an enzyme that tends to attack the artery lining, allowing cholesterol, fats, and lipids to penetrate. The arteries then become clogged with fat, known as plaque, reducing blood flow and increasing the risk of heart disease and stroke. According to Dr. Jeffrey Blumburg, associate director of the U.S. Department of Agriculture's Human

Nutrition Research Center on Aging at Tufts University, vitamin C may prevent the oxidation of blood cholesterol—the first step towards unclogging arteries.

Dr. Matthias Rath, author of *Eradicating Heart Disease,* believes that lack of certain nutrients is the essential cause of most cardiovascular diseases—particularly the thinning of our arterial walls. According to Dr. Rath, vitamin C may be one of the most vital nutrients in maintaining healthy arteries and heart muscle, specifically because of its ability to prevent free-radical damage to the heart and arterial tissue.

Vitamin C acts as a stabilizing nutrient, guaranteeing biochemical balance. Some scientists have likened it to an "iron reinforcement rod in a skyscraper building," due to the tremendous stabilizing effects it has on arterial walls. Blood vessel walls become very fragile when there is a vitamin C deficiency; the endothelial cells fail to "stick" together and collagen fibrils normally present in our bodies fail to develop. Capillaries are more apt to rupture, and in some cases, small hemorrhages occur throughout the body. Furthermore, states Dr. Rath, "A reinforced blood vessel wall is the basic protection against atherosclerotic deposits and cardiovascular disease . . . with low vitamin C in the diet for many years, the repair function goes on and on," resulting in large quantities of fatty lipoproteins being deposited in blood vessel walls, eventually closing them off completely. When this happens, cardiovascular failure is right around the corner.

Enstrom and his researchers at the School of Public Health at UCLA observed that men who took in 300 mg of vitamin C per day lowered their risk of heart disease by 45 percent compared to men who consumed less than 49 mg of C per day. Also noted was that C played a more important role in reducing fatal heart disease than did dietary fat intake or blood cholesterol levels. It is much easier to take a vitamin supplement than it is to reduce dietary fat or cholesterol. And, as we noted before, those who take vitamin C supplements throughout life have been found to live longer, despite smoking, poor exercise and dietary habits or being overweight.

After reviewing data from the First National Health and Nutrition Examination Survey conducted by the National Center for Health Statistics between 1971-1975, researchers observed the relationship between vitamin C and deaths due to cardiovascular disease. It was found that men who consumed the highest amount of C reduced their risk of cardiovascular disease by 42 percent, compared to men who had the lowest intake. In women participants, the difference in cardiovascular mortality was 25 percent. Therefore, by making sure that we are consuming enough key nutrients, vitamin C in particular, our risk of heart attack and stroke may be drastically reduced.

Vitamin C and Diabetes

Diabetics are at particular risk for heart disease because of their bodies' difficulties in getting C to the cell membranes where it can serve its protective function. In diabetics, insulin and glucose are in direct competition for the job of carrying vitamin C to the cell membranes, a competition that may result in insufficient C being carried by either substance. Diabetic specialist Dr. John Cunningham of the University of Massachusetts, Amherst, says diabetics often have a reduced level of C in their tissues even when their dietary intake is far above recommended levels. Therefore it is particularly important that diabetics maintain a high level of C in their bloodstreams to insure that enough reaches their cells.

Diabetics suffer from an excess of blood sugar, which their cells tend to convert to sorbitol (sugar alcohol), a substance that damages their cells. Supplemental doses of vitamin C reduce the conversion of excess blood sugar to sorbitol, thus protecting the cells from at least some effects of the aging process.

Vitamin C and Cancer

Vitamin C is one of the most powerful antioxidants we know. Water-soluble C traps and disarms free radicals in the watery parts of our cells, controlling the permeability of the cell wall and keeping free radicals from entering and destroying cells. C also scavenges free radicals, neutralizing them before they can attack our cells.

Free radicals are essentially aggressive reactive substances we naturally form in our body when we breathe oxygen or burn food for energy. The main difference between a normal molecule and a free radical is that the free radical is missing an electron, therefore making it unstable. It is this state of imbalance and instability that causes the free radical to randomly "attack" other healthy molecules in search of its own missing electron. What happens results in a very fast and destructive chain reaction: when the free radical latches onto a complete molecule, it ends up transforming the healthy molecule into another free radical, which must also look for an electron, which results in yet another complete molecule being attacked and so forth. If not stopped by antioxidants, these free radicals wreak havoc on our cells and our bodies.

The cell is attacked on a variety of levels: first, free radicals attack and oxidize the membranes of the cells, which consist of lipids and proteins. This causes instability in the cell wall, thereby altering how it dumps waste or accepts food and oxygen. Second, the mitochondria of the cell are attacked by free radicals, damaging the cell's primary source of energy. Third, the oxidation caused by free radicals deactivates important enzymes and hormones, interfering with our body's ability to grow, repair itself, and cope with stress. Finally, our DNA can even be attacked by free radicals—up to 100,000 free radicals per day! It is this ravaging statistic that makes us susceptible to so many more diseases as we age.

All free radicals must be neutralized, but some of the worst ones are as follows:

- *superoxide*: Molecular oxygen which has acquired an additional electron; a reactive oxygen species.
- *hydroxyl radical:* The most powerful of radicals, it creates an extremely fast and damaging chain reaction of destruction; consists of the nuclei of one oxygen and one hydrogen atom, plus an extra electron.
- *singlet oxygen:* A reactive oxygen species, this free radical attacks polyunsaturated fatty acids and is deactivated by carotene.

- *ozone:* (same structure and situation as singlet oxygen)
- *hydrogen peroxide:* This ROS has an extremely long life-span, and it can penetrate cell walls and produce harmful hydroxyl radicals.
- *lipid peroxy radical:* When a lipid molecule loses an electron, this type of radical is formed; it too causes a seriously damaging chain of reactions, but it can be quenched by vitamin E.

Vitamin C not only prevents the activation of free radicals, but some researchers believe it to prevent the formation of cancer-causing particles called nitrosamines. It prevents nitrates and other substances from becoming carcinogenic, acting as a kind of first line of defense against the "aging disease" of cancer.

Some 120 studies say that vitamin C is a virtual "vaccination" against cancer: according to Berkeley cancer epidemiologist Dr. Gladys Block, people who take large supplemental doses are only half as likely to get cancer, especially of the stomach, esophagus, pancreas and oral cavity, and perhaps also of the cervix, rectum and breast.

The late Scottish cancer specialist Ewan Cameron was one of the first physicians to notice low levels of vitamin C in his patients. After treating his patients with high levels of C—usually about 10 grams per day—he became convinced of its cancer-fighting benefits. For example, one of his patients had lymphatic cancer and was admitted to the hospital for radiation therapy. However, a two-week backlog for the treatment resulted in the intravenous alternative of 10 g of C per day. By the time radiation was available, it was no longer necessary: the signs of his cancer had vanished and X-rays showed significant improvement.

Dr. Cameron recorded the effect of vitamin C on his patients over time—both its benefits and limitations. Of 100 terminally ill cancer patients treated with this nutrient:

- 45 showed little or no benefit; and of the remaining 55
- 25 had slower cancer growth
- 20 had the growth stopped
- 10 had the growth recede—one being cured completely

While vitamin C is certainly not a sure-fire cure for cancer, reports and studies show it to have obvious positive effects on this debilitating disease.

- In one study, low levels of vitamin C in the blood were shown to correlate with *bladder cancer,* while another study showed that when laboratory animals were given what in humans would be the equivalent dose of 15,000 mg a day, bladder tumors were prevented.
- A study conducted at the Fred Hutchinson Cancer Research Center in Seattle, Washington discovered that high dosages of C were linked with the reduced risk of *cervical cancer*.
- A Finnish study conducted in 1991 concluded that among non-smoking men, those who consumed the least amount of vitamin C were three times more likely to develop *lung cancer* than those who had more than adequate intakes.
- A 1990 study conducted at the University of Toronto analyzed various existing studies, and found that consuming large amounts of vitamin C significantly reduced women's chances of developing *breast cancer*. Compared to those who consumed the least amount of the nutrient, women with the highest intakes were 31 percent less likely to develop breast cancer.
- A study conducted at several U.S. research centers examined 871 men and women with *oral cancer* and 979 individuals who were cancer-free. Their findings showed that vitamin C-rich diets helped prevent oral cancer. Those who consumed the most C reduced their risk of developing the disease by a tremendous 40 to 50 percent.

Countless other studies have also shown positive results relative to vitamin C reducing the risks of cancers of the colon, pancreas, esophagus, and rectum. Some researchers believe that five servings of fruits and vegetables a day—about 200-300 mg of vitamin C daily—is enough to bring about these cancer-attacking affects. But since the majority of Americans don't even consume the meager 60 mg RDA amount of vitamin C in their diets alone, extra supplementation is definitely recommended.

Vitamin C and Anti-Aging

Vitamin C virtually reverses the biological clock by rejuvenating white blood cells in the elderly. A British study found that when senior citizens, average age 76, took only 120 mg of vitamin C daily for two weeks, their white blood cell levels rose to match those of the study's young people, average age 35. Another double-blind study found that only 30 to 50 mg of vitamin C had the same effect on elderly hospitalized patients, while their leukocytes (another immunity agent) became biochemically younger than those of the younger subjects in the study. A USDA study found that even a slight deficiency in C could cause immune functioning to drop precipitously, while only 500 mg of vitamin C a day boosted glutathione (a key antioxidant) in red blood cells by as much as 50 percent.

However, one of the most startling studies concerning vitamin C and longevity was conducted by researchers at the University of California at Los Angeles in 1992. This study examined the dietary habits (including vitamin C intake) of more than 11,000 people over a 10-year period. The results? Men who consumed the most vitamin C (about 150 mg per day) had a 35 percent lower mortality rate than men who consumed only 30 mg per day. Women who consumed the most C had a 10 percent lower death rate than those women with the lowest consumption. Further analysis of this study showed that overall, vitamin C consumption increased life expectancy of women by one year and men by six years.

Other studies suggest that vitamin C improves sperm function, reducing the levels of male-generated birth defects—and restores male fertility, prevents lung diseases such as chronic bronchitis or asthma, combats gum disease, and prevents cataracts.

Taking Vitamin C

Because vitamin C is water-soluble, it leaves the body easily through urination. This means that you can't store C and you can't overdose on it. On the other hand, you must take it frequently to keep your body's C level high. Besides supplements, vitamin C is found in various foods, including citrus fruits and juices, red or green bell peppers, strawberries, tomatoes, broccoli and cantaloupe.

> One kiwi fruit contains 80 mg of vitamin C—that's more than a large orange, which contains about 70 mg. Kiwis are also loaded with potassium as well.

Recommendations for taking vitamin C vary widely. Dr. Pauling recommended 3,200 to 12,000 mg a day. Several other researchers themselves take several thousand mg daily, believing that higher levels of vitamin C convey ever-higher anti-aging benefits. A more moderate recommendation would be 250 to 1000 mg a day, taking more if you're feeling sick or under stress. Many people have found that if they respond to the first warning signs of cold, flu, or other illness with vitamin C—taking, say, 5,000 mg to start with and continuing with 1,000 to 2,000 mg every hour after that—they can "blast" the illness out of their bodies.

Some people may be concerned about the mild diarrhea that high doses of vitamin C sometimes bring on. Others experience the side effects of nausea and heartburn. Everyone's bowel tolerance for C is different, but usually up to 2,000 mg a day causes no reaction.

Dr. Pauling recommended C "salts," that is, vitamin C in powdered form, so that it is possible to take a highly concentrated amount without swallowing a lot of pills.

It's better to take vitamin C supplements throughout the day—twice at least, three or four times if possible—because water-soluble C does leave the body in 12 hours, and even time-release C has been flushed out in 16 hours. However, be careful with chewable supplements: they may cause the loss of tooth enamel or other dental problems. If you choose a chewable, make sure it's sugar-free. It's also a good idea to drink a large glass of juice or water each time you take a high dose of C.

Vitamin C	
Benefits	Strengthens capillaries, promotes healing of wounds, stimulates important hormones and brain chemicals, prevents oxygen damage, stimulates antibodies that help the immune system, protects against nitrosamines (cancer-causing compounds).
Cautions	No known toxicity.
Food sources	Green peppers, broccoli, Brussels sprouts, potatoes, spinach, strawberries, tomatoes, papaya, citrus fruits.

Megadoses: How Much Is Too Much?

For years now researchers and physicians have argued the benefits and risks associated with taking megadoses of vitamin C. While many studies have legitimately found that high doses work efficiently to treat a variety of ills, many physicians and medical organizations contend that megadoses of this vitamin don't have the same health benefits as do the drugs they can prescribe. According to Dr. Stephen Sheffery, this debate exists for several reasons. The first reason is pure economics: if the antiviral properties of vitamin C were fully accepted by the medical society, doctors would be losing income through the loss of prescriptions and possibly loss of patients. Why go to the doctor if you can simply buy large quantities of vitamin C over the counter? Vitamin C is available, nontoxic and inexpensive, which equals competition for most antiviral drugs. Therefore, the virologists who develop these drugs will go out of their way to proclaim C's "toxic side effects."

The fact is, many studies have shown high doses of vitamin C to be extremely beneficial:

- In one study, a gram of vitamin C per hour, including additional doses after sleep, was found to restore a schizophrenic to normal in two days.
- Another study of 60 patients who had high cholesterol and/or a history of heart disease were given one and a half to three grams of vitamin C per day for four to 30 months. Fifty out of the 60 patients reported improvements in their conditions, ranging from moderate to impressive.
- A study done with diabetics showed that one gram of vitamin C per day restored the strength of their capillaries almost up to normal. Another study conducted by Dr. Frederick Klenner, published in the *Journal of Applied Nutrition*, reported that diabetics on 10 grams of C per day could even do without some of their insulin injections.

These are just a few examples of how megadoses of C may help us live longer, better lives and avoid many "aging diseases." The acceptance of these findings, however, may not come so easily. As Sheffery writes, "There's just too much at stake to allow high-dose C to be recognized as the versatile antiviral and antitoxic drug that it is. The system will let you die first."

How Much Vitamin C Do You Need?

One way to tell how much vitamin C you need is to take it up to the level of your bowel tolerance—up to the point where you are getting mild diarrhea—and then cut back slightly, to avoid the symptom. A 1989 report suggested that men take 1.5 mg of C per pound of body weight, and women take 1 mg per pound (i.e., a 150-pound woman would take 150 mg per day). If you are taking high doses (up to 10,000 mg) without diarrhea, you don't necessarily want to take more; rather, you can take your condition as a sign that your system is effectively absorbing this useful vitamin. Diarrhea is how your body rids itself of the excess. People who take high doses of C when they're sick note that they don't have this diarrhetic reaction, even if they do when they're well, presumably because all the extra C is going to fight the illness.

There is no evidence that normal people will get kidney stones from taking high doses of vitamin C. And eight recent studies of people who took up to 10,000 mg of C daily for several years found no serious adverse effects whatsoever. If you have a tendency to oaxalic kidney stones, you must check with your doctor before taking C supplements.

VITAMIN E: KEEPING ARTERIES CLEAR

Vitamin E and vitamin C make a strong anti-aging team: while water-soluble vitamin C is found in the aqueous (watery) parts of our cells, fat-soluble vitamin E is found among the lipids, helping to keep fat cells from peroxidizing (becoming "infected" with oxygen) and turning rancid. Numerous studies have shown that vitamin E offers a long list of benefits, including:

- cutting short the free radical chain reactions that result in the destruction of cells
- blocking the oxidation of LDL cholesterol and other fats that, when oxidized, can damage cells
- preventing heart attack and stroke
- keeping arteries clear of plaque
- increasing our level of immunity
- blocking the growth of cancer cells
- preventing the progress of degenerative brain disease
- easing the symptoms of arthritis
- counteracting cataracts and other eye problems
- preventing "claudication," or decreased blood flow to leg arteries

In a sense, vitamin E is our first line of defense against free radical damage to lipids (fats) in the cell membrane. When a lipid is attacked and "radicalized"—turned into a lipid peroxy radical that is dangerous because it is missing an electron—vitamin E immediately intervenes, sacrificing one of its own electrons to prevent the peroxy radical from stealing an electron from a neighboring layer of fat. With that extra "E" electron, the peroxy radical becomes a lipid peroxide, also a dangerous substance—so the vitamin E works further, with the antioxidant substance glutathione peroxidase, to stop the free-radical chain reaction from oxidizing cell lipids and turning them rancid.

Thus, vitamin E prevents the oxidization and "rancidification" of LDL cholesterol. We now believe that until LDL turns rancid, it poses no particular danger to our bodies. Once it has been chemically altered by its interaction with oxygen, however, it becomes able to infiltrate artery walls, where it builds up as plaque to clog the arteries. By keeping LDL from turning rancid, you can help stop atherosclerosis before it starts.

According to Dr. Ishawlal Jialal of the University of Texas's Southwestern Medical Center at Dallas, subjects who took 800 IU of vitamin E daily for three months cut the rate of their LDL oxidation by 40 percent. In his opinion, you can see benefits in this regard with daily E supplements as low as 400 IU.

A study conducted on primates at the University of Mississippi Atherosclerosis Research Laboratory found that monkeys fed a high-fat diet could nonetheless slow and reverse the blockage of the arteries if they were given vitamin E supplements. Animals fed 108 IU of E daily for three years had only one-fifth as much arterial blockage as animals on a high-fat diet without E supplements. Moreover, when monkeys who were already suffering from blocked arteries were given E, their arterial blockage tended to decrease by about 60 percent: from an average of 35 percent closure of the arteries to only 15 percent average closure in just two years.

Dr. Howard Hodis of the University of South Carolina School of Medicine found that vitamin E also reversed arterial blockage in humans. In his study, middle-aged men undergoing coronary bypass surgery were given 100 IU of E daily, along with their other medications. After two years, their arteries were less narrowed than men who were taking lower doses of E—and angiograms revealed that in some cases, plaque had actually shrunk.

As the large-scale Harvard study showed, vitamin E seems to reduce heart disease as well. The risk of heart disease was found to be 41 percent lower for those taking 100 to 250 IU of E daily than for those who didn't; the E-takers also had a 29 percent lower risk of stroke, and a decrease in overall mortality of 13 percent. In a study of 40,000 middle-aged men, those who were taking more than 100 IU of E daily for over two years had a 37 percent lower risk of major cardiovascular problems, including heart attacks. A World Health Organization study of men in 16 European cities agreed that high levels of vitamin E are even more likely to prevent fatal heart attacks than lowering blood cholesterol, presumably because it's the E that prevents oxidation of cholesterol into its most toxic form.

Vitamin E and Diabetes

Diabetics can find particular benefit in vitamin E, because along with vitamin C, it inhibits an oxidative reaction that leads to protein glycosylation, the linking of excess sugar in the bloodstream to proteins in the body. In a study reported by Dr. Sushil Jain of the Louisiana State University Medical Center and Dr. John Cunningham of the University of Massachusetts at Amherst, diabetics taking 100 IU of E daily for three months had significantly reduced their triglyceride levels, suggesting that E supplements can help to reduce cardiovascular disease in diabetics.

Vitamin E and Cancer

Many studies have also shown a strong link between vitamin E and battling cancer. A study done by researchers at the National Cancer Institute found that when people took an extra supplement of E of about 100 IU, their risk of oral cancer was reduced by 50 percent. A large-scale Finnish study concluded that low blood levels of vitamin E result in a 50 percent higher risk of developing all kinds of cancers. Why is this such a magical cancer-fighting nutrient? Most researchers believe it has to do with vitamin E's tremendous immune-enhancing abilities. According to Dr. Blumberg, Chief of the Antioxidant Research Laboratory at Tufts University, E helps prevent cancer in three steps: it shields the cell from damaging free radicals; it combines with other substances in the intestines and prevents the formation of carcinogens; it enhances the body's immune response system, keeping an eye out for early cancer formations. Blumberg stresses that "Having adequate vitamin E in your blood helps keep your immune cells in a vigorous state, ready to attack the first cancer cells they see, which in fact is your primary defense against cancer."

How Vitamin E Fights Aging

As do many of the anti-aging vitamins, minerals, and hormones we've covered, vitamin E returns an aging person's immunity to almost youthful levels. Dr. Simin Meydani, a Tufts University nutritional immunologist, administered between 400 and 800 IU of E daily to people over 60. Although their immune responses had been declining, the supplemental E reversed that trend, causing many people's responses to rise back to youthful levels. Dr. Meydani found that the white blood cells that fight infection were up by 10 to 50 percent within 30 days. Some other immune functions were up 80 to 90 percent. Meydani notes that her subjects were not people who would be considered E-deficient by normal RDA standards.

In a world where air pollution and other environmental hazards attack our health, we also need the extra protection of the kind that vitamin E affords. The free radicals nitrogen dioxide and ozone—chemical components of air pollution—attack the cells of our lungs, where a high concentration of oxygen already makes us vulnerable to free radical invasion. E short-circuits the creation of lipid peroxide molecules—molecules of oxidized fat— protecting our lungs from the damage they can cause.

Vitamin E

Benefits	Neutralizes free radicals, protects body tissues and cells, prevents oxidation damage
Cautions	Extremely high doses cause fatigue, nausea, headache, intestinal cramps, diarrhea
Food sources	seed oils, green leafy vegetables, liver, whole grains, wheat germ, egg yolks, butter, nuts

Vitamin E and Exercise

Vitamin E supplements are especially important for those who exercise frequently. Ironically, although exercise itself helps to prevent aging, it also increases our risk of aging. When we exercise, we burn fuel, so to speak, engaging the mitochondria, which are the energy-makers of the cells. But the fuel-burning process itself creates free radicals—a kind of cellular toxic waste—which can cause new membrane damage as well as endangering the mitochondria and reducing energy production. E cuts short the free-radical chain reactions that exercise can set off. As a result, people who take E find that their endurance, as well as their general health, improves.

Taking Vitamin E

People who take vitamin E supplements report virtually no side effects, although some people do experience a slight increase in blood pressure when they first start taking higher doses. Although you can get some E in food, if you want to experience this vitamin's anti-aging benefits, you must take supplements. In order to get the 400 IU that most anti-aging specialists recommend as a daily dose, you would have to consume two quarts of corn oil, more than five pounds of wheat germ, eight cups of almonds, or 22 cups of peanuts. If you chose the latter route, you'd also be taking in 22,250 calories and 1,912 grams of fat—hardly a healthy choice!

Even small doses of vitamin E can be effective. Many physicians believe that only 100 daily IU of E will help prevent heart attacks. A preferable dose, however, would be 400 IU. You'll find that the E is more effective taken in two 200 IU doses each day with meals. Up to 800 IU per day is probably a safe dose as well, but doses above 400 IU tend to have a mild anti-clotting effect, like aspirin, so at that level it's not recommended for people already taking anticoagulants facing surgery.

A one-year study of 800 patients found that no one suffered any adverse effects from megadoses of 2000 IU of daily vitamin E; quantities of 3,200 IU daily, however, were found to be toxic, causing headache, diarrhea, and high blood pressure.

A Finnish study was conducted in which daily doses of only 50 IU of vitamin E seemed to contribute to hemorrhagic or "bleeding stroke" in smokers. This overpublicized study was found deficient in many respects, and most nutritional researchers have dismissed it as flawed. U.S. scientists are puzzled, however, as 50 IU of E a day hardly seems enough to alter blood coagulation or to have any positive effect either. Most U.S. doctors are comfortable with a 400 IU daily dose.

Once you start taking vitamin E, expect to continue your dosage as a lifelong regime. Studies seem to indicate that it takes at least two years before the heart-helping benefits of this vitamin reach their optimal level, although other positive effects of the vitamin may be felt immediately.

BETA-CAROTENE: THE SUPREME ANTIOXIDANT

Where vitamin E and C leave off, beta-carotene takes over. First discovered over 150 years ago in the isolated orange pigment of carrots, beta-carotene has become one of the most powerful antioxidants on the market today, responsible for boosting immunity, preventing heart disease, and reducing our chances of cancer. It is also able to convert itself into vitamin A in the body, without displaying any of A's toxic side effects. Beta-carotene holds the promise of many anti-aging benefits, such as:

- preventing lung, stomach and breast cancers
- preventing stroke and heart attack
- blocking the oxidation of artery-clogging cholesterol
- destroying tumor cells
- stimulating and enhancing immune functions
- preventing cataracts and improving night vision

Numerous studies have pointed towards beta-carotene as a key nutrient necessary for not only a longer life, but a healthier, more enjoyable life as well.

Beta-Carotene: Nature's Anticancer Protection

Beta-carotene, the substance that our bodies use to make vitamin A, is a powerful anticancer agent. Dr. Eli Seifter of Albert Einstein College of Medicine in New York conducted studies in which the cancer of some lab animals was treated with radiation alone, while others were given beta-carotene along with radiation therapy. Dr. Seifter found that the radiation treatment worked better when supported by the beta-carotene.

Studies at the Johns Hopkins School of Hygiene and Public Health found that people with low levels of beta-carotene were four times as likely to develop a common form of smoking-related lung cancer as those with higher blood levels of beta-carotene. Studies at China's National Cancer Institute also suggested that daily doses of 15 mg of beta-carotene, along with supplements of vitamin E and selenium, reduced the incidence of lung cancer in smokers. Most scientists feel, though, that it takes twelve years of high doses of beta-carotene to combat the carcinogenic effects of smoking.

Beta-carotene also helps to block cervical cancer. A six-year Australian study found that women who already had breast cancer had a survival rate 12 times higher if they consumed high

Beta-Carotene: A Note of Concern?

Although research has shown that people who eat vegetables high in beta-carotene have the lowest rates in cancers of the cervix, colon, lung, prostate, and stomach, recent studies negating its anticancer ability have brought beta-carotene under scrutiny.

In the Beta Carotene and Retinol Efficacy Trial, funded by the National Cancer Institute and known as CARET, smokers who took beta-carotene supplements actually showed an increase in lung cancer rate of 28 percent, and a 17 percent rise in death rate, compared with the group not using supplements. But many researchers claimed the study was tainted from the start: The 18,000 participants were at a high risk of lung cancer because they smoked, were former smokers, or worked with asbestos, and may have entered the study with pre-existing but undiagnosed tumors. Furthermore, the supplements may have been given too late and six years may not have been long enough to show any benefit from beta-carotene.

A second 12-year study of more than 22,000 nonsmoking male doctors, known as the Physician's Health Study, showed that beta-carotene had no effect—positive or negative—on cancer or heart disease.

And on a brighter note for antioxidants, a new study published in the *American Journal of Epidemiology,* reported that middle-aged men who consume foods rich in vitamin C and beta-carotene have a 31 percent lower risk of dying of any cause than their counterparts who eat less nutrients. And while the study did not include women, previous research such as the Nurses' Health Study from Boston suggests that women benefit as much as men from a diet rich in antioxidants.

Overall, the best advice is to eat a well-balanced diet containing five servings of fruits and vegetables, take a multivitamin/multimineral supplement containing beta-carotene and mixed bioflavonoids, vitamins C and E, and avoid obvious cancer initiators like cigarette smoking.

levels of beta-carotene; the beta-carotene actually seemed to block the proliferation of the cancer cells.

A U.S. study of men with colon cancer found that only 30 mg of beta-carotene a day inhibited certain cancer-promoting activities of the cells by 44 percent after only two weeks; the preventive function had increased to 57 percent after nine weeks. The cancer-promoting activity stayed low even six months after the men had stopped taking beta-carotene.

Beta-Carotene and Heart Attack

A Harvard study conducted by Dr. Charles Hennekens found that male doctors who took 50 mg supplements of beta-carotene every other day for six years had only half as many fatal heart attacks, strokes, and other heart disease incidents as doctors who took a placebo during the same period. It seemed that after only two years, beta-carotene's protective function could be felt, perhaps because like vitamins C and E, it helped slow the buildup of arterial plaque.

Another Harvard study of 90,000 female nurses found that those who had taken more than 11,000 IU (about 7 mg) of beta-carotene a day had a 22 percent lower risk of heart disease than women who were getting less than 3,800 IU (about 2.25 mg) of daily beta-carotene. Those who ate larger amounts of beta-carotene also had a 37 percent lower risk of stroke.

How Beta-Carotene Fights Aging

Like vitamins C and E, beta-carotene helps to protect the integrity of cells against free radical attacks. Singlet oxygen—oxygen with a missing electron—corrupts our genes, turns cell fat rancid and therefore toxic, and destroys the cell's structure. Beta-carotene, though, is a very efficient "quencher" of singlet oxygen. It protects cells, preventing the corrosive effects of aging.

Beta-carotene is used by our bodies to manufacture vitamin A, which prevents aging by boosting our immune responses. Vitamin A helps keep skin stay smooth and young-looking as well as strengthening bones.

The improved immune response in those who take beta-carotene has been noted in numerous studies. Dr. Ronald Watson of the University of Arizona worked with 60 older men and

---

Beta-Carotene

Benefits	Essential to growth and functioning of tissue linings of body's surfaces, essential to bone growth an development, increases immune system responsiveness, reduces risk of cancer
Cautions	No known toxicity for beta-carotene, BUT high doses of Vitamin A itself may have bad side effects, including liver toxicity
Food sources	Carrots, dark yellow or orange vegetables, sweet potatoes, pumpkin, spinach, broccoli, papayas, oranges, peppers, apricots

---

women, whose average age was 56. He found that those who took 30 to 60 mg of beta-carotene daily for two months had more natural "killer" cells, T helper cells, and activated lymphocytes—all needed to help protect the body from cancer as well as from viral and bacterial infection. Dr. Meydani discovered that Harvard doctors who took 50 mg of beta-carotene every other day had a significant increase in their levels of natural killer cells.

Taking Beta-Carotene

It is easier to get adequate daily beta-carotene in your diet than it is to get enough of vitamin C or E. The National Cancer Institute suggests eating five servings of dark yellow, orange, or dark green vegetables or fruits a day, as these colorful foods are high in beta-carotene. (As the name hints, this is the substance that gives carrots their yellowish color.) However, the USDA states that the human body can more easily absorb the beta-carotene in supplements than in natural foods.

If you do prefer to get your beta-carotene entirely through diet, lightly cooked foods will be easier for your system to digest than raw. However, heavy cooking destroys beta-carotene, even in foods like sweet potatoes, carrots, greens, and spinach, that are otherwise high in it. (For more on foods high in beta-carotene, see Chapter 13, "The Long-Life Diet.")

Most doctors recommend 10 to 15 mg a day of supplemental beta-carotene, taken in divided doses and with meals, as you need fat to be able to digest it. Taking beta-carotene in divided doses three times a day gives you three times greater benefits than taking the same total amount only once a day.

Beta-carotene appears to be absolutely nontoxic. Even though high concentrations of vitamin A can have adverse effects, the body never manufactures its own toxic quantities of A, no matter how much beta-carotene you take. And the only noticeable side effect is a slight yellowing of the skin, which only happens at extremely high doses.

A controversial 1994 Finnish study appeared to discover one adverse effect of beta-carotene. In this study, long-time heavy smokers who were taking 20 daily mg of beta-carotene had a 28 percent greater risk of lung cancer than those who took no supplements. Most scientists greeted this finding with extreme skepticism, however. As Harvard researcher Julie Buring put it, "The idea that the equivalent of seven or eight carrots a day causes cancer just doesn't make sense biologically." In our opinion, smokers should maintain high levels of beta-carotene, because the predominance of scientific studies support its anti-aging and anticancer properties.

VITAMIN C, E, AND BETA-CAROTENE: THE THREE-WAY ANTIOXIDANT THREAT

If any one of these vitamins has powerful antioxidant properties, the three in combination are even more effective, both in combating aging and in preventing cancer, heart disease, and other diseases.

For example, in the Harvard study of 87,000 female nurses

already cited at the beginning of this chapter, women with a high intake of all three antioxidant nutrients had a 54 percent lower risk of stroke. Likewise, animal studies at Harvard's School of Dental Medicine found that treating animals with vitamin C, E and beta-carotene and the antioxidant glutathione combined was the most effective way to bring about the regression and/or disappearance of cancer.

> Increased intakes of antioxidant vitamins (beta-carotene, vitamin C, vitamin E) could potentially prevent or postpone 50 to 70 percent of cataracts.

Apparently, the three antioxidants work together to fight LDL cholesterol, which, as we've seen leads to damaging attacks on the arterial walls and adds to the build-up of arterial plaque. Vitamin C is water-soluble, while E and beta-carotene are fat-soluble, allowing both the fat and watery parts of our cells to be protected from free-radical attacks which lead to both aging and cancer.

Therefore, vitamin supplements, taken in the proper dosages have a wide range of both short- and long-term benefits without harmful side effects. As scientists become more educated about the role of free radicals in relation to the development of chronic diseases, the role of these vitamins can become more specifically targeted to enhance our health and our lives. Therefore, adding more of these crucial nutrients to your anti-aging program now can help you stay young and healthy for years to come.

COENZYME Q-10: THE MIRACLE HEART MEDICINE

Although many people in the United States have never even heard of coenzyme Q-10 (also known as CoQ-10, ubiquinone, and vitamin Q), millions of people in Japan, Europe, and Israel take it for congestive heart failure and a variety of other illnesses. Some 15 percent of all Swedes and 20 percent of all Danes take it as a nutritional supplement and/or as a medication.

Natural vs. Synthetic Vitamins

Is there really a difference between natural and synthetic vitamins? Maybe not. Critics claim that at the very best, a synthetic vitamin interacts with the human body as a mere drug or a pharmaceutical agent—*not* a supporting nutrient. At worst, synthetic vitamins can damage the functioning of the human body through biochemical imbalances. A basic guideline to follow when vitamin shopping is that cheaper is *not* better; if it's cheap it's usually synthetic, which means it was manufactured by poor quality control standards. Also, synthetic vitamin complexes cannot be utilized to the fullest extent that natural complexes can. Their bioavailability and metabolise may be lacking, which means that our bodies can't absorb them. Jim Fixx, a famous runner and widely quoted fitness guru, died early in life of a heart attack and an autopsy was found to have large amounts of undigested vitamins within his intestines. If you decide to start supplementing your diet with vitamins and minerals, make sure to buy them in the best bioavailable formulation possible.

Advantages of natural vitamins
- natural complexes are protein in nature, in the form of an enzyme or co-enzyme.
- natural complexes carry trace mineral activators necessary for the vitamin to act as a biochemical catalyst.
- synthetic vitamins are only a fraction of the real biologically active nutritional complex, therefore helping repair our cells and tissues in only a fraction of the way a natural complex would.
- natural vitamins contain all auxiliary ingredients, whereas synthetic complexes usually contain one or two active co-factors.

Remember:
If it's a high-quality vitamin, you should be able to break it in your fingers or with a dull knife. Another quality test is seeing if it will dissolve in a warm glass of water. If a vitamin doesn't pass these tests, it probably won't break down in your system. If your body has trouble digesting in general, try gelatin-encapsulated vitamins.

Vitamins lose potency with age. It's best to keep them in the refrigerator or in a dry cool place.

If your body is absorbing the vitamin's nutrients, especially B-vitamins, urine will be a bright yellow color.

Vitamins that contain as little as 50 mg of niacin may cause temporary tingling, hot flashes and redness of the skin. Don't worry; this reaction is normal and may discontinue as the body becomes accustomed to the nutrient. Try to take it with meals or a fiber supplement. This slows the rate of absorption, which reduces side effects. Above all, don't use niacin in conjunction with alcohol, spicy foods or anything else that causes vasodilation (opening of the blood vessels).

Avoid low-priced generic brands, as they are sometimes poorly formulated. Do buy name brands backed by a known physician or Ph.D., made by companies who have a good reputation to protect.

Where can I find natural vitamin complexes?
Natural vitamin complexes can be found at most health food stores. However, it is important to shop in places that have knowledgable staff and salespeople who can provide you with accurate information.

Dr. Greg Fahy, formerly chief scientist at the Organ Cryo-preservation Laboratory at the American Red Cross Jerome Holland Laboratory in Rockville, Maryland, sees CoQ-10 as "a nutrient that is made by virtually every living organism and is thus an unavoidable component of human diets. CoQ-10, like vitamins C and E, simply helps to maintain and improve overall health."

It was first discovered back in 1957 by F.L. Crane in beef heart mitochondria. CoQ-10, a highly fat-soluble molecule, is usually found in these mitochondrial membranes where it manufactures adenosine triphosphate (ATP). ATP is the basic energy molecule of the entire human body. Therefore, some scientists believe that CoQ-10's health benefits lie in its ability to enhance the functions of our mitochondria.

Researchers claim a number of cardiovascular and anti-aging benefits for this enzyme, which appears naturally in most of the cells in the human body. But because CoQ-10 is so important to energy manufacturing in the human body, it is found in some tissue cells more abundantly than in others.

For example, because our heart beats constantly throughout our lives, CoQ-10 is needed in greater quantities in cardiac tissue cells. Extra CoQ-10 is also needed in the organ doing our daily dumping and purifying, the liver. Most importantly, it has been found to be plentiful in the immune system, the system that continually fights and attacks various diseases and viruses that we become more susceptible to as we age.

Like many key body chemicals, CoQ-10 declines rapidly beginning at 20 and dropping almost 80 percent by the end of middle age. Some researchers believe that loss of CoQ-10 is related to the increase in degenerative heart disease after age 50. Other possible reasons for the body's depletion of this enzyme could be attributed to free radical damage to mitochondrial membranes, or perhaps the process of "lipid peroxidation"—the same process that makes butter rancid—that damages other membranes in our cells.

Studies have shown that there is one-quarter less CoQ-10 in the blood of patients with heart disease than in healthy individuals. One study showed that 75 percent of heart disease patients had serious deficiencies of CoQ-10, while another found that 75 percent of the elderly cardiomyopathy (heart failure) patients in the study improved significantly after being treated with CoQ-10. Supplementation alone is not the only way to increase one's supply, as many studies point to rigorous exercise as a way to boost our levels of this enzyme.

Various animal studies have shown that endurance training helps to strengthen out heart muscles, mainly because it increases our levels of essential CoQ-10. Training was also found to help patients who had already experienced a heart attack.

In a 1993 patient study published in *The Clinical Investigator,* scientists reported that after treating 115 heart patients with CoQ-10, diastolic function improved and myocardial thickness decreased—a state which may reduce one's chance for a future heart attack.

CoQ-10 also lowers blood pressure. According to Texas cardiologist Dr. Peter Langsjoen, working with colleagues at the University of Texas at Austin, about 85 percent of 109 patients with high blood pressure managed to bring their blood pressure down after taking 225 mg of CoQ-10 a day. (The other 15 percent saw no improvement, and one patient's blood pressure got worse.) Those patients who improved found that systolic pressure fell from an average of 159 to 147, while diastolic pressure dropped from an average of 94 to 85, usually within three or four months. Moreover, echocardiograms (ultrasound tests of the heart) found improvement in heart function as well. Although at the beginning of the study, nearly all were taking one or more drugs for hypertension, by the end of the study, 25 percent were taking no drugs at all, and 51 percent had managed to stop taking from one to three of their medications.

Like many other anti-aging supplements, CoQ-10 helps cleanse and strengthen the arteries, fighting atherosclerosis and preventing oxidation of blood cholesterol. According to Boston University researcher Balz Frei, CoQ-10 prevents the artery-destroying oxidation of LDL cholesterol even more efficiently than vitamin E or beta-carotene.

CoQ-10 also makes the cardiac muscle stronger, can treat and prevent cardiac arrhythmias, reduces the risk of heart attack, reduces the injury caused to myocardial tissue due to chemical wastes (ischemia) or lack of oxygen (hypoxia), and helps treat and prevent other circulatory problems, as well as chronic obstructive pulmonary disease.

How CoQ-10 Prevents Aging

Scientists don't know exactly how CoQ-10 works, but they do know that it's an antioxidant, like vitamin E. Apparently, it protects fat molecules from being oxidized by the free radicals that continually attack fat cells. CoQ-10 helps to stabilize cell membranes, which keep cells intact. It also supports the activity of the mitochondria, those tiny entities that burn oxygen to manufacture energy within cells. Our heart muscles need an enormous amount of energy to keep pumping blood throughout the body, which may be why CoQ-10 is in such high concentration in the cardiac region.

Because this enzyme protects the mitochondria, it also seems to protect the brain from damage. Researchers speculate that such degenerative brain diseases as Alzheimer's and Lou Gehrig's disease are related to low levels of CoQ-10 and might be susceptible to treatment by this extraordinary enzyme.

Like other key anti-aging vitamins and minerals, CoQ-10 boosts the immune function. Almost 30 years ago, in 1968, Emile Bliznakov demonstrated the healthy effects of CoQ-10 on the immune system. Bliznakov injected rats with a closely related variant of CoQ-10, called CoQ-6, and observed the rate of phagocytosis, or foreign substance removal. It was discovered that CoQ-6-treated rats removed foreign antigens twice as fast as the untreated rats. These rats also experienced a dramatic increase in their production of antibodies—a 247 percent increase! One study of older mice found that they initially produced only one-third the antibodies against foreign invaders that young mice generated. After treatment with CoQ-10, however, their antibody production jumped by a factor of two and a half, bringing them up to 80 percent of the young mice's antibody production level.

Human immune systems also respond positively to treatment with CoQ-10. When Dr. Karl Folkers of the University of Texas gave humans 60 mg daily doses of CoQ-10, they experienced a significant increase in the production of immunoglobulin, the major antibody in human blood. It seemed to take only one to three months for the treatment to take effect.

Mice that had been treated with CoQ-10 also seemed to look and act younger, to stay more active into old age, and to live far longer than mice that had not been treated. According to Dr. Stephen Coles, an anti-aging specialist at the California Institute of Technology, mice who receive CoQ-10 supplements "look terrific, their coats are better, they groom themselves better—they look a few months younger." (Remember, mice only live for about two years, so a few months younger in a mouse's life translates into a few decades in human terms!)

Dr. Coles points out that the effects of CoQ-10 aren't really noticeable on younger mice. It's only when the mice start to age that you can tell the difference: "Halfway through life all the mice look alike. But when they get to the very end of their life span, the differences suddenly jump out at you. The CoQ-10 mice begin to look better and better."

Pathologist Dr. Steven Harris of UCLA found that giving mice CoQ-10 did not set any records for mouse life span. However, 30 percent of the mice who had been treated lived two

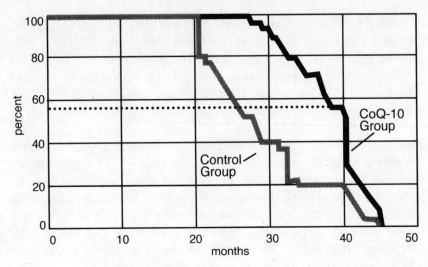

CoQ-10 survival curve for rats.

months longer than the mice who had not been treated. In another study, the mean survival rate of female mice injected with 50 mg of CoQ-10 per week increased 56 percent over mice who had not been treated.

Other benefits of this enzyme include a reduction in periodontal (gum) disease and a general boost in energy for sedentary people, but we're only just beginning to learn about other possible benefits of this nutrient.

Dr. Coles sees taking CoQ-10 as a long-term process: "You should not start taking it on grounds that you're going to instantly look better, feel better and be happier," he warns. "CoQ-10 is an insurance policy, an investment in the future, and the payoff will only happen at the end of life."

CoQ-10 Prevents Surgical Complications

CoQ-10 has also been found to be beneficial in reducing postoperative cardiac complications. In a study of 40 patients undergoing artery bypass surgery, half were administered 150 mg of CoQ-10 per day for seven days before the operation, while the control group was given none. The findings suggested that pretreatment with CoQ-10 may lower the risk of surgical complications during bypass grafting, simply because of the enzyme's ability to reduce peroxidative damage.

Taking CoQ-10 Supplements

Generally, it's advisable to take CoQ-10 supplements if you're age 50 or older, particularly if you're prone to heart problems or at high risk for them. Healthy people should begin with a 30 mg daily supplement; people with specific problems might want to take from 50 to 150 mg a day, depending on their physician's advice.

Unless you have a severe deficiency of CoQ-10, you probably won't notice its effects right away. It takes one to three months for the enzyme to begin to affect your heart; its impact on your energy level or immunity system may be even more subtle. Vitamin E seems to intensify the effects of CoQ-10, as does selenium.

Of course, your body manufactures CoQ-10 by itself as well. For this process, it requires B vitamins: B6, B12, niacin, and folic acid. You can also find natural sources of CoQ-10 in many types of foods—eggs have been found to be a prime nutritional source—in addition to rice bran and wheat germ. Other food sources include fatty fish, like mackerel and sardines, organ meats like heart, liver, and kidney, soy oil, and peanuts. How-

CoQ-10	
Benefits	Helps prevent cardiovascular disease, enhances immune system, reduces periodontal disease, boosts energy levels, acts as an antioxidant, lowers blood pressure
Cautions	No known toxicity
Food sources	Eggs, rice bran, wheat germ, fatty fish, organ meats, peanuts

ever, you'd have to eat a whole pound of sardines or two and half pounds of peanuts just to get 30 mg of CoQ-10, so if you really want to raise your enzyme levels, supplements are probably your best bet.

Supplements come in many forms, all of which are acceptable. Just be sure that you are either taking an oil-based capsule or adding a little fat (olive oil or peanut butter) to the dry tablets. Without some kind of oil, the dry tablet could pass right through your system totally intact, providing you with no benefit at all.

Chapter 10

Thyroid

All too often in our society, a slowing down of physical or mental functions is accepted as the normal course of old age, rather than being diagnosed as an illness or condition that may be treated with nutrition, hormones, exercise, or a change of lifestyle. Perhaps one of the most pernicious "masks" for old age is hypothyroidism—an insufficient production or absorption of the thyroid hormone that won't allow our metabolism to function at its peak efficiency.

WHAT IS THE THYROID?

The thyroid is a small, butterfly-shaped gland located in the neck, over the trachea, or windpipe, just below the larynx. Despite its tiny stature, the thyroid has tremendous responsibilities, as it is the gland that affects virtually all metabolic processes. It does this by releasing certain hormones, which in turn regulate the body's metabolism, temperature, and heart rate. If the thyroid isn't functioning at its optimal level, neither are you.

167

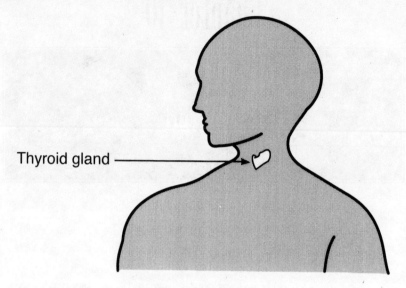

The thyroid gland.

The following are some of the most common symptoms of thyroid deficiency. Many of them will sound to you like physical maladies that are supposed to be expected and tolerated as old age approaches.

Common Symptoms of Hypothyroidism

- fatigue and general loss of energy; moving more slowly
- weakness
- susceptible to colds, viruses, and respiratory ailments
- heavy, labored breathing
- muscle cramps
- persistent low back pain
- bruising easily
- mental sluggishness, poor memory
- headache
- emotional instability—crying jags, mood swings, easily upset, temper tantrums, and the like; more easily made nervous or anxious
- getting cold easily, particularly in the hands and feet

- dry, coarse, or leathery skin; pale skin
- coarse hair and/or loss of hair
- brittle nails
- loss of appetite
- stiff joints; mild arthritis
- reduced interest in or energy for sex
- atherosclerosis (arteries clogged with fat, or plaque, leading to other cardiovascular problems)
- decrease in heart contractility; that is, the heart doesn't pump blood with sufficient force, leading to insufficient circulation, particularly to the brain

The detection of hypothyroidism is especially important for older individuals. One study found that in a population of elderly people, ages 60 and over, who attended a senior citizens' center, 5.9 percent suffered from hypothyroidism. Another study, published in 1993 in the *Journal of Endocrinology and Metabolism,* found a noticable decrease of thyroid activity and a very low prevalence of thyroid auto-antibodies in healthy centenarians (individuals 100 years old or over).

Despite its prevalence in older individuals, hypothyroidism is one of the most overlooked conditions in this age group. In fact, telltale symptoms are diagnosed in as little as 25 percent of elderly hypothyroid patients. In one instance, laboratory confirmations of hypothyroid patients were compared to these individuals' initial clinical examinations. The results? Only 10 percent of people with the disease were properly diagnosed in their primary clinical examination.

Some studies indicate that as many as 15 percent of people over age 60 have subclinical hypothyroidism.

Of course, it's possible that these symptoms may be the inevitable outcome of the aging process—but they are far more likely to result from a combination of low thyroid and nutritional deficiencies.

Correcting hypothyroidism can restore your energy, endurance, body heat, sexuality, mental vigor, and emotional resilience. It can boost resistance to colds and other respiratory conditions, protect against heart and arterial disease, and raise your defenses against cancer. Restoring the proper levels of thyroid can even make your hair, skin, and nails smooth, strong, and healthy.

Case Study: The Debilitating Effects of an Overlooked Thyroid Problem

Dr. Murray Israel tells of a patient whose story illustrates the powerful anti-aging effects of thyroid—and the overwhelming aging effects of hypothyroidism. Dr. Israel was called to see an old woman who was so debilitated that the priest had already been summoned to give the last rites. Her breathing was shallow, her heartbeat faint, and her blood pressure was dangerously elevated. Examination had shown her coronary arteries were clogged with severe atherosclerosis. Her hair had turned totally white, and her skin was dry and marked by dead patches.

Dr. Israel treated the woman with 10 mg of thyroid and brewer's yeast (the best source of B vitamins then available) three times a day. Within two weeks, the woman was mentally alert and physically strong enough to walk to church. Soon after, her dead skin peeled off, revealing a smooth, pink complexion underneath. Black hairs even appeared amidst the white. The woman went on to live an active, energetic life for another 20 years.

Clearly, hypothyroidism had created many of the signs of aging we've come to expect and consider normal! And treatment with thyroid and vitamin supplements had in effect reversed the aging process.

HOW YOUR BODY MAKES THE THYROID HORMONE

In order to be sure you're getting all the thyroid hormone (TH) your body needs, it's helpful to understand how your body makes it. The whole process begins with the hypothalamus, the body's "thermostat" which regulates many hormonal activities. When the hypothalamus determines that blood levels of TH have fallen too low, it sets a chain of activity in motion by discharging thyroid releasing hormone (TRH). TRH signals the pituitary to release a second hormone, thyroid stimulating hormone (TSH). Finally, TSH tells the thyroid gland to get to work, and the thyroid gland produces TH. When levels of TH have risen high enough for the body to function properly, the pituitary responds by ceasing to release TSH and the process stops—until the hypothalamus determines that it's time to start again.

There are two ways that the body can come to suffer from insufficient thyroid hormone. One is when the thyroid itself has difficulty producing it. Lack of iodine, a tumor or some other thyroid problem may result in a gland that doesn't properly carry out the orders given by the hypothalamus and the pituitary. This is known as *primary hypothyroidism*.

The other way that TH levels can fall is when the hypothalamus and/or the pituitary aren't functioning properly. This is known as *secondary hypothyroidism*.

The thyroid itself needs iodine to function. Lack of iodine will cause the thyroid to swell, a condition known as goiter—a visibly enlarged thyroid gland on the front and side of the neck. You only need a very tiny amount of iodine, however: a daily dose of 100 micrograms (mcg) for women and 120 mcg for men. Most people get that in iodized salt or seafood.

Many people think that if they don't have goiter, their thyroid glands are getting everything they need to function. Unfortunately, that's not the case. Adequate iodine will keep you from getting goiter, but by itself, it's not enough to assure efficient production of TH.

THYROID AND VITAMIN DEFICIENCIES

Sometimes vitamin deficiencies result in either primary or secondary hypothyroidism. The B vitamins are particularly key to efficient thyroid production:

- A shortage of vitamin B2 will depress the function of ovaries and testes and will prevent the thyroid and adrenal glands from secreting necessary hormones.
- Vitamin B3 (niacin) is necessary not only for TH production but also for respiration and for the metabolism of proteins, carbohydrates, and fats.
- We don't know whether vitamin B6 (pyridoxine) is necessary for the thyroid or the pituitary gland, but we do know that without sufficient quantities of it TH production falls.

On the other hand, TH itself is necessary for your body to make use of vitamin B12 (cyanocobalamin). A severe B12 deficiency could result in anemia (possibly fatal), mental illness, neurological disorders, neuralgia, neuritis, or bursitis—all symptoms that might be confused with the "normal" aging process. Since B12 can't be produced by the body itself, you have to ingest it in your diet or in vitamin supplements. But without adequate TH levels, your body can't absorb this essential vitamin, no matter how much you ingest.

THYROID AND VITAMIN C

Vitamin C is also a key supplement that can facilitate the production of TH, and vitamin C deficiencies can cause gross disorders in TH production. Guinea pigs, like people, don't manufacture vitamin C in their own bodies. When experimental guinea pigs were deprived of vitamin C, the capillaries in their thyroid glands began to bleed, a condition that worsened as the scurvy—the shortage of C—also got worse.

Long-term deficits in C vitamins can cause hyperplasia, in which normal thyroid gland cells begin to multiply at at abnormal rate, producing too much TH, a condition known as hyperthyroidism. The pituitary is supposed to regulate the production of TH, monitoring hormone levels so as to tell the thyroid when to start and stop. Insufficient vitamin C, though, seems to interrupt the pituitary's governing function.

On the other hand, as soon as the guinea pigs were given adequate supplies of C, all the thyroid gland problems disappeared. Taking a vitamin C supplement, then, can benefit your thyroid as well as performing many other functions (see Chapter 9).

THYROID AND VITAMIN E

Vitamin E deficiencies also affect TH production. In one experiment, rabbits deprived of vitamin E experienced a range of TH problems, including the rapid multiplication of certain thyroid gland cells and insufficient TSH synthesized by the pituitary gland. Rats deprived of E had a similar response, and in addition, they transmitted hyperplasia to their litters.

THYROID AND VITAMIN A

Thyroid and vitamin deficiencies tend to interact with one another, so that insufficient vitamins keep the body from producing thyroid, while insufficient thyroid keeps the body from making proper use of vitamins. The thyroid gland has a particularly powerful interactive relationship with vitamin A. On the one hand, if your thyroid is underactive, it can't properly convert beta-carotene into this essential vitamin, and carotene may accumulate. This accumulation can cause the carotene to bind to the cells of the corpus luteum, preventing vitamin A from forming the vital hormone progesterone. Some people with hypothyroidism may evidence a slight yellowish tinge on their skins, revealing that the beta-carotene they're consuming—in food sources or in daily supplements—is remaining unconverted within their systems.

On the other hand, a body with a low level of vitamin A can't produce TSH. Studies by Dr. Isobel Jennings on cattle and sheep revealed that the basophils of the pituitary gland—the actual cells where TSH is produced—degenerate with insufficient

According to studies by Dr. Isobel Jennings of University College, University of Cambridge, England, when animals were denied vitamin A, not only did they produce less thyroid stimulating hormone, but their pituitary gland basophils (cells where thyroid stimulating hormone is synthesized) degenerated as well.

vitamin A. The pituitary's release of TSH is the final step in the thyroid-producing chain, and if the pituitary isn't producing TSH, the thyroid gland won't do its job either.

A deficiency in vitamin A also reduces the ability of the thyroid to take up iodine. The research of Danish scientist B. Palludan showed that after only two weeks of severe vitamin A deficiency, the thyroid secretion of pigs dropped by 40 to 50 percent.

That means that even if you are getting enough iodine in your diet, insufficient levels of vitamin A may be preventing your thyroid from making use of it, causing your thyroid to produce lower levels of TH, and leading to hypothyroidism.

Abnormal thyroid has all the makings of a vicious circle: if your thyroid can't help convert beta-carotene to vitamin A, neither your pituitary nor your thyroid will be getting enough vitamin A to do its job—and your thyroid will become even less able to help your body manufacture the vitamin A that it needs.

THYROID AND THE "AGING DISEASES"

The symptoms of hypothyroidism mimic many of the conditions that people associate with aging. Mental problems that resemble Alzheimer's disease and other degenerative brain diseases may also result from low TH production. In fact, hypothyroidism may be responsible for cases of treatable dementia, and has been related to negative changes in cognitive function in elderly patients. Without adequate TH, your heart pumps less vigorously, sending less blood—and less of the essential nutrients and oxygen that blood carries—into the brain. Many patients find that memory problems, confusion, loss of concentration, and similar symptoms clear up when TH levels are back to normal.

Depression may result from the changes of life that come with growing older. But hypothyroidism may also produce emotional reactions, including a loss of energy that impedes making positive changes. Crying jags, antisocial behavior, phobias, insomnia, anxiety, and a sense of helpless confusion may result both from hypothyroidism and from a related condition, hypoglycemia (low blood sugar). Many patients have reported an immediate change in mood and energy level as soon as they started taking TH supplements.

THYROID AND DIABETES

Proper levels of TH are essential for the body to maintain appropriate levels of blood sugar. Thus, hypothyroidism may be implicated in diabetes, particularly mature-onset diabetes, a condition in which the body has extreme difficulty regulating blood sugar levels. Essentially, thyroid allows us to convert glucose into energy. In cases of hypothyroidism, however, glucose cannot be utilized and this results in glucose waste and hypoglycemia. Hypoglycemia then leads to the secretion of adrenaline, which causes toxicity of the circulatory system. These circulatory problems are prevalent in diabetics, but they may be reduced or avoided with thyroid supplements. TH supplements have also been shown to reverse other symptoms of diabetes, and in some cases have reversed mature-onset diabetes itself.

THYROID AND METABOLISM

TH governs your body's metabolism. So if TH levels are unnaturally low, you will have an unnaturally hard time losing weight and will find yourself gaining weight with unusual ease. The weight gain—or difficulty with weight loss—often associated with aging may be logically due to reduced TH levels that can be corrected. (Often, too, weight gain in age results from a drop in physical activity, so in addition to checking your TH levels, read Chapter 11, "Exercise of the Immortals.")

Low thyroid levels have been related to high levels of cholesterol, with the attendant increased risk of heart disease and vascular problems. In fact. elevated cholesterol is a classic symptom of extreme hypothyroidism, and studies show that administering two grains of thyroid can reduce the levels of cholesterol and triglycerides in patients.

THYROID AND CANCER

Finally, a number of studies have associated hypothyroidism with increased risk of cancer. Dr. J.G.C. Spencer of Frenahay Hospital in Bristol found that the so-called "goiter belts" (regions where goiter is extremely prevalent, due to low levels of iodine in the water and diet) had higher than average cancer rates, a finding that extended over 15 nations on four continents. According to Dr. Bernard Eskin, director of endocrinology at the Department of Obstetrics and Gynecology at the Medical College of Philadelphia, iodine deficiencies are associated with breast cancer in both rats and humans. As the thyroid gland needs iodine to function, we may infer that thyroid problems are somehow related to the cancer. Moreover, the *Neurology Journal* and the *Southern Medical Journal* have both reported cases in which thyroid supplements actually reversed certain types of cancer.

DETECTING A THYROID PROBLEM

According to Dr. Stephen Langer in his book *Solved: The Riddle of Illness*, some 40 percent of the population is deficient in thyroid in some way. Most hypothyroidism isn't clear-cut on standard medical tests, but there is a simple way to find out if this is a condition from which you suffer. Take the *Barnes Basal Temperature Test*:

1. Before you go to bed at night, shake down a thermometer and leave it by your bed.
2. As soon as you awaken the next day, place the thermometer in your armpit and leave it there for 10 minutes before getting up.
3. Record the temperature. A normal temperature will be 97.8 to 98.2 degrees Fahrenheit. If your temperature is lower on two consecutive days, you are very likely suffering from a degree of hypothyroidism. (Note: menstruating women should not take this test on the first day of their periods, when temperatures are likely to fluctuate more than usual.)

Another test that does a particularly good job of detecting any malfunctions is a new, highly sensitive TSH assay. TSH is an excellent indicator of thyroid hormone action at the tissue level, and many doctors believe that these TSH assays will provide the best indication of deficient thyroxine production, or hypothyroidism.

Serum TSH levels are measured by radioimmunoassay and many experts believe it is the best available test not only for revealing primary hypothyroidism, but also for distinguishing secondary hypothyroidism. The test is conducted as follows: a synthetic thyroid releasing hormone (TRH) is injected intravenously, which causes the release of the thyroid stimulating hormone from the anterior pituitary. TSH levels are measured both before and after the injection of TRH, and by comparison of these levels, thyroid function can be monitored. The higher our TSH concentration, the more likely you are to be suffering from primary hypothyroidism, whereas in secondary hypothyroidism, TSH levels are usually low.

Recent widespread use of this highly sensitive TSH assay has not only eliminated the need for TRH stimulation tests in patients with thyroid cancer or goiters, but it has also allowed physicians to better monitor thyroid hormone replacement therapy in their patients so that TH is not over-replaced.

THYROID AND OSTEOPOROSIS

Women may have more reason to measure their TSH levels than men, since nearly all women who are diagnosed with high levels of TSH have some form of hypothyroidism. In fact, hypothyroidism is much more common in females than in males. Treatment, however, has certain complications.

Studies have shown that thyroid hormone increases bone mineral resorption, increasing the risk of osteoporosis, especially in postmenopausal women. One study found that women being treated with enough thyroxine to suppress TSH for 10 years or more had a nine percent decrease in bone density. Patients with conditions such as goiters or thyroid cancer must receive TSH-suppressive doses of thyroxine, and therefore are at a particularly high risk for osteoporosis.

Women who want to check the functioning of their thyroid or who are presently taking thyroid replacement hormones—especially older women—should be screened with this highly sensitive TSH assay around the age of 45, and then follow up with a screening every two years; this is to ensure, primarily, that their thyroid is functioning properly, and secondly, that there is no over-treatment with TH, which would increase the risk for osteoporosis.

TAKING THYROID SUPPLEMENTS

If your home self-test suggests that hypothyroidism may be a problem for you, we urge you to see your physician and discuss the possibility of thyroid supplements. It is important that your health-care provider adjust the dose until you've found the level that is right for you. Also, adjust your diet and vitamin supplements in such a way as to support your thyroid needs.

You may be one of the 60 percent of U.S. residents whose thyroid is functioning normally. If you're in the other 40 percent, however, you may be surprised at the extent to which TH supplements seem to restore your youth.

PROTECTING YOUR THYROID

In a sense, your first line of defense against hypothyroidism is to take a good multivitamin along with vitamin B complex and vitamin C supplements. Some cases of hypothyroidism may be treated in this way, without the affected person ever having to take thyroid supplements.

On the other hand, if your thyroid problem is caused by something other than a vitamin deficiency, your body won't be able to make use of the vitamin supplements you are taking. In that case, you may need TH supplementation.

Not only vitamin deficiencies sabotage your TH production. Here are some other common causes of this problem:

- environmental pollutants, particularly fluoride in water
- barbiturates and other drugs that contain cyanide
- certain medications, such as sulfa drugs and antidiabetic medications
- prednisone
- supplemental estrogen, such as is found in birth control pills and hormone replacement therapy
- some cough medicines
- amiodarone HCl (Cordarone)
- lithium
- aspirin and other painkillers that contain salicylates
- oil of wintergreen (found in rubbing liniment)
- cigarette smoke, primary or secondary

Even if your TH production has been adequate all your life, the circumstances associated with aging may lead you to take medications that create a thyroid problem, or push an already

Thyroid Supportive Supplements

The following thyroid hormone cofactors and thyroid gland stimulants have been reported as helpful in those suffering from hypothyroidism. Consult your physician before beginning any therapy.

Supplement	Suggested Dosage	Comments
L-Tyrosine (amino acid)	500 mg twice daily on an empty stomach with small amounts of B6.	Low plasma levels have been associated with a hypothyroid.
Sea kelp	As directed by physician.	Contains iodine, the basic substance of the thyroid hormone.
Raw thyroid glandular (Armour extract)	As directed by physician.	Available by prescription only. Synthetic thyroid hormones are often ineffective.
Vitamin B complex including riboflavin (B2) and B12 lozenges	100 mg with meals. 50 mg twice daily. 15 mg dissolved under the tongue 3 times daily or as directed.	Improves cellular oxygenation and energy. B12 is absorbed better in lozenge form.
Brewer's yeast	As directed on label.	Rich in basic nutrients (B vitamins, etc.).
Iron chelate or Floradix formula	As directed on label.	Essential for enzyme and hemoglobin production.
Unsaturated fatty acids	As directed on label.	For proper functioning of the thyroid gland.

Supplement	Suggested Dosage	Comments
Vitamin A plus beta-carotene	15,000 IU daily.	Included in a multivitamin complex.
Vitamin C	500 mg 4 times daily.	Do *not* take extremely high doses—this may affect the production of the thyroid hormone.
Vitamin E	400 IU daily.	Avoid larger amounts.
Zinc	50 mg daily.	An immune system stimulant.

existing problem into a major deficiency. Unless you and your physician identify this as an easily correctable thyroid condition, you are both likely to mistake it for the "inevitable" process of aging. Arriving at the proper level of thyroid for your system can actually determine how long—and how well—you live.

Chapter 11

Exercise of the Immortals

As many gerontologists and researchers have found, exercise is the closest thing to an anti-aging pill that exists. People who are physically fit, eat a healthy, balanced diet, and take nutritional supplements, can measure out to be 10 to 20 years biologically younger than their chronological age—this is what makes an immortal. An immortal doesn't necessarily live forever, but can be free from mental and physical disease and degeneration for years longer than an unhealthy individual. And exercise is an extremely important part of achieving this "immortality."

Remember, it doesn't matter if you were once physically active in your younger years; if you're not currently engaged in a physical activity program on a regular basis, your body is not receiving the innumerable health-related benefits of exercise.

Here are just *some* of the reasons to exercise:

- Improves immune system functioning
- Helps you lose weight—especially fat weight
- Improves survival rate from myocardial infarction
- Improves body posture
- Reduces risk of heart disease

- Improves the body's ability to use fat for energy during physical activity
- Helps the body resist upper-respiratory tract infections
- Helps relieve the pain of tension headaches
- Increases maximal oxygen uptake
- Increases muscle strength
- Helps preserve lean body tissue
- Reduces risk of developing high blood pressure
- Increases density and breaking strength of ligaments and tendons
- Improves coronary heart circulation
- Increases levels of HDL cholesterol and reduces LDL cholesterol
- Helps improve short-term memory
- Sharpens dynamic vision and controls glaucoma
- Reduces risk of developing Type II (non-insulin dependent) diabetes
- Reduces anxiety
- Assists in quitting smoking
- Slows the rate of joint degeneration (osteoarthritis)
- Enhances sexual desire, performance and satisfaction
- Helps in the management of stress
- Improves quality of sleep
- Reduces risk of developing colon cancer
- Reduces risk of developing prostate cancer
- Reduces risk of developing breast cancer
- Reduces risk of developing stroke
- Reduces susceptibility to coronary thrombosis (a clot in the artery that supplies the heart with blood)
- Helps alleviate depression
- Helps alleviate low back pain
- Improves mental alertness and reaction time
- Improves physical appearance
- Improves self-esteem
- Decreases resting heart rate
- Helps in relaxation
- Helps prevent and relieve the stresses that cause carpal tunnel syndrome
- Helps relieve constipation

- Protects against "creeping obesity"—slow weight gain that occurs with age
- Improves blood circulation, resulting in better functioning organs, including the brain
- Increases productivity at work
- Improves balance and coordination
- Helps to retard bone loss as you age, thereby reducing your risk of developing osteoporosis
- Improves general mood state
- Helps in maintaining an independent lifestyle
- Allows more energy and vigor to meet the demands of daily life
- Increases overall health awareness
- Improves overall quality of life

PHYSICAL EFFECTS OF AGING

Over 48 million adults in the U.S., who are otherwise healthy and able-bodied, can be classified as sedentary. An inactive lifestyle only places extra strain on the body, increasing risk for cardiovascular problems, cancer, and many other diseases. More and more, scientists are finding that an adequate exercise program, coupled with a healthy diet, can recapture youthful vitality by slowing or reversing many of the physiologic changes that are associated with aging.

An aging metabolism is less able to use fatty acids properly, thus burdening our systems, depressing our immune system and possibly leading to atherosclerosis. Exercise uses free fatty acids for 80 percent of the calories needed to complete an activity, essentially converting them to energy. As we learned in Chapter 4, the production of growth hormone improves our immune system, build up our muscles, burns off fat, and generally contributes to overall well-being. Although our bodies manufacture less of it as we grow older, accounting for a 40 percent loss with a 30 percent decrease in strength by age 70, exercise stimulates and increases production of this vital hormone.

Not only does it result in a reduced ability to function physically, but the less muscle you have, the less energy you burn while you're resting (metabolic rate). As your metabolic rate and your activity level go down, you need fewer and fewer calories to maintain your body weight. But most people don't decrease their calorie intake to match their declining needs.

Light weight lifting may be an effective method to burn off at least some of these excessive calories. A small study done at Tufts University took 12 volunteers 56 and older and set them on a 12-week strength-training program. The group worked out for 30 minutes three times a week. Researchers found that the volunteers' bodies were burning more energy, allowing them to consume an average of 300 additional calories a day without gaining weight.

After age 35, there is also a decline in total bone mass of up to one percent per year. Women going through menopause may begin to lose their bone density at an even higher rate of up to three percent per year. With low bone density, there is an increased risk of breakage and of developing osteoporosis. Victims of osteoporosis have brittle, porous bones that fracture easily and can result in such deformities as the curved spine "dowager's hump." These conditions are not only debilitating but can be fatal. Weight bearing exercise is the key to building maximum bone mass before age 40 and in retarding the gradual loss of bone mass after age 40. For women, treatments like estrogen replacement therapy (see Chapter 6) can also help overcome bone loss.

Flexibility is yet another factor that diminishes with age. Older people are more prone to stiffness and orthopedic injury than younger people because of physical inactivity. Muscles become stiffer and joints degenerate, producing less joint-lubricating synovial fluid. Connective tissues gradually lose their elasticity and muscle fibers shorten. This loss in flexibility can make common daily tasks such as bending over a chore and fool the mind and body into thinking that it is unable to embark on any exercise. However, about 80 percent of all lower back pain results from poorly conditioned muscles. A simple exercise program can help strengthen the back and eliminate most of these pains, even after a few weeks. By strengthening these joints and muscles, you may eventually be able to participate in other activities and reduce your risk of injury.

Along with the physical changes that the aging process brings on, most people experience a decline in their ability to memorize, concentrate and learn new things. Although these changes do have a physiological basis, many experts believe that they are not ordained by any biological clock. Rather, older people begin to lose certain physical and mental abilities because they are not using them.

In fact, scientists believe that the decline in strength and muscular endurance is due more to disuse of the neuromuscular system than to aging. Small, gradual decreases in strength take place because of a loss in muscle fiber until about age 60, when a more marked decline occurs. Yet elderly people who are put on a program of strength training produce increases in strength, and suffer a loss of strength with age that is considered "hardly noticeable."

> In the United States, as many as 250,000 deaths per year are attributable in part to a lack of regular physical activity.

According to Waneen Spirduso, author of *Physical Dimensions of Aging*,

> Chronic resistance strength training enables individuals to maintain high levels of strength for many years and also provides individuals who have not been involved in strength training an opportunity to reverse many of the age-related deterioration processes that are observed in the muscles of sedentary people.

Recent studies have shown that exercise may also fight aging mentally as well as physically. Tests revealed that highly aerobically fit adults tend to have higher cognitive abilities than sedentary people who are not particularly fit; they seem to process information more quickly and more easily than their inactive counterparts. Researchers speculate that this is because exercise has a beneficial effect on the circulation of blood to the brain, on certain brain chemicals, on the neuroendocrine system (involved in information processing), and on one's ability to get restorative sleep.

Because exercise helps normalize brain chemistry and restore mental equilibrium, studies are pointing to regular physical activity as an effective alternative or counterpart to psychotherapy for people who suffer from mild to moderate depression. And unlike many medications, exercise delivers positive side effects. Physical activity calms the nerves of people who feel anxious and agitated, and invigorates those who feel lethargic and tired. It can also improve appetite for people who don't feel like eating, and reduce food cravings in those prone to overeating.

Finally, health and fitness are not the same. Consider two elderly people who have similiar states of health—that is, they are similiar as far as presence or absence of certain diseases. Yet a person who is fit—strong, flexible, and with a high degree of stamina—will be able to stay more active and enjoy life more than the person who is not fit, even if that nonfit person is, by medical standards, "healthy."

MODERATE EXERCISE: PROLONGING LIFE

If you're a sedentary person, any regular exercise of moderate intensity—even if it's mowing the lawn, gardening or climbing the stairs—will allow you to live longer. Even if you're 60 or 70, it's important to realize that it's never too late!

The Centers for Disease Control and the American College of Sports Medicine recommend that you accumulate 30 minutes a day of exercise in addition to your normal daily activities—and it doesn't have to be 30 minutes consecutively. People who have busy schedules often have to exercise intermittently. *The Journal of the American Medical Association* lists brisk walking, cycling, swimming or calisthenics, racket sports, golf (if you pull your cart or carry your clubs), housecleaning, and raking leaves as some of the options of moderate-intensity physical activities. Thirty minutes a day of exercise is what is recommended for a significant improvement in life expectancy. To improve your fitness and quality of life, you need to perform at least 20 minutes of sustained aerobic exercise that increases your heart rate at least three days a week.

Sedentary persons have approximately twice the risk of acute myocardial infarction and death from coronary heart disease compared to people who are physically active.

Perhaps the most impressive study demonstrating the life extending benefits of exercise was conducted by the American Cancer Society, which followed more than one million American women and men for 20 years. Their conclusion: "Physical exercise lengthens life and wards off heart disease and stroke," particularly for men.

The Cancer Society's findings are supported by a number of other studies. In 1972, T. Khosla of the Department of Medical Statistics at the Welsh National School of Medicine found that exercise had a beneficial effect on his subjects' health. He concluded that because people who exercised were less likely to be obese or to start smoking at an early age, they were not only spared these health hazards but also gained the overall benefits of exercise.

According to the *American Journal of Clinical Nutrition*, exercising while you diet not only improves your mood and self confidence, but may actually help you stick to your regimen. Researchers found that obese women who exercised 45 minutes per day, three times per week during a 12-week diet program lost an average of 19.3 pounds of fat, while non-exercisers only lost an average of 13.4 pounds of fat. Those who exercised also reported reductions in anxiety and depression and an increase in positive feelings.

A study conducted by Dr. Ralph Paffenbarger and his colleagues focused on nearly 17,000 Harvard male alumni with similar demographic characteristics. Men who used up fewer than 500 calories a week on exercise were the group with the highest death rate. The men who expended 500 to 1,000 calories a week on exercise (the energy burned in, say, walking five to ten miles) had a 22 percent lower risk of death, while the men who expended up to 3,500 calories a week on exercise (the equivalent of five to 10 hours of intense exercise) had a 54 percent improvement in longevity.

Interestingly, both the Paffenberger study and another Harvard alumni study found that while a certain amount of exercise is good, more is not necessarily better. In the Paffenberger study, men who used up more than 3,500 calories a week (more than 10 intense hours weekly) had a slightly lower improvement in longevity than their moderately exercising counterparts. While the moderate exercisers had a 54 percent improvement in longevity over the no-exercise group, the intense exercisers had only a 38 percent improvement.

> If you have high blood pressure and exercise, you'll have a greater life expectancy than if you have normal blood pressure and don't exercise.

A 1977 study of Harvard graduates conducted by Anthony Polednak and Albert Damon compared men who were major athletes (a letter in one or more sports), minor athletes (participation but no letter), and nonathletes. They found that ". . . minor athletes generally and, for the most part, lived significantly longer than major athletes and nonathletic classmates. . . . In percentages of men still alive and in percentages of men reaching ages 70 and 75, minor athletes were consistently and for the most part significantly higher in [lifespan]."

When you think about exercise that will prolong life and health, your goal should be to find vigorous, demanding physical activity—but not overly intense, highly competitive, or physically abusive patterns of exercise, which can create negative stress, generate excess adrenaline, or divert energy from the body's normal maintenance processes.

Vigorous exercise creates lactic acid, which can greatly benefit the heart, as well as binding and removing toxic metals that accumulate in our bodies. Yet excess lactic acid can make our muscles stiff and sore. So our goal in exercise, as in all aspects of anti-aging, is *balance*—enough exercise to win the enormous benefits to our health, but not so much as to put an undue strain on our bodies or our spirits.

PREPARING FOR EXERCISE

To begin a regular exercise program we recommend the following test to determine your level of fitness and to help set your exercise goals. However, if you're over 35, haven't exercised for a year, or have any type of heart trouble, *be sure to consult your physician* before beginning this test!

The Step Test

- Find or build a step that is eight inches high.
- Practice until you can step up and then down with each foot—two "up-down" cycles—in five seconds. (You might want a partner to help time you.)
- For three minutes, step up and down with alternate feet, at a rate of two cycles per five seconds. Then wait 30 seconds and take your pulse for 30 seconds.
- Check the following table to find out how to rate yourself.

Poor or Fair. You are at increased risk for cardiovascular disease and *need* an aerobic exercise program. Find the exercise that best fits your lifestyle or seek out a personal trainer from the National Academy of Sports Medicine, 699 Hampshire Road, Suite 105, Westlake Village, CA 91361, phone: (805) 449-1330. Remember, always start at a beginning level.

Average. You need to exercise more regularly to gain the full anti-aging benefits. Make sure you exercise for at least 20 minutes a day three times a week.

Good. You are in good shape, but there is still room for improvement. Increase the intensity or duration of your aerobic workouts.

Classification Age	20-29	30-39	40-49	50+
Men	Number of beats/30 seconds			
Excellent	34-36	35-38	37-39	37-40
Good	37-40	39-41	40-42	41-43
Average	41-42	42-43	43-44	44-45
Fair	43-47	44-47	45-49	46-49
Poor	48-59	48-59	50-60	50-62
Women	Number of beats/30 seconds			
Excellent	39-42	39-42	41-43	41-44
Good	43-44	43-45	44-45	45-47
Average	45-46	46-47	46-47	48-49
Fair	47-52	48-53	48-54	50-55
Poor	53-66	54-66	55-67	56-66

Excellent. Congratulations! You're in the top of your class based on age range. Your time is best spent focusing on body contouring and increasing your flexibility and balance. There is *always* room for improvement.

The first step in choosing the type of exercise that's right for you is to determine your target heart rate. Generally, you should aim for raising your heart rate to about 80 percent of its maximum capacity. Subtract your age from 220 and multiply the result by .75 (75 percent). This is your target heart rate, which will give you the greatest benefits available while not straining your heart or depleting the necessary energy for maintaining your system.

You should aim for raising your heart to its target rate and keeping it there for 30 minutes at a time, for a minimum of about two hours a week. In other words, you're looking for four half-hour sessions of vigorous exercise per week.

However, if you haven't exercised in a while, plan on working up to this ideal gradually, over a period of three or four months. To determine your level of vigor, try talking while exercising. If you're so out of breath you can't talk, you're working too hard. Slow down. And don't start with half-hour workout sessions—try ten or even five minutes at first—until your stamina increases.

If possible, though, try to exercise at least four times a week, even if only for five minutes at a time. Repeated attempts at exercise will build up your muscles as well as your heart and lungs. The more often you exercise, the more easily exercise will come to you.

Finally, don't be discouraged! Although building up your strength and stamina is a gradual process, most people experience fitness as a series of quantum leaps. One day you can barely drag yourself around the block—the next day, jogging seems so easy and natural, you feel like you're floating. Exercise can also vary so that after that "floating" day, you may again experience one or two days of difficulty before moving back up to your new, higher plateau. You'll soon find that regular, appropriate exercise will help you create a new sense of power and well-being that is well worth any times of difficulty or frustration.

> Older individuals have a low proportion of total body water and are more susceptible to dehydration. Therefore, it is important to drink water regularly before, during, and after exercise.

CHOOSING YOUR EXERCISE

It is very important to warm up before embarking on any physical activity to lessen the chances of pulling a muscle, ligament, or tendon. The warmup can be compared to a balanced breakfast that fuels your body and mind in the morning, preparing it for a hard day of work. A proper warmup will take a good 10-15 minutes and will loosen nuts and bolts that, left tight, can cause injury. An easy way to warm up is to mimic the exercise you are planning to engage in. For example, low-level walking may be the precursor leading to the more demanding brisk walking or slow, light stretching of the arms over the head and to the sides can eventually lead into a vigorous game of tennis. *Never* overexert yourself during the warmup, for it can cause fatigue by building up an oxygen debt. This is called an "anaerobic" state, which can end up tiring you out before you've even begun

Walking Workout Tips

Walking is an excellent exercise in itself. It not only improves health and aerobic fitness, but is also one of the safest ways to exercise. Studies have shown that walking decreases risk of coronary heart disease by raising HDL cholesterol levels and increases maximal oxygen consumption. Dr. Kenneth Cooper of the Aerobics Institute in Dallas ranks walking as one of five top aerobic activities—along with jogging, cycling, swimming, and cross-country skiing. It is the perfect initial step for the beginning exerciser, which can eventually lead to other higher endurance exercises. Don't underestimate the power of walking though, as very fast walking can actually be more beneficial aerobically than jogging or slow running at the same speed.

1. **Try to walk at least once every day.**
2. **Walk to your favorite music.** Many studies have shown that when people exercise to music, they exercise harder, longer and better.
3. **Walk faster, farther, and more frequently,** and those extra calories will start to burn off.
4. **Walk wherever and whenever you can.** Don't sit when you can stand or walk around.
5. **Keep a walking journal.** Jot down not only what you eat, but each mile you walk. This will help you chart your progress and give you an idea of how many calories you are using.
6. **Set goals for yourself,** both short- and long-term. Goals give us something to shoot for and keep our motivation high.
7. **Reward yourself** with non-food presents for making these goals—a new piece of clothing for a small goal, or a weekend trip when you complete a long-term goal.
8. **Walk with a friend.** The support is not only comforting, but it helps people stay focused and motivated.
9. **Practice moderation.** Exercise should be enjoyable, not a hassle or an obsession. If you can't walk one day, don't punish yourself. There's always tomorrow.
10. **Practice positive thinking during your walks.** Use walking time as personal time for yourself. Meditate. Think about how good you feel when you exercise, and about how much healthier you are mentally and physically. You'll end your walk with a positive and upbeat attitude.

to really exercise. Remember, treat the warmup like a slow-motion exercise, a light, essential step that can make planned exercise a safer and more enjoyable activity.

If you've been inactive for a long time, however, we recommend beginning with just daily light stretching exercises to help regain functional range of motion in certain joints and to avoid risk of injury. After you feel ready to exert yourself more, start with an exercise that is aerobic in nature—one that requires a high use of oxygen. (You'll find examples of aerobic exercises listed below, under "endurance and cardiorespiratory function.") Swimming and other water exercises are excellent starters because they don't place a lot of stress on the joints. Similarly, stationary cycling places less stress on the joints than other activities and is recommended for beginners over outdoor cycling because of the hazards of the road. You'll see that many exercises contribute towards two or three different aspects of fitness.

The Six Aspects of Fitness

1) Endurance and cardiorespiratory function	brisk walking, hiking, jogging, running, bicycling, aerobic's classes, cross-country skiing, swimming, rowing, trampolining
2) Strength and muscular development	weight training, sprinting, swimming, rowing, tennis, yoga, isometrics, martial arts, squash, basketball
3) Speed and reaction time	sprinting, tennis, Ping-Pong, racquetball, baseball, handball, martial arts, Frisbee throwing, soccer, football
4) Coordination and balance	dancing, golf, squash, sailing, tennis, trampolining, bowling, horseback-riding, baseball, Tai Chi, basketball, football, badminton, billiards, skating, martial arts, yoga
5) Flexibility	dancing, stretching, Tai Chi, meditation, yoga
6) Neuromuscular relaxation	gardening, golf, Frisbee throwing, kite flying, martial arts, Tai Chi, yoga

Find a way of working different types of physical activity into your week, as well as choosing an exercise that affords more than one fitness benefit. For example, you might jog or walk briskly four times a week for a half an hour, followed by a session of light, strength-oriented weight training. On the weekend, you might go dancing, throw around a Frisbee, or play a game of golf.

Try combining exercises for even better all-over body conditioning. For example, if your favorite exercise is jogging, try something completely different like yoga to trigger head-to-toe relaxation. Do both workouts and you get the yin and the yang of exercise benefits: a strong heart, a limber body and a calmer outlook. Another combination might be to look on popular hobbies such as gardening and bicycling as part of your workout. Many people become so engrossed in gardening that they are not aware of the muscles that are being toned, and bicycling afterwards is a great way to cool off and burn off calories. The options are so endless that you could literally turn the great outdoors into your own personal gymnasium!

All exercise programs, no matter how light or hard, need an adequate cool-down period that includes stretching and relaxation. Not doing so can cause discomfort and in some cases, cardiac abnormalities. The cool-down allows the body to return to a resting state. Take at least five minutes to walk around at a slow pace, swinging your arms back and forth. Breathe deeply and release everything from your mind, except for how good you feel from exercising.

EXERCISES FOR IMMORTALITY

There are many components of physical fitness. Health-related components include cardiovascular endurance, muscular strength and endurance, muscular flexibility and body composition. Skill-related components include agility, balance, coordination, power, reaction time and speed. It is very important to gradually work on *all* of these areas in order to achieve the anti-aging benefits as well as all-round physical conditioning.

Too often people and personal trainers buy into the aging

Warning Signs to Stop Exercising

If you should exhibit any of these signs, don't wait. See your physician immediately!

• nausea or vomiting
• chest pain
• excessive fatigue during or after exercise
• pain in the neck or jaw area
• palpitations (irregular heartbeats)
• shortness of breath
• severe, unrelenting pain in muscles and joints

myth and accept becoming weaker, slower and clumsier with age as inevitable. Essentially, we give up on ourselves and assume that our bodies aren't capable of taking great strides or even small strides. Older people get stuck doing only low-aerobic activities such as walking (not to say walking isn't a great way to exercise), ignoring other vital areas. It is important to realize that no matter what your age or current condition, it's likely that your body *can* reach new limits of performance.

When pursuing any kind of physical fitness, always obtain medical clearance, especially individuals with preexisting cardiovascular disease or cardiac problems, chronic obstructive pulmonary disease (emphysema, asthma, chronic bronchitis), uncontrolled diabetes, osteoporosis and arthritis. *Always* start out slowly and increase your level of exercise gradually. You should never feel any strange discomfort. Also, it's a good idea, especially for those with osteoporosis or arthritis, to perform any kind of exercise on a mat or padded floor to protect against serious injury. Here are 10 anytime/anywhere exercises that will help get you started on the path to immortality.

1) The Tai-Chi Breath of Life

This fluid breathing exercise is adapted from Daniel Reid's book, *The Tao of Health, Sex and Longevity*. It incorporates your body, breath and mind and the four distinct stages of breathing: inhalation, retention, exhalation and pause. Breathing exercises help relax the nerves, calm the heart, boost circulation and enhance energy reserves.

- Stand with your heels together and toes splayed at a 45 degree angle, knees bent, spine erect. Bring hands together

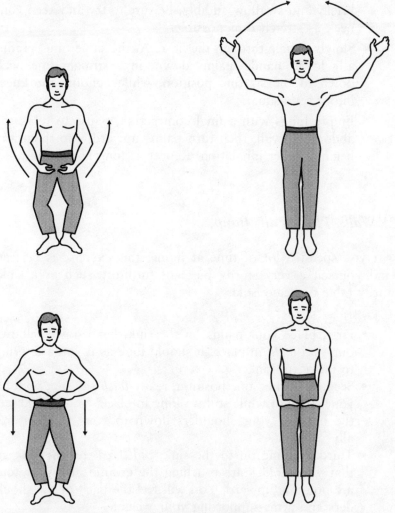

The Tai Chi Circle

A four-stage breathing exercise, for energizing, relaxing and calming.

in front, below the navel, palms up, with the right hand cupped in left.

- Empty your lungs and slowly inhale. As you inhale, slowly raise the hands out to the sides, palms up, and make as wide a circle as possible as you raise them above your head. At the same time, slowly straighten the knees, hands still raised above and lungs full. Tuck in the pelvis, retain briefly and swallow audibly. Be sure to try and keep your neck as stretched as possible.
- Slowly exhale through the nose. At the same time, gradually lower hands, palms down, in a straight line back down to the starting position, while bending the knees into a semi-squat.
- Empty lungs with a final contraction, pause to relax the abdominal wall, then turn palms upward, cup them and begin another inhalation. Repeat as long as you wish.

2) *Walk, Push, Pull, Jump*

If you spend a lot of time at home, this exercise is perfect. Find yourself a very sturdy piece of furniture such as a sink, sturdy table or heavy sofa.

- First, place your hands on the sink, head down, elbows out, and *walk* in place. It should look as if you are trying to move the sink.
- Second, in the same position, really *push* the sink with all your strength while still walking in place. You should feel the back of your shoulders down to your forearms really working.
- Third, holding on to the sink, *pull* back on the sink so that your ankles are touching the ground and your toes are pointing upward. You will feel the back of the shoulders and arms supporting your weight.
- Fourth, lean forward, transferring all your weight on top of the sink and onto your forearms and calf muscles, *jump*

Walk, Push, Pull, Jump

You can use your kitchen to get fit just as easily as you can use it to get fat.

up off the ground. Repeat. This little number proves that exercise can still be fun, and in a practical way!

3) *Mountain out of a Molehill*

This stretching exercise will help alleviate sore muscles and joints and improve muscle tone in the upper body.

- Your body will be face-down to the floor. It will be supported by the hands, palms down against the floor, and the toes in a flexed position, spaced about two feet apart, and the arms and legs should be kept straight.

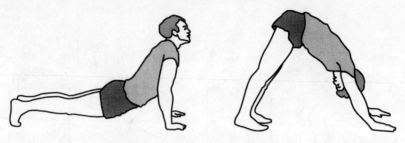

Mountain Out of a Molehill

A stimulating stretch to relieve soreness and invigorate muscles.

- Start with your arms perpendicular to the floor, and the spine arched, so that the body is in a sagging position. Bring the head back as far as possible. You will feel the stretch in the neck and pectoral muscles.
- Bring the chin forward, tucking it against the chest. With feet flat on the floor, raise buttocks up in the air, while bringing body into an inverted "V." Return to original position, and start all over again. You will feel the stretch in the back of the thighs, legs and calves. Remember, breathe in deeply as you raise the body. Breathe out fully as you lower it.

4) *Pelvic Push-Up*

Yoga works the body and the mind. It can strengthen the immune system, improve flexibility and strength, sharpen mental focus, provide relief from back pain and other discomforts and improve overall well-being. This yoga-like exercise not only benefits the spine and many other inner organs, it also effectively releases muscular tension in the shoulders.

- Lie on your back with your hands by your sides, knees bent and feet about hip-distance apart and flat on the floor.
- Inhale and press down on your feet and raise your pelvis slightly upward, squeezing your buttocks.

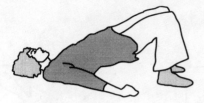

Pelvic Push-Up

A center-body toner and shoulder relaxer.

- Maintaining this position, raise the rest of your torso off the floor as far as is comfortable.

Keep pressing down with your feet as you hold the pose. In addition to releasing tension in the pelvic region, you will also feel the front of the thighs working. Repeat several times.

5) Cat-Man-Do!

This hyperextension exercise strengthens the lower back allowing increased flexibility of the neck, shoulders and spine.

- Kneel on all fours.
- Inhale as you lean your head back slowly.
- Exhale as you bring your head down and slowly arch the spine. As you become fluent in this exercise, try and make the movement rhythmic.

Cat-Man-Do!

Copy cats' sinuous stretches for lower-back strength, and more.

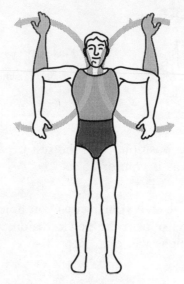
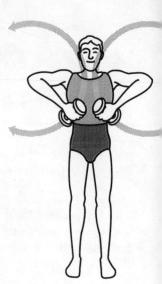

Symphony No. 5

Tune up with a harmonious hum.

6) *Symphony No. 5*

- Start humming or counting. This will increase concentration and help you warm up, just as an orchestra tunes its instruments before a performance.
- Standing with feet slightly apart, arms out, and elbows high and out to the side, trace two C's that are back to back with your forearms. Repeat this motion as many times as possible, being careful not to overstrain the arms. This exercise increases mobility in the elbow joints as well as works the entire arm.
- Try holding light weights or soda pop cans while doing the exercise to help build upper arm strength. Gradually increase weights.

7) Towel Tug of War

- Using a towel, grasp it firmly at both ends, pulling it taut. Wrap it around your forehead, holding one side with your left hand. Forcefully pull your head in the opposite direction, against the towel, while still grasping on tightly. Change sides and repeat. Do the same exercise with the head going backward and forward. This position works all of the neck muscles and helps release accumulated stress and tension.

- Another way to perform this exercise is to keep the taut towel parallel to the floor and pull it slowly to the left while resisting with your right hand. Then pull the towel slowly to your right while resisting with your left hand. Start with six pulls in each direction and gradually increase repetitions. Now, keeping the towel taut, take a deep breath and start with arms in front of you. Move your arms in a huge circle stretching over the head and down again, and exhale slowly. Inhale and repeat. You will feel the shoulders rotating and the entire upper body working together in every direction. Make sure to maintain a good range of motion.

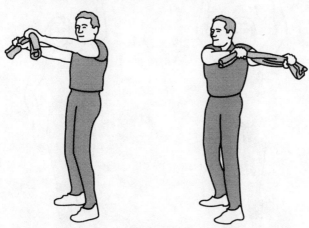

Towel Tug-of-War

You're on both sides of this contest, so you can only win, with stress release as the prize.

8) Flamingo Dance

Most falls in older people are due to weak ankles. This exercise builds strength in the ankles for increased support. The ultimate goal is to gain maximum balance and equilibrium, while reducing risk of injury.

- Stand on a hard floor, wearing shoes, legs slightly apart. Raise up on your tiptoes and then come back down to position. Do this until you don't feel wobbly and your balance is secure.
- Now raise both arms over your head while standing on tiptoes. Still on tiptoes, raise one arm only, then the other only. Continue until you feel that your balance is secure.
- Keeping the left leg firmly planted on the floor, raise your right leg on tiptoe. Switch sides. Repeat, raising an arm and a leg. Close both eyes while on tiptoe. Close one eye. This exercise can be done in a variety of combinations. After mastering it in shoes on a hard floor, move up to

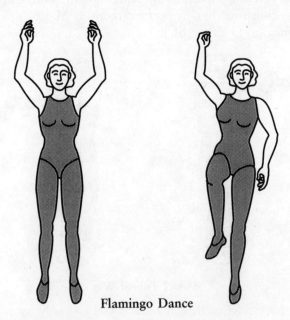

Flamingo Dance

Balancing tips from the birds.

shoes on plush carpet or another uneven surface. Next, try the exercise with bare feet on floor and carpet. For safety precautions, you may want to place a big chair on either side of you.

9) Leg Drops

This exercise is beneficial for the lower abdomen, the hip flexors, and front thigh muscles.

- Find a heavy, sturdy chair and place it against the wall. Sit forward on the chair, gripping the sides and lean your shoulders backward.
- With the left leg straight, lift your right leg as straight as possible into the air. Alternate to the left leg. Repeat about four times and gradually work your way up.
- Once proficient with this movement, try lifting both legs together up and down. You will feel your arms working along with the stomach muscles tightening. Remember, just because you may not be able to straighten your legs all the way, doesn't mean you aren't getting the benefits of the exercise.

Leg Drops

Keep at this exercise and see the payoff in a tighter abdomen and more powerful legs.

Sock 'em Knock 'ems

For when you're not gonna take it any more!

10) Sock 'em Knock 'ems

Sock 'em Knock 'ems are a great way to get out extra frustration while building up your upper body and cardiovascular system.

- Stand erect with feet shoulder-width apart. Flex the knees slightly and visualize a punching bag in front of you.
- Clench your right fist and punch the invisible bag with all your might, then punch with the left fist. Move your arms in a complete motion, bringing them all the way forward and all the way back. Use your whole body. Remember to breathe deeply. Alternate right and left 20 times.
- You can try doing the same exercise overhead by aiming the punches toward the ceiling, bringing the elbow down toward the floor with each punch. This position is especially good for posture and arms. Try alternating positions. Start out slowly and increase speed to burn off even more calories!

MAKING THE MOST OF YOUR EXERCISE

All experts agree that older people especially should check with their physicians before embarking on any exercise program. After that, the key is to get moving and have fun doing it! Give yourself feedback! For example, wear a pedometer so you can chart a progress report and reward yourself for the effort. If you look upon exercise as one more miserable chore that an unfair world demands of you in order to prevent the effects of aging, you may become somewhat more fit, but the added emotional stress of this "unpleasant task" may very well wipe out any possible anti-aging benefits that you might expect. If, on the other hand, you view exercise as a time of joyous communion with your body, a time of testing your limits or of experiencing your physical place in the world, the sense of fitness that you can expect will be enhanced by a new sense of empowerment and accomplishment that can literally take years off your age. It may take you a while to find the type and routine of exercise that's right for you—but once you grasp on to it, you'll discover that exercise is not only the most effective anti-aging medicine you can acquire, but also a pleasure in its own right. After all, why bother reaching 100 years or more if you can't have a positive mental outlook *and* an active lifestyle?

Chapter 12

The Immortals: Successful Athletes Over 60

Johnny Kelley finished his sixtieth Boston Marathon at the age of 83.

Ada Thomas started jogging after she retired at the age of 65. At age 68, she ran her first marathon; at age 69, she finished first in her age group in the women's division. At age 72, she was still running five miles during the week and playing tennis on the weekends.

Ivor Welch didn't start his athletic activity until he was 83. Five years later, at age 88, he had run in five marathons. At age 90, he ran in two half-marathons.

Ruth Rothfarb and Ida Mintz, both over 80, each ran the Boston Marathon in a little over five hours in 1991.

Most of us may not match the athletic feats of these senior athletes—perhaps not at any age! The remarkable accomplishments of these athletes, however, are not just personal triumphs; they're also tributes to the amazing resilience of the human body. They demonstrate that whether you start your exercise program early or later in life, you can still enjoy the physical strength and vigor that most people attribute only to the young.

A MAN AHEAD OF HIS TIME: JACK LALANNE

Jack LaLanne is truly a testament to the virtues of lifelong exercise. Born September 26, 1914, LaLanne grew up as a sickly child. By the age of 16 he suffered from failing health: he was underweight, ridden with acne, and a sugarholic. It was after his mother took him to a seminar given by Dr. Paul Bragg, one of the founding fathers of the natural health movement, that LaLanne was "reborn." After speaking with Dr. Bragg, LaLanne began his lifelong quest to promote good nutrition, diet and proper exercise throughout his community and the world.

In 1931 LaLanne opened a spa in his home—actually, it was on his front lawn and in his basement—where he began working with local policemen and firemen in order to train them for physical tests. It was this spa, named "Jack LaLanne's," that started it all.

By 1936 LaLanne had opened the first commercial health club in Oakland, California. This was just the first of many firsts. LaLanne was the first to put weights in the hands of women; he was the first to invent sectionized weight machines; he was the first to put men and women together in the gym; he was the first to turn the gym into a comfortable, pleasant place where anyone could work out, not just your typical male sweatbox.

Even though LaLanne began his healthy lifestyle early in life, winning the title of Mr. America in his forties, as the years go by, the rewards of physical fitness do not seem to leave him. In fact, as LaLanne ages, the more amazing his athletic feats become:

- At the age of 60, LaLanne swam from Alcatraz Island to Fisherman's Wharf, handcuffs on his wrists and shackles on his feet, while towing a thousand-pound boat. Why, people asked? LaLanne's response: "To give the prisoners hope."

- At the age of 62, LaLanne swam the length of the Golden Gate Bridge underwater, against treacherous tides, this time towing a 2,000-pound boat!
- In 1976, at the age of 61, LaLanne wanted to do something special to commemorate the Spirit of 76 for the country's bicentennial celebration. He did this by swimming the length of Long Beach Harbor, approximately one mile, handcuffed and shackled, towing 13 boats, one for each of the original colonies, containing the appropriate number of people—76.
- By age 65, LaLanne was swimming in Lake Ashinoko, Japan, handcuffed and shackled, towing 65 *boats*, which coincidentally were loaded with 6,500 pounds of Louisiana wood pulp!
- Again, at age 70, once again handcuffed and shackled, fighting blustery winds and currents, LaLanne hit the water and succeeded in towing 70 boats and 70 people (one person on each boat,) for an unbelievable one and one-half miles.

So how does a 70-year-old tow 70 boats through rough waters? LaLanne's daily regimen consists of about 450 vitamin and mineral supplements, including liver and yeast, which he believes helps him build strength. He eats natural foods in their natural states, being sure to avoid red meats, and includes fresh poultry, like turkey. And of course, everything is very low in fat. LaLanne does not live on diet alone, however. He trains two and one-half hours daily as well, combining both weights and aerobics. In fact, when training for a swimming feat, LaLanne has been known to practice treading water against the weight of a harness in his pool for up to five hours at a time!

Today, at the ripe age of 81, LaLanne is currently training for yet another amazing athletic feat to take place within the next few years: a 26-mile underwater swim—literally an underwater marathon—from Los Angeles to Cattalina Island. And with LaLanne's incredible track record, it looks as if his next feat will not be his last.

BOB DELMONTEQUE: A MAN STILL IN HIS PRIME

At the age of 16, Bob Delmonteque stood at six feet tall and weighed in at 195 pounds. Today, at age 75, nothing has changed. Delmonteque still boasts the same toned, muscular, athletic frame he sported in his teenage years.

His committment to exercise and good health began in childhood, growing up on a Texas ranch. He remembers running to school—eight miles one way and another eight miles coming back. These daily "sprints" sparked Delmonteque's interest not only in track and field, but in a variety of other sports, including basketball and football. His initial reasoning for buying a set of barbells was not to bulk up, but rather to improve his athletic abilities and simply "be the best athlete in Texas." He achieved this remakable goal, gaining all-star status in every varsity sport he played throughout school.

Now at the age of 75, Delmonteque is still considered one of the greatest athletes in the country, let alone Texas, with one of the most impressive physiques of his generation. Just this past year, Delmonteque ran the Sante Fe marathon in an amazing five hours and 23 minutes—and he did this without heavy training. When really training seriously, he has finished marathons in as little as three hours and 19 minutes! He also plans to compete in the Senior Olympics in the spring of 1996—a decision he speaks about with the utmost confidence and enthusiasm.

When asked his secret of such amazing physical and mental health, Delmonteque believes it's all a person's mind-set. In fact, meditation and yoga-inspired breathing exercises are a large part of his daily routine. For 20 minutes every morning, noon, and evening he meditates, during which he practices both deep breathing and self-hypnosis exercises. These sessions, he feels, help him release any negativity, stress or toxic bodily poisons, while supercharging him physically, spiritually and mentally.

Aside from his daily meditations, Delmonteque doesn't believe in obsessive or regimented exercising. Instead, he does "whatever he feels like doing," be it jogging, skiing, weight lifting or sprinting. But he *does* believe in a basic three-faceted longevity exercise program, consisting of:

- *aerobic activity* to strengthen the cardiopulmonary system and build endurance.
- *weight training* to build lean muscle mass and reduce the risk of osteoporosis.
- *stretching* to build pliability of the tendons and ligaments.

Delmonteque eats the same way he trains, insisting that an individual should not get too fanatical or obsessive. Instead, he opts to "eat things as close to nature as possible," and he firmly believes in the famous old adage, "you are what you eat." His daily goal, is to keep his weight at 195 and his waist at 32 inches. If he goes above or below these markers, he works to regain his goal.

At 75, Delmonteque is a true role model for other men and women looking to get back into shape and regain some of the spirit and vitality of youth. His advice? "Well," he says, "there's a saying: man who sit on bottom get up on bottom." The best thing to do is to *just do it*. In fact, Delmonteque believes that "lack of physical activity is the biggest contributing factor to the increased risk of disease and illness as we age." However, he warns that people who haven't exercised in a while should always consult with their physician before starting a program.

Delmonteque is living proof that by taking care of ourselves spiritually, mentally and physically, we can attain a sense of well-being at *any* stage of our lives.

The following six profiles are based on stories appearing in *Growing Old Is Not for Sissies* by Etta Clark (Pomegranate Calendars and Books, Corte Madera, CA), an inspiring text-and-picture survey of senior athletes.

BODY-BUILDING FOR LIFE: BILL PEARL

Looking at Bill Pearl today, it's difficult to believe that he actually retired from competitive body building almost 24 years ago. A four-time Mr. Universe, at age 65 he's still in the fabulous shape he was in during his competitive years, and his training schedule is definitely not that of a weary old man.

Since the age of 10, Pearl has worked out four to five times every week. That's 55 years of exercise—and proof that weight training has some serious implications for extending human life, both in years and in quality of health.

Pearl, currently living on a farm in Oregon, still religiously continues to body-build. Following the advice of the the old adage, "Early to bed, early to rise, makes a man healthy, wealthy and wise," Pearl credits his good shape to his sleep schedule. Being in bed by 8 each night allows Pearl the freedom to do what he loves most: train hard, and train early. He'll wake at 2:30 in the morning starting his workout with 30 to 45 minutes on the stationary bike, stair climber or rower. He then proceeds to weight train from about 4:15 until 6. One hundred and twenty minutes of serious training, four to five times per week: a workout not many 25-year olds can keep up with.

Pearl's philosophy on life is one we all should strive for. He states, "At 65, my goal is to have a productive lifestyle. I want to put in 17 to 18 waking hours, all of which are productive."

SWIMMING AGAINST THE TIDE:
TOM RICE AND GEORGE FARNSWORTH

Like LaLanne, Tom Rice and George Farnsworth are also proof of the benefits of long-term exercise.

Both men are lifelong athletes: Farnsworth, a competitive swimmer, and Rice a professional wrestler also known as "The Masked Marvel." In 1966 they began swimming together virtually every day, inside San Francisco Aquatic Park and out into the bay. Farnsworth has continued his vigorous physical regimen into his late sixties and Rice into his early seventies. When wrestling injuries forced Rice into the water to strengthen his legs, he found he liked water sports. He continued to use swimming as a body-building exercise, occasionally towing boats attached to a belt around his torso. Once he even towed a 200-ton ship some 400 yards as a publicity stunt!

Both Rice and Farnsworth have suffered health problems that might have led less dedicated athletes to stay out of the water. At age 68, Farnsworth had a triple bypass; a year later, Rice had a quadruple bypass. Nevertheless, they both found their way back to health and continue to swim together. Rice says that swimming is one of the best ways to fight off the physical miseries of age: "If you work out in the water you can beat whatever ailments you have—even if you just walk in a swimming pool."

POWER LIFTING: HELEN ZECHMEISTER

At age 81, Helen Zechmeister could lift weights that men and women several decades younger might find themselves unable to budge. The national age-group power-lifting records she has held include 245 pounds for the deadlift, 94½ pounds for the bench-press, and 148 pounds for the squat. The only reason that Zechmeister's scores were not considered world records was because the International Power Lifting Federation had no age classification for senior citizens. (Zechmeister was in effect competing against women in their thirties.)

Even most women in their thirties, however, would be proud to match Zechmeister's strength and endurance. At age 81, she was working out in a daily regimen of running, swimming, and lifting. She even competed in a men's 35-years-and-older contest. And guess what—she won.

OVERCOMING ADVERSITY: A.J. PUGLIZEVICH

Sometimes people take A.J. to athletic activity as a response to illness or physical hardship. Puglizevich had known life-threatening illness as early as age 13, when a doctor told his mother that he would be dead within the year. He survived then, only to hear, at age 35, that a hip problem would take away his power to walk unaided within a matter of months.

Fortunately, Puglizevich did not accept these prophecies. He went on to become a renowned senior athlete who at age 76 was competing in the International Senior Olympics. Puglizevich's events are sprinting, the shot put, the discus and javelin throws. He has also won several Senior Olympic boxing competitions.

GRACEFULLY DEFYING GRAVITY: KENT DIEHL

You wouldn't expect a fine-arts appraiser and the owner of a successful antiques business to be a world record trick roper— but Kent Diehl has been roping since he was only nine years old. At age 63, ten years ago, he still called himself "a part-time cowboy," and commented, ". . . with plenty of business pressures, it is most gratifying to pick up a length of rope and spend some time with a good clean sport. The concentration required to keep a limp rope in the air going at full speed clears the head and muscles of everything but the job of rope spinning."

In fact, Diehl is living proof that fitness at an older age is not only rejuvanating physically, but it can be mentally stimulating as well. Sports such as rope spinning not only get the blood flowing, but can hone concentration, preciseness and overall mental agility.

At age 63, Diehl held a world record for five years in a difficult roping event: the largest loop ever thrown and spun while lying down. In the course of his rope-spinning career, Diehl has met such personalities as Will Rogers, Tom Mix, and President Franklin D. Roosevelt. He speaks of his rope-spinning much as a dancer might speak of body movement, as a physically demanding art form that requires immense stamina, skill, concentration—and grace:

"People are fascinated with trick roping because to take a very limp length of rope and keep it going smoothly, defying gravity with graceful flowing loops suspended in the air, inanimate but seemingly endowed with life—to perform intricate figures, mystic patterns of flowerlike arrangements in ever-changing sizes and designs at will—all of this takes consummate skill."

DIVING IN: LUELLA TYRA

As we look forward to growing old, many of us hope to feel physically healthy into our seventies, even into our eighties. But imagine staying physically active into your nineties! At age 92, Luella Tyra was still engaged in competitive swimming. At the 1984 Nationals in Mission Viejo, she entered in several races, diving into the water and swimming 100-meter courses in the backstroke, breaststroke, butterfly and freestyle. Although her coaches had to help her out of the water at the end of every race, she completed every contest by herself. She was the oldest competitor that day at Mission Viejo—perhaps giving some of the other swimmers something to look forward to.

FIGHTING FOR THE LEAD: THE WORLD VETERANS GAMES

In the last few decades, a new category of athlete has been developed—the "masters" athlete. Masters are active athletes who exceed the age limit that's considered necessary for world-class success in a particular sport: in swimming, 25; in track and field, 35; in race-walking, 40. Various masters' competitions have sprung up over the years, including the National Senior Sports Classics (formerly the Senior Olympics), which is open to top athletes over age 50, and the World Veterans Games, a track-and-field event for men over age 40 and women over age 35. As the baby boomers grow older, we can expect a growing interest in masters' athletic events.

SENIOR ATHLETES: BREAKING THE BARRIERS

Part of the reason senior athletes are so inspiring is because they allow us to realize what the human body is truly capable of. They are pushing the limits of the possible. In most athletic events, there's a kind of "barrier of the possible"—the utmost boundary that one can imagine. Runners, for example, thought for years that the four-minute mile was the *ne plus ultra* of athletic achievement. But once Roger Bannister broke through the time barrier, several runners began turning in lower times. Our physical limits seem to be just as much a function of the imagination as of the body.

Senior athletes help us redefine what we expect of our bodies with age. Of course, there are huge genetic variations among the human population, plus environmental factors (pollution, bright sunlight, high levels of noise) and lifestyle choices (smoking, high-fat diet, sedentary life) which are all relevant deciding factors to future physical health. But overall, the healthier your choices in youth, the greater your reserves in age. And as the athletes profiled demonstrate, these reserves can be much greater than we're used to thinking.

You may not break a world weight-lifting record or run the Boston Marathon at 80, but perhaps you will discover a regimen of healthy eating, a regular exercise program, and vitamin supplementation that will allow you to enjoy physical longevity for many years to come. These senior athletes prove that such a choice is possible, at any age, for anyone who chooses to make it.

Chapter 13

The Long-Life Diet:
Nutrition for Longevity

... the cornerstone to your health is diet. Most problems affecting our aging are the chronic degenerative diseases and we have to recognize that three-fourths of the people on Earth don't get these diseases. When we eat a diet that is sparse in meats and fats we do a lot better.
——Dr. WILLIAM CASTELLI,
director of the Framingham Heart Study

A good diet can make an enormous difference to how quickly we age. Among other benefits, a good diet

- provides the food, water, and oxygen that your cells need to reproduce, transmit information, and repair damage
- assures the body a continuous supply of usable fuel, which improves your emotional stability and energy levels
- helps you to purge toxins and waste products, retention of which can increase your risk of cancer and other degenerative diseases
- decreases your risk of cancer, arteriosclerosis, hypertension, heart disease, osteoporosis, senility, and depression

218

- synchronizes your body rhythms, helping you to function physically, mentally, and emotionally at peak efficiency
- adds years to your life—and helps make those years more healthy

Of all the topics covered in this book, diet is probably the most emotionally charged. For most of us, food is much more than just a source of nutrition. It's also a source of comfort, a symbol of love, a recreational pastime, a connection to family and community, and, occasionally, the ground for potent emotions such as anger, fear, anxiety and depression. Moreover, despite the healthful changes in diet that have become increasingly fashionable over the past two decades, many of us have much farther to go before we are able to maintain a true anti-aging regimen. Encountering a long list of "do's" and "don'ts" can be overwhelming, especially where food is concerned.

Less than one-third of Americans meet the U.S. government's *Healthy People 2000* goal of eating five or more servings of fruits and vegetables per day. According to the American Journal of Public Health, studies show that people eat only 1.2 servings of fruits and 3.1 servings of vegetables daily.

Our advice to readers of this chapter is to take it one step at a time. Once you've understood the basic principles on which our anti-aging diet recommendations are based, you can evolve your own system for making the changes that will be most helpful to you. Some people find it easiest simply to overhaul their eating habits once and for all. Other people are more comfortable making one change at a time. Likewise, some people find that once they give up a "forbidden" food, they never miss it. Others work out a system of allowing themselves occasional tastes of the sweet desserts or high-fat foods that are no longer a regular part of their diets. Whatever your modus operandi, remember that dietary changes can be both immensely difficult— and extremely rewarding. Following the right diet can literally add years to your life.

THE HAZARDS OF FAT

Over the past two decades, our society has become increasingly preoccupied with both health and thinness. The popularity of gyms, health clubs and personal trainers, along with the extremely svelte silhouettes of beauty queens and fashion models, attests to the ideals of fitness and slenderness.

> An estimated one-third of Americans are clinically obese or 20 percent over their ideal weight.

At the same time, more Americans are obese than ever before. According to the National Health and Nutrition Examination Survey, some 58 million American adults—over 33 percent of the population—are obese by medical standards (at least 20 percent over the desirable weight range for one's height, with fat constituting 30 percent or more of the body in women and 25 percent or more in men). The U.S. obesity figure of 33 percent is up from a rate of 25 percent in 1980 and 24 percent in 1962.

Although no one knows exactly what the health hazards of obesity are, excess weight seems to be implicated in some 300,000 deaths a year.

> Heart disease aside, there is overwhelming evidence that a high-fat diet increases the risk for cancer of the colon, breast and prostate.

More significantly, excess weight prevents a person from extending his or her life, and contributes to many of the diseases of aging: high blood pressure, heart disease, stroke, diabetes, cancer, digestive disorders, gallbladder complications. High weight is correlated with high cholesterol, which in turn is a predictor of cardiovascular problems.

Fat in men tends to settle in the stomach, creating the so-called "apple" shape, whereas fat in women most often settles around the hips, giving overweight women a "pear" shape. Men seem to be at higher risk for most obesity-related conditions than women.

To determine whether your shape is dangerous to your health, measure your waist at its narrowest point and then measure your hips and buttocks at their widest point. Divide the waist measurement by the hip figure. If your waist-to-hip ratio is higher than .8 (for women) or .95 (for men), you probably need to lose weight.

Another way of finding out whether your weight is in a reasonable range is to look at the chart on page 222.

THE FRUSTRATIONS OF DIETING

Most people who look to dieting as a means of losing weight consider the whole process a rather Sisyphean experience. Just when they seem about to lose those last few pounds or maintain their new desired weight, they fall off their diets, begin to gain, and the whole dieting cycle starts all over again. A 1993 issue of *Consumer Reports* put the recidivism rate for dieters at 75 percent. Dr. Xavier Pi-Sunyer of St. Luke's Hospital in New York puts the figure even higher, at about 85 percent.

Nutritionists, scientists, and dieters themselves have long quarreled over why weight should be so hard to lose and so easy to gain, especially after one has already established a certain higher-than-optimal weight. The most persuasive theory speaks about the set point, the body's predetermined comfort zone for weight, which represents a complex negotiation of genetic factors, the amount of food available in infancy, and eating patterns as a child and adult. Once the body decides on a set point, however, it mobilizes all of its resources to maintain weight at that level. If weight drops below the set point, the body, fearing starvation, lowers metabolism to burn fat more slowly while at the same time increasing appetite. As weight approaches the set point, metabolism picks up again and appetite decreases.

According to this theory, frequent dieting followed by regular regaining of lost weight confuses the body and causes it to

WEIGHING IN

Men

Height Inches	Small Frame	Medium Frame	Large Frame
62	128–134	131–141	138–150
63	130–136	133–143	140–153
64	132–138	135–145	142–156
65	134–140	137–148	144–160
66	136–142	139–151	146–164
67	138–145	142–154	149–168
68	140–148	145–157	152–172
69	142–151	148–160	155–176
70	144–154	151–163	158–180
71	146–157	154–166	161–184
72	149–160	157–170	164–188
73	152–164	160–174	168–192
74	155–168	164–178	172–197
75	158–172	167–182	176–202
76	162–176	171–187	181–207

Women

Height Inches	Small Frame	Medium Frame	Large Frame
58	102–111	109–121	118–131
59	103–113	111–123	120–134
60	104–115	113–126	122–137
61	106–118	115–129	125–140
62	108–121	118–132	128–143
63	111–124	121–135	131–147
64	114–127	124–138	134–151
65	117–130	127–141	137–155
66	120–133	130–144	140–159
67	123–136	133–147	143–163
68	126–139	136–150	146–167
69	129–142	139–153	149–170
70	132–145	142–156	152–173
71	135–148	145–159	155–176
72	138–151	148–162	158–179

Preferred weight-height ratios.

stick ever more stubbornly to its set point. The less the frequent dieter eats, the lower his or her metabolism drops, so that losing weight becomes extremely difficult and gaining weight seems to take place with virtually any intake of food.

In addition to the frustrations of so-called yo-yo dieting, health professionals have recently raised concerns that frequent weight gains and losses might actually be dangerous to the dieter's health. These fears, however, seem to be largely unfounded. According to a recent survey by the National Institutes of Health task force of 43 different studies of dieting, "Obese individuals should not allow concerns about hazards of weight cycling to deter them from efforts to control their body weight."

Even if you're not worried about the dangers of dieting, what about the more basic problem of finding an effective way to reduce body fat? The bad news is that there is no easy answer. The good news is that with the proper combination of exercise (see Chapter 11) and dietary change, you can alter both your body weight and your chances for a long and healthy life. The dietary changes we'll explore in this chapter aren't so much "diets" as long-term approaches to eating. And the stakes aren't just a slender figure or a chance to wear last year's jeans, but rather a new lease on life.

EAT RIGHT FOR LONG LIFE

Basically, the diet that will most support healthy longevity follows these principles:

It's nontoxic. That means it contains hardly any preservatives, additives, pesticides, growth hormones (routinely given to livestock and poultry), antibiotics (likewise), food coloring, chemical flavoring, and other substances that tax your liver, your digestive system, and your heart.

It contains enough nutrients and fuel to satisfy your daily needs. Since most fresh fruits and vegetables lose much of their nutritional value within hours after being picked, you'll probably have to augment even the healthiest diet with vitamin and mineral supplements. Nevertheless, the more you can obtain basic

---

The American Heart Association Dietary Guidelines

1. Dietary fat intake should be less than 30 percent of total calories.
2. Saturated fat intake should be less than 10 percent of total calories.
3. Polyunsaturated fat should not exceed 10 percent of total daily calories.
4. Cholesterol intake should not exceed 300 mg per day.
5. Carbohydrate intake should represent 50 percent or more total calories with emphasis on complex carbohydrates.
6. Protein intake should constitute the remainder of the calories.
7. Sodium intake should be limited to less than three grams per day.
8. Alcohol consumption is not recommended, but if consumed, should not exceed one ounce a day of ethanol or eight ounces of wine or 24 ounces of regular beer.
9. Total calories should be consumed with the goal of achieving and maintaining a person's recommended body weight.
10. Consumption of a wide variety of foods is encouraged.

---

nutrients from natural sources, the healthier your diet is likely to be.

It consists of foods that are easy to digest and eliminate. Evidence dating back to prehistoric times indicates that humans were originally vegetarians, with meat-eating developing as a later, acquired taste. Certainly our digestive systems bear this theory out, for they process and eliminate meat and poultry with far greater difficulty than high-fiber foods, complex carbohy-

A high plasma level of the amino acid homocysteine is an independent risk factor for coronary artery, cerebrovascular, and peripheral vascular diseases. According to researchers at the University of Washington, increasing folic acid through fruits and vegetables or supplementation can lower these risks, preventing "13,500 to 50,000 deaths per year."

drates, and fresh produce. Although occasional consumption of meat—say, twice a week—is probably a key ingredient of a healthful diet, there's mounting evidence that more frequent consumption increases your risk of colon and pancreatic cancer.

In short, your diet should consist of the following:

- raw or lightly cooked whole-grain cereals
- raw or lightly steamed vegetables and sprouts
- raw fresh fruit, including the skin because of the fiber and pectin it contains
- lightly cooked beans, lentils, and peas
- raw nuts and seeds (unsalted)
- a certain amount of nonhomogenized dairy products, particularly cultured products like yogurt
- fresh meat, fish, and poultry about two times a week

A recent report in the Journal of the American Medical Association, estimated that up to 50,000 deaths from heart disease could be prevented each year if Americans consumed more folic acid.

Along with this healthy diet, you may want to take the vitamin and mineral supplements discussed in Chapters 8 and 9, if only because it's so difficult, in our mechanized, nonagricultural society, to find uncontaminated, truly fresh food. For example, frozen vegetables have 25 percent less of the common vitamins (A, C, B1, B2, and B3) than cooked fresh vegetables, while canned vegetables have two to three times fewer vitamins than frozen. (Canned peas, for example, have lost 96 percent of their vitamin C.) Yet fresh produce that has sat in a truck or on a grocery shelf for a few days may have even fewer nutrients than frozen food. Exposure to oxygen, carbon dioxide, heat, cold, moisture, and light all cause food to degenerate, as does physical damage.

We all need a certain amount of fat, protein, and carbohydrates. Yet the typical American diet maintains entirely the wrong balance of these essential nutrients: it's 40 to 45 percent fat, 15 to 20 percent protein, 20 to 25 percent simple carbohydrates (refined sugar and related foods), and 20 to 25 percent complex carbohydrates (whole grains, vegetables, and fruits). A healthier balance would be only 10 to 20 percent fat and a similar amount of protein; 0 to 5 percent simple carbohydrates; and at least 65 percent complex carbohydrates.

You'll notice that some foods are conspicuous by their absence from the "healthy diet list." Sugar, salt, alcohol, caffeine, and foods high in preservatives, as well as high-fat foods, will all contribute to making you old before your time. American staples such as pre-sweetened cereals, luncheon meats, bacon and pork products, white flour, cola and other sweet drinks (even if made with aspartame), sweetened fruit drinks, potato chips and pretzels, roasted nuts and seeds, instant foods of all types, fried foods, coffee, tea, and (alas) chocolate all tend to age the body; they put a strain on your organs, your digestive system, and your cardiovascular system, and in many cases, they actively introduce free radicals into your body.

> According to research conducted by the Human Environmental Sciences department at the University of Kentucky, bagged vegetables in the supermarket not only stay fresher longer than unwrapped vegetables, but they also retain vitamin C and beta carotene better because of the controlled amounts of water, oxygen and carbon dioxide inside the bag.

In the rest of this chapter, we'll go into more detail about some of the more common health hazards in the American diet, as well as offer some positive suggestions for what to eat instead. Before we move on, though, a word of caution: don't become a food fanatic! If it works best for you to eat a basically healthy diet, with occasional treats of chocolate ice cream or beer and pretzels, by all means, go ahead. If the one indulgence you can't bear to give up is your morning cup of coffee or a few glasses of wine with dinner, let yourself go—if that makes it easier to maintain good nutrition elsewhere in your diet.

Some people find that once they experience the benefits of healthier eating, it's worth it to them to give up the caffeine, sugar, fat, and salt that, in both the long and the short run, drain your energy and strain your system. Other people find that they can only maintain a healthy diet if they are occasionally eating certain favorite foods. The point is not to achieve a rating of "100 percent correct," but to make some basic changes and adopt a diet that primarily consists of whole grains, fresh fruits, and vegetables.

THE SOYBEAN SOLUTION

Acting as one of nature's own antioxidants, the soybean may be one of the most important foods we add to our long-life diet. Some nutritionists call soybeans a natural "anti-aging pill," because they may interfere with free radical damage and enhance our cells' defenses against aging and age-related diseases.

In a study conducted by Dr. Denham Harman, father of the free-radical theory of aging, laboratory animals that consumed soybean protein drastically reduced free-radical damage to their cells, more so than animals fed casein, a dairy protein. In addition, the animals that ate soybean protein extended their life spans by 13 percent!

The effect soybeans have on longevity is not restrained to laboratory animals, however. It is a known fact that the Japanese, who eat the highest daily amount of soybeans in the world, live longer lives than any other group of people on the planet. The Japanese consume about an ounce of soybeans per day— almost 30 times more than Americans—and they have far fewer cases of heart disease, cancer, diabetes and osteoporosis.

Scientists at the University of Pennsylvania School of Medicine found that soybeans contain a protease inhibitor called the Bowman-Birk inhibitor, which is so versatile against various cancers that it has been dubbed "the universal cancer preventive agent."

Perhaps the key ingredient that makes soybeans such powerful antioxidant food is a substance called genistein. Genistein is a rare, vital antioxidant that has immense anti-aging biological activity. Some of genistein's potent anti-aging effects include:

> Soybeans contain an anti-disease agent called genistein which has
> been shown to interfere with fundamental cancer processes at virtually
> every stage.

- interfering with cancer activity at every stage, including breast, colon, lung, prostate, skin and blood (leukemia) cancers
- reducing plaque build-up in artery walls and reducing the risk of heart attack, stroke and atherosclerosis

Exposure to the chemical genistein reduces breast cancer in animals by 40 to 65 percent, according to Dr. Stephen Barnes, professor of pharmacology at the University of Alabama at Birmingham. Japanese women (who eat soybeans regularly) have only one-fourth as many instances of breast cancer as American women, whose soy consumption is extremely low. Soybeans fight breast cancer in two ways: they have a direct anticancer effect on our cells; and they prevent estrogen from causing malignant changes in breast tissue. This phenomenon is seen in both pre- and postmenopausal women.

As with breast cancer, soybeans also help prevent prostate cancer. Observing the differences between Japanese and American males, the power of the soybean is quite evident. While Japanese men are still prone to prostate cancers, their cancers don't grow fast enough to become as deadly as most American cases of prostate cancer do. And according to Finnish researcher Herman Adlercreutz, eating soybeans and soy products has been shown to reduce prostate cancer in laboratory animals.

Other amazing effects of this little bean on the human body include boosting HDL cholesterol levels and lowering triglycerides, keeping blood sugar at healthy levels—thus reducing our risk for mature-onset diabetes and heart disease—and increasing bone mass by helping our systems retain calcium.

In order to reap the anti-aging benefits of the soybean, you must make sure you are eating the beans' *protein* (i.e., soy sauce or soybean oil contain very little protein, and therefore exhibit very few life-giving properties). According to Dr. Mark Messina, author (with Virginia Messina and Kenneth Serchell) of the book

The Simple Soybean and Your Health (Avery, 1994), some of the best sources for good soy protein are:

- soy flour: 1/2 cup—50 mg
- soy milk: 1 cup—40 mg
- tofu: 1/2 cup—40 mg
- soy nuts: 1 ounce—40 mg
- miso: 1/2 cup—40 mg
- tempeh: 1/2 cup—40 mg

Obviously, you don't have to eat *all* of this soy product once a day—Dr. Messina recommends perhaps one cup of soy milk and three to four servings of tofu daily. That would equal what the Japanese normally consume—about 50 to 75 mg per day. It's also important to remember that to see any of these anti-aging effects, you must eat soy every day; studies have shown that chemicals like genistein only remain in our bodies for 24 to 36 hours at most. Therefore, daily servings are needed to keep our cells fully stocked with the power of soy.

THE USES AND ABUSES OF FAT

In the current focus on low-fat foods and the dangers of cholesterol (to some extent related to fats in the diet), it's important to remember that the body needs a certain amount of some kinds of fat. Natural fats provide a concentrated form of energy and create the environment in which fat-soluble vitamins, such as A and E, can be digested. They also provide the essential fatty acids, which the body uses to maintain its cellular structure.

Fats come in two forms: saturated, from dairy, meat, and fish products; and unsaturated, from vegetable and fish oils. Here are some forms in which fat can be useful to your body:

- *Cod liver oil* This form of fat contains essential fatty acids that convert into chemicals that protect your heart.
- *Evening primrose oil* Available in health food stores, this substance also contains essential fatty acids, including

The Pritikin Diet

The Pritikin Diet, named after the late Nathan Pritikin, has become not only an influential and popular diet program used by the American Heart Society, but is also now a common household phrase. Through a strict regimen of diet and exercise, Pritikin dieters boast the ability to maintain their ideal body weight, quit smoking, and improve their blood pressure levels. Most importantly, the Pritikin diet promises a significantly decreased risk of heart disease.

The main concept of the program is to keep one's daily food consumption high in complex carbohydrates and low in fat—a smart concept indeed. However, the Pritikin diet is also known for its strict guidelines, and those who can actually stick to it have an iron willpower.

Two diets are recommended by the Pritikin Longevity Center:
1) the regression diet
2) the maintainance diet

The regression diet, called "regression" because it helps our chances of heart disease "regress," is usually followed at the Pritikin Center, as this diet allows for a total daily cholesterol intake of only 25 mg per day. Since it is so restrictive, patients find it easier to follow in a structured setting.

The maintainance diet can be done outside the Center, as a continuation of the regression diet, and it allows a daily cholesterol intake of up to 100 mg, making it a little more lenient. Both diets are composed of 80 percent carbohydrates, 10–15 percent protein, and only five to 10 percent fat.

Despite its somewhat difficult and restrictive nature, this diet has proven beneficial for many patients afflicted with heart disease. And according to Pritikin himself, "Many patients recommended for bypass surgery could control their heart disease just as effectively with drugs and a diet and exercise program."

gamma-linoleic, which lowers cholesterol and blood pressure, heals eczema, eases hangovers and premenstrual tension, and helps to control weight.
- *Olive oil* This is probably the most beneficial form of fat to use for cooking, as olive oil lowers LDL cholesterol without affecting HDL cholesterol. It is known as a mo-

nounsaturated fat. The best olive oil is extra-virgin and hand-pressed, as hydraulic presses may generate heat that in turn damages the oil.

- *Polyunsaturated fats, such as sunflower seed oil and sesame seed oil* Like their cousin, the monounsaturated olive oil, both these fats lower LDL cholesterol, but they also lower HDL cholesterol. They're also more susceptible to turning rancid than olive oil—a process known as "auto-oxidation," which, as the name suggests, introduces those free radicals that antioxidants must then combat.

Olive oil especially has been shown to have numerous health benefits. A new study reported in the *British Medical Journal* found that the traditional Mediterranean diet, rich in olive oil and moderate amounts of wine, may have significant long-life benefits. The six-year study of 182 rural Greek men and women

Studies have shown that the risk of developing lung cancer is up to five times higher in nonsmoking women whose diets are heavy in saturated fats as in those women who avoid cigarettes and eat leaner foods.

over age 70 found that those who consumed a diet including olive oil, whole-grain breads and fresh fruits and vegetables significantly reduced their chances of dying during the study, compared to those who ate diets rich in red meats and saturated fats.

The study broke down the Mediterranean diet into eight components:

- a high ratio of monounsaturated to saturated fats
- moderate ethanol consumption (alcohol)
- high consumption of cereals, fruits and vegetables
- low intake of meats and dairy products

According to these components, for every unit increase there was an astounding 17 percent reduction in overall mortality.

Fish Oil and Heart Disease

Observations of the diet and lifestyle of Greenland Eskimos show that a high fat diet composed of Arctic foodstuffs and low in cholesterol results in a population with:

- very low incidence of heart disease
- very low incidence of hypertension
- very low platelet aggregability

The reason? Fish oil. Actually, it's because of eicosapentaenoic acid, or EPA, which is found in high concentrations in fish and marine life. Unlike the damaging prostaglandins found in animals (like thromboxane, which constricts arteries), when we consume EPA we experience less vasoconstriction in arteries and less platelet aggregation. Therefore, we reduce chances of blood clots, atherosclerosis, stroke, and heart attack. Consuming fish oil can also help lower serum cholesterol and triglyceride levels.

However, a word to the weight-conscious: fish oil is not calorie-free. If you want to start taking fish oil daily, you might want to reduce your daily food consumption by about 300 calories, or else you'd be putting on about 25 extra pounds per year.

On the other hand, several types of commonly used fat are relatively dangerous to your system and should be avoided:

Hydrogenated fats, such as margarine and shortening These are fats created through the process of hydrogenation, which converts a liquid (unsaturated) fat to a solid (saturated) fat by exposing the fat molecules to hydrogen. Hydrogenated fats interfere with the body's production of prostaglandin, a substance that helps create a resistance to pain and helps produce healthy cells and tissues.

Highly heated or reheated fats Unless you're buying cold-pressed oils (available in health-food stores and some gourmet stores), you're buying fat that has already been heated, which oxidizes it and increases its ability to oxidize in the body. Fats heated to more than 300 degrees Fahrenheit are more likely to be highly oxidized.

According to a recent study conducted at the University of Washington in Seattle, eating 5.5 grams of omega-3 fatty acids a month, (the equivalent of four three-ounce servings of salmon) may reduce the risk of cardiac arrest by 50 percent.

Here are some additional suggestions for healthy uses of fat in your diet:

- Buy small bottles of oil with narrow necks and tightly closed lids; refrigerate after opening. This will limit the fats' exposure to oxygen.
- Use saturated fats, such as butter, rather than unsaturated fats, such as margarine. Use nonhydrogenated fats, such as butter, olive oil, sunflower oil, or sesame oil, rather than hydrogenated fats, such as margarine or shortening. Margarine is doubly dangerous to your body because it is a hydrogenated fat. The unnatural molecules it contains raise your blood cholesterol, even though margarine itself contains less cholesterol than butter. Hydrogenated fats also tend to deposit fats in your arteries, interfering with the circulation of your blood. Finally, hydrogenated fats increase your body's exposure to free radicals.

Recently a study reported in the medical journal *Cell* announced the discovery of a hormone that may trigger the formation of fat cells in the body. According to Dr. Ronald Evans of the Salk Institute in La Jolla, California, the hormone triggers a receptor that causes normal cells to change into fat cells.

Although development of a possible "anti-hormone" may take five years or more, the discovery of this hormone has enabled researchers to better understand the origin of the fat cell, which according to Dr. Evans is "the most important part of the process."

Stop That Fat

The easiest way to lose weight is to cut out dietary fat.

Choose	Instead of
pita or bagel	croissant
crispbreads or flatbreads	regular crackers
graham crackers/fig bars	chocolate-chips
plain whole-grain cereal	granola
low-fat breads or muffins	cake and doughnuts
farmer cheese	cream cheese
nonfat frozen yogurt	ice cream
low-fat or nonfat yogurt	sour cream
low-fat or skim milk	whole milk
low-fat cottage cheese	ricotta cheese
fruit spreads or jam	butter and cream cheese
pretzels	chips and nuts
hot-air popped corn	microwave/oil popcorn
cod, flounder or scrod	salmon and mackerel
water-packed tuna	oil-packed fish
baked or boiled fish	breaded and fried fish
tomato sauce	cheese sauce
part-skim mozzarella	muenster or cheddar
mustard or ketchup	mayonnaise
baked turkey or chicken	bologna and salami
turkey ham or smoked ham	hot dogs and sausage
Canadian bacon	bacon
extra-lean ground beef	regular ground beef
sirloin tip roast	T-bone or chuck
skinless light-meat poultry	dark meat w/skin

The Cholesterol Issue

Evening primrose oil, cod liver oil, and olive oil actually reduce total and/or LDL cholesterol in your body. Lecithin, L-carnitine, vitamins C and E, dietary fibers such as oat bran, and deodorized garlic also lower cholesterol and/or triglycerides. In addition,

According to the Second Report of the National Cholesterol Education Program, niacin typically reduces low-density lipoprotein cholesterol by 10 to 25 percent and triglycerides by 20 to 50 percent, while
boosting cardioprotective high-density lipoprotein cholesterol by 15
to 35 percent.

vitamin E, oat bran, and garlic increase your body's level of
HDL cholesterol.

Cholesterol remains a somewhat mysterious term to many
health-conscious Americans. We've all heard about the striking
dangers of this bodily substance: its relationship with deadly
heart disease and other cardiovascular disorders, its dangers to
the immune system and its possible correlation with certain types
of cancer. What many people do not know is that more than 90
percent of blood cholesterol is actually manufactured by one's
own body. Reducing dietary cholesterol will therefore have relatively little effect on blood cholesterol levels.

This is not to say that your blood cholesterol levels are
outside of your control. On the contrary, many factors tend to
increase your cholesterol level: smoking, high blood pressure,
liver problems (exacerbated by a diet high in toxic additives and
preservatives), inadequate exercise, carrying too much body fat,
stress, and depression. Because consuming too much fat tends to
aggravate these other factors, it will indirectly raise your cholesterol level.

On the other hand, you have many options for reducing
your cholesterol level: substituting vegetable for animal protein
(vegetable proteins contain sterols, which block your blood's
ability to absorb cholesterol from your intestines and may also
help your liver better regulate cholesterol production); eating

Currently, the American Heart Association and the National Cholesterol Education Project recommend the "prudent" diet for everyone,
regardless of sex, race or age: 300 mg of cholesterol daily, 65 mg
total fat for the average 2,000 calorie-eating person, 22 g saturated fat.

A Word About Cholesterol ...

What *is* cholesterol and *why* do we need it?

Cholesterol is a crystalline substance made up of fats. Naturally, it is found all throughout our bodies—in the brain, liver, blood and bile. Produced mainly in the liver, cholesterol is needed for the body to function properly; it is used by the cells to build membranes, it's needed to make bile salts, hormones and vitamin D, and it also aids in digestion. As cholesterol travels through the body, cells take what they need and leave the excess in our bloodstreams. It is this excess cholesterol that can "stick" to our arteries as plaque and lead to various forms of heart disease.

What are triglycerides?

Triglycerides are fats attached to a glycerol molecule, which are made up of three fatty acids. They are essentially the major transport and storage form for fats in our bodies, but high levels of triglycerides in the body have been associated with heart disease and diabetes.

The good and the bad

Researchers have discovered two different types of cholesterol: low-density lipoproteins (LDL "bad" cholesterol) and high density lipoproteins (HDL "good" cholesterol). Our bodies can't use LDL cholesterol because it's obtained through animal products, and our cells usually reject it. Therefore, LDL cholesterol usually ends up as plaque that clogs our artery walls, while the body produces its own serum cholesterol, which it can utilize. HDL cholesterol, however, actually helps remove excess cholesterol from tissues and the bloodstream. Studies have shown that those individuals who have high levels of HDL's and low levels of LDL's also have a lower risk of heart disease. And if a person has already experienced a heart attack, increasing HDL levels and decreasing LDL levels brings improvement in arterial plaque.

more fiber (fiber blots up excess fat); making sure you get the essential fatty acids that will regulate your blood fat; and exercising regularly (see Chapter 11).

Fiber: The Answer to Fat

Fiber tends to soak up fat. A high-fiber diet can be an effective anti-aging tool, improving your digestion, relieving the strain on your liver and gall bladder, and reducing the risk of large bowel cancer, gallstones, diabetes, arteriosclerosis, colitis, hemorrhoids, hernia, and varicose veins.

Fiber is the structural material that gives plant cell walls their integrity. Hence, fresh fruits and vegetables, whole grains, nuts, seeds, and legumes are all good sources of fiber.

Fiber is also an important part of the human digestive process. It gives volume to the food we ingest, so that our intestines can more easily pass along their contents. Both absorption of nutrients and the elimination of waste are eased by fiber, with consequent benefits to your intestines.

There are many different types of fiber, and your body will benefit from absorbing some of each. Broccoli, green beans, and lettuce contain cellulose, which swells to increase the weight of food ingested. A high cellulose content helps food move more quickly through the intestines, reducing the amount of time that bacteria can breed. It also eases pressure on the colon.

Cereals, brans, and whole grains contain hemicellulose, which increases the bulk of fecal matter, also relieving pressure on the colon. Hemicellulose reduces the possibility of gallstones, it lowers cholesterol levels, it generally absorbs and neutralizes many harmful toxins, and, by moving food more quickly through the system, reduces the amount of time that bacteria and carcinogens may breed within it.

Pectin is a type of fiber found in apple peel and carrots. It is known to lower cholesterol and generally to act as an antitoxin. Mucilage, found in legumes and seeds, also lowers cholesterol, as well as speeding the process of food through the system.

Lignin, found in wheat bran and apples, helps bind the heavy metal trace elements in our food, preventing their oxidizing effects, as well as producing other antitoxic effects.

However, if you're depending on bran as your major source of fiber, be aware that it can leach calcium, magnesium, and zinc from your system. As with most nutritional elements, it's a good idea to get fiber from many sources, and to avoid "megadoses" of any one type of food.

PROTEIN: A DOUBLE-EDGED SWORD

The right place for protein in a healthy diet is a problematic concept for many Americans to grasp, for virtually all of us have been brought up with the notion that "more is better" where protein is concerned. In a sense, traditional nutritional ideas about protein have been oriented toward an outmoded model of building up muscles and body mass—useful for a short-lived people facing the physical dangers of a hunting society or the enormous physical demands of agricultural labor, but not particularly useful for the prevention of aging and age-related disease that concerns us now.

The very name protein comes from the Greek word for "of first importance," and protein is truly vital for human life itself. Our bodies use the 22 amino acids of protein to build muscles, skin, hair, nails, and blood, as well as to nourish the heart, the brain, and other organs.

Yet excessive consumption of protein not only puts an unwarranted strain on our digestive and eliminative systems, but it also reduces our immunity, increases cholesterol levels, and causes calcium to be leached from our bones.

How much protein your body needs depends on your lean body weight, as protein is the substance used to maintain that weight. A number of factors may increase your need for protein. A child's growth requires protein, as muscles, organs, and other parts of the body rely upon that substance for their ability to expand. Exercise and weight training use protein to increase muscle mass. Alternately, stress, serious illness, and wasting diseases deplete the body's protein intake, requiring increased consumption to make up the loss.

Many nutritionists believe that the recommended daily allowance for protein in the American diet is vastly inflated. And, even given these high standards, the average American male eats nearly twice the recommended amount, while the American female likewise overconsumes.

Studies of centenarians, on the other hand, show that they tend to have a low intake of protein, and to favor vegetable sources over animal protein. A diet high in rice, beans, and other grains and legumes, supplemented by small amounts of dairy products and fish, is far healthier than one that relies on red meat and chicken for protein.

SENSIBLE SALT

By now, most Americans have heard the warnings about a high salt intake: it tends to raise blood pressure, increases the risk of prostate problems, heightens premenstrual tension, and contributes to heart attack and stroke. Yet salt is so widely used in American cooking that, unless you cook all your own food from fresh and natural sources, you are likely to be exposed to salt without knowing it.

Here's a list of some common high-sodium foods that a person on an anti-aging diet would do well to avoid:

Beverages	commercial buttermilk, tomato juice, V8 juice
Fats	gravy, peanut butter, prepared salad dressings
Protein foods	canned salmon and tuna, cheese, luncheon meats, ham, bacon, smoked fish, other cured meats and fishes, frozen dinners
Snacks	(unless unsalted) pretzels, potato chips, popcorn, crackers
Vegetables	virtually all canned vegetables, sauerkraut, olives, pickles

Soups	virtually all canned, dried, or instant soups
Condiments	virtually all commercially prepared condiments, including ketchup, soy sauce, meat sauce, barbecue sauce, chili, prepared mustard, seasoned salt, MSG, meat tenderizers

There are some healthy alternatives to salt. Even though you should use these substances, too, in moderation, they are likely to be easier on your system than commercial salt:

- *Sea salt*—only 75 percent sodium chloride (the basic elements in table salt) and 25 percent trace minerals

---

Chlorella

Chlorella is a therapeutic green algae that's been in existence since the Pre-Cambrian period—almost 2.5 billion years. It consists of 60 percent protein, 20 percent carbohydrates, and contains unsaturated (good) fats. In addition, chlorella contains an abundance of vitamins, minerals, and antioxidants including: vitamins A, B-2, B-6, C, K, E, calcium, magnesium, iron, zinc, phosphorus, iodine and beta-carotene. Proponents of this nutritional superfood speak of its ability to ward off disease and slow the aging process. Chlorella has also been credited with:

- boosting immunity
- reducing high blood pressure
- reducing the risk of diabetes
- helping reduce symptoms of premenstrual syndrome
- reducing symptoms of menopause
- reducing the risk of anemia
- promoting cell growth
- healing wounds

Chlorella contains chlorophyll, which can help speed the cleansing of the bloodstream. And its high content of DNA and RNA has been found to protect against the effects of ultraviolet radiation.

- *Kelp*—only 18 percent sodium chloride; many trace minerals
- *Miso*—a fermented soybean product, only 12 percent sodium chloride, 15 to 20 percent protein, 5 to 8 percent fat, and 12 to 22 percent carbohydrates.

GARLIC AND ONIONS

Two of the most valuable foods on the planet, which can be used as delicious spices in place of salt, are garlic and onions. For centuries, people have recorded the healing and life-giving properties of these two miracle foods.

Pyramid builders ate garlic daily for endurance and strength.

Since Biblical times, garlic has been used to cure a variety of ailments:

- it lowers blood pressure by dilating blood vessel walls
- it thins blood by inhibiting platelet aggregation, thereby reducing the risk of blood clots and heart attack
- it lowers serum cholesterol
- it aids in digestion
- it stimulates the immune system
- it acts as an antibiotic

The Russians refer to garlic as a natural antibiotic. Garlic actually contains an amino acid derivative called alliin, which when consumed, releases an enzyme called allicin. Allicin is capable of killing 23 kinds of bacteria—including 60 types of fungi and yeast, and salmonella. This enzyme has such a powerful antibiotic effect on the body that some say it is equivalent to penicillin.

Garlic has also been reported to protect against certain types of cancer, especially stomach and colon cancers. Studies done at

Garlic was also used in treating wounds and infections during World War I to prevent gangrene.

the Memorial Sloan-Kettering Cancer Center found that garlic compounds stifled the growth of cancer cells. John Milner, a garlic researcher at Pennsylvania State University reported that garlic was found to inhibit cancer in all tissues, including breast and liver.

Garlic also has many antioxidant properties. Like vitamins C, E and A, garlic blocks free radicals from oxidizing LDL cholesterol, so it won't clog arteries. Therefore, it subsequently helps arteries damaged by atherosclerosis heal, and it protects against other forms of heart disease. Studies have shown that a mere clove and a half of garlic daily can reduce cholesterol levels by as much as nine percent! However, not everyone enjoys the robust flavor (or pungent odor) of a whole clove. In that case, odorless garlic capsules are available as supplements at most health food stores. The following conversion table can be used as a reference if you choose not to eat garlic fresh:
Two to three fresh cloves equals

- one teaspoon garlic powder
- four 1,000 mg garlic tablets
- four gel capsules of Kyolic* garlic
- one teaspoon of liquid Kyolic* garlic

Onions play a similar role in fighting against age-related diseases. A close kin of garlic, onions (red and yellow, not white) are full of antioxidants, the most important being quercetin, an antioxidant that has been reported to inactivate many cancer causing agents, especially in the stomach as well as inhibit enzymes that spur cancer growth. Quercetin also prevents oxidation of LDL cholesterol. And much like garlic, onions help thin

*Kyolic garlic: Kyolic garlic is a specific brand developed by Japanese aging researcher Dr. Hiroshi Saito. Kyolic is one of the most thoroughly tested garlic supplements on the market today. An overwhelming 80 percent of research on the benefits of garlic has been done with the Kyolic brand.

the blood to prevent clotting, boost HDL cholesterol levels and lower triglyceride and LDL levels, and therefore prevent stroke.

In Africa, garlic is used to treat typhus and cholera.

The best way to reap the benefits of these two foods is through your daily diet, and both can be used freely and easily in cooking—in salads and salad dressings, as spices, or in marinades and sauces. And in powder form, they can be combined into just about any meal you wish to prepare.

Many people find success in substituting other herbs and spices for salt, including basil, red pepper or lemon. Others have discovered that, after a few weeks on what seems like an impossibly bland no-salt diet, suddenly, food takes on a whole new range of flavors and the palate actually rejects the salty taste it used to crave.

SUGAR: SWEET AND DEADLY

We've saved the worst news for last: sugar is terribly bad for you. Whether you take your sweetness in the form of table sugar, brown sugar, turbinado, raw sugar, honey, glucose, dextrose, or corn syrup, it puts an enormous strain on your system and acts as a cross-linking free radical to damage your cells.

One of the most common results of overconsumption of sugar is hypoglycemia, or low blood sugar. Some 35 percent of all Americans suffer from some form of this condition, in which a craving for sugar is followed by a swift high and then a painful crash as sweet foods are consumed. Fatigue, trembling, rapid heartbeat, inability to concentrate, memory problems, and emotional instability are only some of the symptoms of this troubling condition, which feels so familiar to many hypoglycemics that they don't acknowledge it as a "condition" at all. Only after they have given up or greatly reduced their consumption of sugar do they realize what reserves of energy and calm might routinely be within their reach.

Sugar addicts who drink caffeine experience a double rush—and a double crash. Ironically, the very substance that seems to perk you up also drains you, so that you're caught in a vicious cycle of needing coffee to wake up and sugar to keep yourself going. Reducing or eliminating your intake of sugar and caffeine, on the other hand, beside prolonging your life, will enable you to feel more energetic, alert, and productive on the same amount of sleep—or less!

Most Americans consume 22 percent of their calories in sugar, which is added to virtually all prepared and packaged foods, including many vegetables, meats, and whole-grain products as well as the more obvious sweetened cereals and breads. Yet sugar leads to fat gain, the degeneration of one's muscles, dysfunction of the immune system, cardiovascular problems, arteriosclerosis, and premature aging, as well as diabetes and hypoglycemia.

If you would like to cut down on your sugar consumption, here are a few suggestions:

- Read food labels. Ingredients are listed in the order of amount, with the most plentiful substance first, so if "sugar" is anywhere in the top three or four, you know you're eating something far too sweet. Read carefully, as many manufacturers break up their sugar counts by listing "sugar," "dextrose," "corn syrup," and other forms of sweeteners in a single list, making each element look less significant than it really is.
- Substitute artificial sweeteners, such as NutraSweet, and increase your consumption of whole grains. The former may satisfy your cravings, while the latter will reduce them.
- Pay attention to when, how, and why you need sweet foods. Sometimes the need for a sugary treat is more psychological than anything else, and you may be able to learn to meet those emotional needs in a way that's gentler to your system and better for your health.

Top 25 Healing Foods	25 Foods to Avoid
Garlic	Soft cheeses
Soybeans	Ice cream
Yams/sweet potatoes	Peanuts, salted/roasted
Kiwi	Fried or pickled eggs
Bananas	Alcohol
Beans (dry and green)	Bacon
Broccoli	Processed lunch meats
Tuna (water-packed)	Pork*
Turkey (skinless breast)	Gravies*
Oat bran	Saturated fats
Potatoes (baked)	Canned soups*
Bell peppers (red and green)	White, brown or raw sugar
Carrots	White rice
Papaya	Processed/sweetened oatmeal/cereals
Cantaloupe	Canned, bottled or frozen fruit with
Rice (brown)	sweeteners
Greens (spinach, kale, turnip	Yogurt with fruit/syrup
greens, Swiss chard, curly endive)	Tuna, canned in oil
Onions	Vegetables, canned or frozen with salt
Yogurt (nonfat)	or additives
Apricots	Anchovies
Garbanzos	Soft drinks
Oranges	Chocolate
Lamb	White vinegar
Pasta (whole-wheat)	Processed cheese products
Tomatoes	White-flour products
	Fried foods

*Selection based on usual ingredients. Exceptions for low-fat, low-sodium or other healthful modifications would apply.

H₂O: WETTER IS BETTER

Water is the most essential nutrient for human life. Our bodies are composed of two-thirds water, and the brain alone is made up of 85 percent water! It is present in every cell and tissue of the body and plays a vital role in almost every biological process including digestion, absorption, circulation, and excretion. Water also is the foundation of blood and lymph, regulates body temperature, helps maintain youthful skin and strong muscles, and lubricates our joints and organs to keep them in working order. Yet, despite our need for a constant fresh supply of water, many people—especially the elderly—do not consume and maintain enough of it for good health and long life. In the elderly the most consistent biomarker of aging is intercellur dehydration and one contributing factor may be a loss of thirst sensitivity with age.

When you are dehydrated, your body temperature increases and you lose not only water but valuable electrolytes such as the essential minerals potassium and sodium. Dehydration can creep up on you especially when exercising. It's a good idea to keep a bottle of water near you at all times.

Dehydration warning signs can include:

- Dizziness
- Headache, heaviness in the head
- Flushed skin
- Weakness, fatigue
- Dry mouth, loss of appetite

Advanced signs can include:

- Blurred vision
- Hearing loss
- Dry, hot skin
- Rapid pulse, shortness of breath
- Unsteady gait
- Extremely frequent urination without drinking fluids

You cannot replace the health benefits of drinking water by substituting beverages such as soft drinks, coffee, alcohol and juices. Many alcohol and caffeinated drinks actually act as diuretics, causing us to urinate more frequently than normal. This can cause a general state of dehydration resulting in urinary tract infections and cellular damage. Everyone should drink at least eight eight-ounce glasses of water per day (64 ounces total), but not just any water. Not all water is the same nor is it all good for you.

Types of Water: Which Is Best?

Steam-distilled water. The best water a person can drink is pure water—water that contains nothing but molecules of two hydrogen atoms and one oxygen atom. Pure water is easily energized; It begins to attract other substances that end up destroying its pure state. Therefore, the best state of drinking water we can hope to find in supermarkets is called steam-distilled water. Distillation involves vaporizing water by boiling it. As the steam rises, it leaves behind most of the bacteria, viruses and chemicals. The steam is then condensed and cooled where it becomes distilled water. Drinking steam-distilled water actively removes inorganic and toxic materials that are rejected by our cells and tissues from the body. An added benefit is its ability to chelate or attach to other toxic molecules and minerals and eliminate them. It is important to realize that steam-distilled water is devoid of minerals which over a long period of time can become a problem if your diet is mineral deficient. Read your supplement labels carefully to see if they include necessary trace minerals and supplement if needed. *Tip:* Adding fresh lemon juice to the water improves both taste and adds trace minerals.

Natural spring water. Another popular bottled water sold today is termed "spring" water. Natural spring water means that the water has risen to the earth's surface from some type of underground reservoir. Spring water's mineral content is not altered, but it may or may not have been filtered or otherwise treated. Therefore, you may want to read the labels of these bottled waters carefully and find out if what you're drinking is really natural.

Tap water. The worst water you can put in your body is, unfortunately, the most accessible: tap water. This type of water comes out of household faucets and in many communities is highly contaminated with chemicals such as chlorine, flourine, biological poisons, and various pollutants. Tap water has very little benefit to the functioning of our cells and tissues, and it may do more harm to our bodies than good.

NOURISHING YOURSELF

One of the best ways to change your diet to promote your health and longevity, is to listen closely to your body. Paying attention to your cravings and reactions, to the way things taste and feel inside your mouth, to your sense of hunger or satiety. Sometimes we keep eating long past the point of hunger, just out of habit, or from nervousness or anger. Listening to your body and your emotions can help ease this habit. We often expect foods to be sweet or salty simply because we've forgotten to pay attention to how else they might taste or because we don't take the time to identify what we're craving: a sweet food or simply a soft one? A salty food or just something to crunch between our teeth? Honoring your appetites and cravings will actually make healthy eating easier, as well as enabling you to get more satisfaction out of both your healthy and your "treat" consumption.

The Long Life Diet may not be easy. But take heart. It will pay off—in more vigorous and exciting years of life and health.

Chapter 14

Mind Over Matter: Anti-Stress Tips For Anti-Aging

Throughout this book we've looked at the aging process and factors that can contribute to it: poor diet, exposure to pollution, a sedentary lifestyle, heavy consumption of alcohol, smoking, etc. We've also explored a range of nutritional supplements, lifestyle choices, and hormonal treatments that can slow, ease, or even reverse the aging process. But perhaps the most powerful anti-aging weapon that you have is your mind.

> A hormone produced by stress, cortisol, is associated with a dozen or more serious degenerative diseases and has been found in some studies to be present in elevated levels in the last days of life.

Numerous studies have shown that your health is greatly affected by how you react to stressful events in life—setbacks or deadlines at work, conflicts and losses at home. By the same token, changing your reactions, learning to meditate or other relaxation techniques, and generally committing to a positive, open attitude towards life can help make you younger, reducing your biological age and expanding your abilities to maintain a vigorous and energetic lifestyle.

WHAT IS STRESS?

More than half a century ago, Dr. Hans Selye recognized the mind-body connection involved with stress, as all of his patients had similar physiological and psychological characteristics. Two of which were loss of appetite and increased blood pressure. Further studies with laboratory rats found that these same physical responses existed with animals when they were put under stress. He came to the conclusion that stress is "the non-specific response of the body to any demand placed upon it." However, according to Selye, it is not stress that harms us but *distress*. Distress occurs when when we prolong emotional stress and don't deal with it in a positive manner.

Selye referred to our body's response to stress—or distress— as the general adaptation syndrome (GAS). GAS consists of three different stages: alarm, resistance and exhaustion. The alarm stage is comparable to the well-known "fight or flight" response, during which the body releases the hormone cortisol and prepares to either battle whatever is threatening it or retreat.

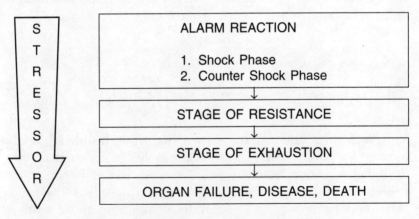

Diagram of the general adaptation syndrome.

However, since many modern-day stressors aren't physical things we can run from and escape immediately, the alarm stage is lengthened, leading up to the next phase, resistance. This stage allows us to adjust our body to counteract the physiologic changes in response to the stress. However, if the stress factor does not disappear, the third stage occurs, exhaustion. It is during exhaustion that the body creates a situation of distress, and responses can range from extreme fatigue to disease and possibly death.

STRESS AND AGING

Stress in itself is not necessarily a negative thing. The term stress simply refers to any situation—physical, emotional or both—that requires any bodily response more active than equilibrium. A slight change in temperature is experienced by the body as stress, i.e., a demand from nature to mobilize the body's resources and raise or lower body temperature. A new love affair is stressful even while it is blissful, as it evokes your intense attention to a new person and creates powerful emotions that demand a new kind of attention to yourself. Playing tennis, negotiating a big deal, planning a birthday party for your child, even reading an exciting mystery novel, are all sources of stress in that they demand physical or emotional responses from you, pleasurable though these activities may be.

Where stress becomes negative is in our responses to it. If your reaction to negotiating a big deal is not pleasurable suspense but a killing anxiety, than your body will probably respond with a headache or stomach ache, and your immune system may become weaker as well. If the daily drive to work is the occasion for a hundred little explosions of temper, you're creating a level of negative stress that will affect your body quite differently than if you enjoy the challenge of driving skillfully through crowded city streets.

This type of negative stress creates a number of ailments, from mental frustration, anxiety, and depression to headaches, allergies, ulcers and heart disease. In the long run, negative responses to stress can wear down the immune system, potentially leading to cancer and other diseases traditionally associated with aging.

Doctors at King's College Hospital in London found that out of 100 women diagnosed with early stage breast cancer, 50 percent had experienced at least one severe adverse event, (e.g., the breakup of a marriage or the death of a close family member) in the past year.

Many studies have been done on the physical stress response in the elderly, and it was found that when placed under stress, elderly people experienced loss of appetite, weight loss, a lowered lymphocyte count—which impairs immune function—and an increase in psychological distress and in serum cholesterol levels.

Moreover, negative stress increases our body's production of free radicals. In response to a stressful situation, the hypothalamus releases neuropeptides that keep the body in a perpetual state of excitement. This in turn causes the pituitary to stimulate the adrenal glands, which in turn produce the stress hormones: cortisol, epinephrine, and norepinephrine. It's as though our cells' furnaces were stoked, causing them to burn energy at a higher rate—with free radicals as a kind of polluting by-product. These chemical reactions set off a chain reaction resulting in still more free radicals.

Cortisol may be a particularly dangerous catabolic hormone as far as aging is concerned. In "Stress Cortisol, Interferon, and Stress Diseases," an article for *Medical Hypotheses*, Dr. Sapolsky of Rockefeller University in New York cites studies that point to the increased presence of cortisol some two to seven days before death. High cortisol levels, according to Dr. Sapolsky, are associated with many of the degenerative diseases of aging: hypertension, ulcers, myocardial infarction, diabetes, infections, arthritis, cerebral vascular accidents, psychosis, psoriasis and other skin conditions, Parkinson's disease, multiple sclerosis and Alzheimer's disease. Studies have also shown high levels of cortisol to inhibit muscle growth. In addition, acne, alcoholism and obesity are also to some degree associated with elevated levels of cortisol.

Apparently, high cortisol levels, generated by negative responses to stress, interfere with our immune system as well as actively encourage disease. Cortisol not only interrupts our body's production of antibodies, it may actually destroy antibodies already in circulation. Although stress-induced cortisol levels affect people of all ages, the loss of cortisol receptors in the brain—a sign of aging—may be responsible for the generally higher levels of cortisol among the elderly, and consequently their heightened vulnerability to diseases. Furthermore, laboratory studies have shown that the duration of the stress reaction is longer in older animals, possibly explaining the decreased rate of cortisol elimination with age.

> Researchers at Harvard Medical School interviewed 1,623 heart attack victims four days after the attack, and discovered that angry episodes doubled their risk of a heart attack—which often occurred a mere two hours after the outburst.

There are a number of ways we can combat the destructive effects of a negative response to stress. Diet and exercise play a large part in our responses. The B vitamins in particular help our mind and body cope with stress, while regular exercise, particularly aerobic exercise, enables us to meet life's challenges with a more relaxed and healthy attitude—and fewer symptoms of negative physical stress.

MEASURING OUR INTERNAL AND EXTERNAL STRESS INDEX

In order to determine your current stress level, we've come up with a quick and simple life stress quiz you can take on your own. It's a test based on both external and internal stress factors and events that affect us daily.

For the first part of the test, you will be examining external events that may affect your personal stress index. Simply circle each of the following events which have occurred in your life during the past six months and add up the appropriate values:

I. EXTERNAL STRESS INDEX

Life event	Value
Death of a spouse	100
Divorce	73
Marital separation	65
Jail or imprisonment	63
Death of close family member	63
Serious personal injury or illness	53
Marriage	50
Fired at work	47
Marital reconciliation	45
Retirement	45
Change in health of family member	44
Pregnancy	40
Sex difficulties	39
Business readjustment	39
Significant change in financial state	38
Death of a close friend	37
Change to a different line of work	36
Foreclosure of mortgage loan	30
Change in number of arguments with spouse	31
Change in responsibilities at work	29
Son or daughter leaving home	29
Trouble with in-laws	29
Outstanding personal achievement	28
Spouse begins or stops work	26
Begin or end school	26
Change in living conditions	25
Trouble with boss	23
Change in work hours or conditions	20
Change in residence	20
Change in schools	20
Gain of new family member	39
New mortgage or significant loan	17
Change in sleeping habits	16
Weight gain or loss over 10 pounds	15

Total score of external stress events   _____

Now add up your values to determine your external stress index and rate yourself as follows:

50 points or less = Clean, virtually stress-free living.

100 points or less = Average stress index for modern life.

150 points or less = Warning! Take steps such as the strategies discussed later in the chapter to limit stress-related illness.

155 points or more = Danger! Real problems in your home and work environment may be taking its toll on you and placing you at a genuine risk for premature illness and accelerated aging. Don't be brave—GET HELP. Your longevity is at stake.

2. INTERNAL STRESS INDEX

This index deals more with thoughts and emotions, rather than external forces. Read each of the following statements and mark the response that best describes yourself:

1) I feel unhappy or depressed:
   a) none of the time
   b) some of the time
   c) most of the time

2) I don't lead a full life:
   a) none of the time
   b) some of the time
   c) most of the time

3) Without trying, I'm losing weight:
   a) none of the time
   b) some of the time
   c) most of the time

4) The things I once did easily, I now have difficulty with:
   a) none of the time
   b) some of the time
   c) most of the time

5) I have more energy early in the day:
   a) none of the time
   b) some of the time
   c) most of the time

6) Constipation is often a problem:
   a) none of the time
   b) some of the time
   c) most of the time

7) I am hyperactive:
   a) none of the time
   b) some of the time
   c) most of the time

8) I feel I have no purpose in life:
   a) none of the time
   b) some of the time
   c) most of the time

9) I find myself crying spontaneously:
   a) none of the time
   b) some of the time
   c) most of the time

10) The future seems hopeless:
    a) none of the time
    b) some of the time
    c) most of the time

11) I don't seem to enjoy the same things I once did:
    a) none of the time
    b) some of the time
    c) most of the time

12) I have trouble sleeping at night:
    a) none of the time
    b) some of the time
    c) most of the time

13) My thoughts are not as clear as they were last year:
    a) none of the time
    b) some of the time
    c) most of the time

14) Lately, I am more irritable:
    a) none of the time
    b) some of the time
    c) most of the time

15) I feel I have no contribution to make to society:
   a) none of the time
   b) some of the time
   c) most of the time

16) I sometimes think I need professional help:
   a) none of the time
   b) some of the time
   c) most of the time *

17) I use alcohol, drugs, food and/or tobacco to help me feel better about life:
   a) none of the time
   b) some of the time
   c) most of the time *

18) I have thoughts of suicide:
   a) none of the time
   b) some of the time *
   c) most of the time *

For each question you answered (a) give yourself one point; for each question you answered (b) give yourself two points; and for each answer you circled (c), give yourself three points. Now add up your score for your final internal stress index. You can rate yourself as follows:

If your score was:

18-26 points = A-O.K. Internal stresses seem well under control.

27-36 points = Something is missing, and you may want to take a closer look at how you handle some of the internal stress-related events in your life. Try to incorporate some of the strategies for coping with stress discussed later in the chapter.

37-54 points (or *any* answers marked*) = There are some real stress-related problems involved here. *You should seek outside help immediately*. After all, what's the point of living beyond 100 if you feel that life is miserable? If we allow the affects of stress-related illness and aging to go unchecked, we allow stress to control and destroy our lives. Life is a precious gift, and it is meant to be enjoyed. There are answers out there, and help is available if you need it.

25 STRATEGIES FOR COPING WITH STRESS

Now that you've identified your strengths and weaknesses in dealing with stress, what other options do you have for responding to frustration and anxiety? We've already discussed diet and exercise as great stress-busters. You're probably also aware of simple but effective things you can do for yourself, like making time to relax each day, giving yourself frequent treats and positive reinforcement, and finding new ways of expressing and asserting your feelings with loved ones and living companions.

Besides these daily changes, however, there are some long-term habits and practices that can generally lower the level of stress in your life. The following 25 stress-relieving, anti-aging strategies can help you to function at a biological age that is far lower than your chronological age, so that you can live longer and enjoy life more:

1. Get a regular medical checkup. Not only can checkups be comforting if the doctor confirms that you're in good health, but they are also an indispensable method of preventing any minor health problems from becoming worse. *Note*: Be sure not to waste your time and money on "turn your head left and cough" basic physical exams. Your annual life extension physical exam should be thorough and inclusive, paying particular attention to the very early detection of cancer, heart disease, diabetes, stroke, and metabolic disorders. See Appendix B for a recommended list of physicians.

2. Tie the knot! Studies show that married people are healthier than single people. In fact, married people have been reported to reduce their risk of illness, accidents and death by up to 50 percent!

3. Take a siesta—that is, a short nap. These 20- to 30-minute naps are best taken midday, since it is at this time that the body's metabolism is at its lowest. Taking afternoon naps also fits in with your body's natural circadian rhythm.

4. Don't ever assume that your children's success or failure is completely the result of your parental influence. By not accepting our children for who they are, a stressful burden is placed not only on you as a parent but on the entire family unit.

5. Spend high-quality time with friends. Social relationships are not only fun, they're necessary for good mental health. When our internal resources are depleted, the comfort of close friends can help lessen our worries and burdens.

6. Become more spiritual, either through an organized religion or through your own personal meditations. People who are affiliated with a religious or spiritual group are usually tapped into three powerful stress reducers: forgiveness, hope and understanding.

7. Adopt a pet. Various studies have shown pet owners to live not only longer lives, but happier, more fulfilled lives as well, and like human friends, a pet can show devotion and bring necessary companionship, closeness and comfort to anyone's life.

8. Take up a hobby or develop a new interest. If you're truly enjoy doing something, stress will evaporate on its own.

9. Use of time-management techniques, such as a daily planner or a daily list of "things to do" can not only be very productive but can relieve stress as well. By listing what we need to accomplish, we reduce our risk of trying to do too many things at once, thus burning ourselves out physically and mentally.

10. If you feel the source of your stress is coming from where you live, for example, a major city or urban area, you might want to consider moving to a calmer, quieter place of residence. However, if moving is not an option, perhaps forming a closer sense of community with your neighbors may help ease some of the stresses related to your living situation.

11. Sometimes something as simple as a mere change in the way we think about things can help reduce stress in our lives. For example, start perceiving your commute to work—be it by train, plane or automobile—as an opportunity to relax, reflect, prepare or meditate, rather than as an aggravation.

12. Keep a careful check on your finances: money, whether we have too little or too much, can become a huge emotional strain. Be prudent and be smart. Try to realize that you have value and quality as a human being. More important, the quantity of your life is not determined by how much cash you have. Ultimately, material items become a burden, and many wealthy people find they are slaves to their posssessions.

13. Practice the art of meditation and relaxation (discussed later in this chapter). Studies have shown that people who take time out of the day to devote to these activities have lower blood pressure and a reduced risk of heart disease.

14. Smile! Scientists have actually discovered a connection between the facial muscles used when smiling and an area of the brain that releases "feel-good" neurochemicals.

15. By improving your communication skills, you can reduce not only stress but unneeded frustration, anger and resentment in your life. Mixed signals are never pleasant to give or to receive. It is not only important to be a better communicator, but a better listener as well.

16. Exercising more will not only lower your anxiety levels, but will decrease any feelings of depression and low self-esteem. It is probably one of the most essential elements of any stress-reducing program (see Chapter 11).

17. Change your diet. Perhaps the extra pounds you're carrying around is adding to the extra internal or mental pounds you've been carrying as well. A healthy change of diet will help you feel more alive, more energized, and happier overall.

18. Cut back on alcohol consumption. While many people view alcohol as a way to escape from stress, it never reduces it. In reality, drinking more than two ounces of alcohol daily has been shown to raise blood pressure, inflame tempers, damage brain cells and eventually increase stress levels.

19. Say no to that second cup—caffeine is one of the most agitating substances your body can consume. By substituting

a decaffeinated beverage for that usual cup of coffee, you'll remain much calmer and reduce the jitters associated with caffeine.

20. Stop smoking! By quitting *right now*, you can significantly improve your current state of health and live a longer life. Quitters can expect to notice improved lung function within days, a decreased risk of coronary heart disease within a year, and a diminished risk for cancer within three years.

21. You may not want to be an eternal optimist, but do try to avoid being a perpetual pessimist. For maximum stress control, try being a little bit of both, so as neither to overextend yourself nor become a total cynic. Negative thinking can cost you added years of a healthy lifespan.

22. Don't second-guess past mistakes or failures. By dwelling in the past, we only end up harboring feelings of guilt and remorse that should be let go. If you're going to remember past mistakes, try to evaluate them in a positive way. Life is an education. Sometimes negative events are our best learning experiences.

23. Learn to assert yourself positively. Speak from your own point of view and help others understand what you are trying to convey.

24. Learn to express your anger positively and respectfully: don't scream or act hostile. Positive anger can actually help us change stress into strength; destructive anger, on the other hand, when turned inward can lead to stroke, high blood pressure, and heart disease.

25. Convert feelings of low self-esteem, not into forms of stress but into forms of strength. Everyone experiences personal defeats and losses, and a key element to stress reduction is not to allow these setbacks to control our lives.

MEDITATION

Perhaps the single most effective way of coping with stress—and a true anti-aging technique—is meditation. Transcendental Meditation in particular, founded by the Maharishi Mahesh Yogi, has been the subject of numerous studies that have validated its amazing physiological and emotional effects. Transcendental Meditation, or TM, must be learned from a practitioner, but it is relatively easy and inexpensive to do. Most cities now have people who will gladly teach you this life-enhancing practice. (If you're not sure where to find a teacher, ask at your local health-food store or health-food restaurant.)

We are all familiar with three states of consciousness: waking, sleeping, and dreaming. Meditation apparently creates a fourth state of consciousness, in which the mind is awake, but still. During meditation, muscles relax, the metabolism of red blood cells slows down, breathing and heart rate are lowered, and the blood flow to the brain increases.

Daily meditation seems to have the long-term benefit of lowering anxiety, improving mental functioning, and, in the long run, lowering a person's biological age. According to a literature review conducted by Dr. Kenneth Eppley, TM lowered anxiety more than twice as much as any of the other relaxation techniques studied by researchers. Studies conducted by Dr. Hari Sharma and his colleagues at Ohio State University and the Maharishi International University at Fairfield, Iowa, found that lipid peroxides (indicators of free radicals in the blood) were significantly lower in elderly people who meditated regularly. Comparing meditators to non-meditators, with both groups maintaining a similar fat content in their diet, meditators aged 60 to 69 had 14.5 percent fewer lipid peroxides in their blood, while meditators aged 70 to 79 had 16.5 percent fewer. According to Dr. R. Keith Wallace's study of meditators, people who had meditated for over five years had a biological age averaging 12 years younger than a control group who did not meditate. In some cases, the meditator's biological age was actually younger than his or her chronological age on the day he or she learned to meditate!

PROGRESSIVE RELAXATION

Progressive relaxation, intended to create deep muscle relaxation was originally developed by E. Jacobson, and is currently a very popular method used in most physical and occupational therapy programs. This technique works by combining tension and gradual relaxation in a series of muscle groups. For example, you would begin by contracting the biceps muscles for five seconds, then gradually relaxing them for the next 45 seconds. This would be followed by the same contraction and relaxation of the triceps muscles. The complete sequence of muscle groups starts at the head and continues downward to the feet, or vice versa. Once the technique is learned, you will be able to recognize which muscle groups need relaxing, and can then progress more quickly through the sequence to those specific muscles that need attention.

SELECTED AWARENESS

Selected awareness involves utilizing the biologic limitations of people to respond to a small number of stimuli simultaneously. This means that by directing ourselves to concentrate on just a few selected stimuli, relaxation is induced. There are several selected awareness techniques currently used today:

- *Hypnosis*: With hypnosis, a therapist can induce relaxation by providing you with either a mental task or a repetitive stimulus. By doing so, your perception is altered, allowing the hypnotist to restrict your awareness. Hypnosis can be learned by the patient, and once learned, this state can be achieved without the aid of a hypnotist.
- *Autogenic training*: This method is similar to hypnosis in its use of a therapist to help direct awareness. However, instead of focusing on a mental image or task, autogenic training concentrates on physical stimuli—sensations of the relaxation response. You are taught how to imagine

physiological sensations, such as warmth or heaviness, that evoke relaxation.

- *Guided imagery*: This method concentrates solely on your imagination. The place can be anything, from an exotic island to one's own bedroom, real or fantasy. The relaxation response evoked from this image can then be retrieved whenever needed.

BREATH CONTROL

Breath control originated as an essential component of yoga, and ranges from simple to complex. This technique can be employed any time, anywhere—if you're stuck in traffic or even when you're in a board meeting.

Simple breath control consists of a modification of the breathing pattern. By lengthening the expiration phase of breathing, relaxation occurs. During breath control, you should think of something positive or calming, which will enhance the overall feeling of relaxation.

> According to Dr. Neil Schachter, pulmonologist at Mount Sinai Medical Center in New York City, taking a full, deep breath every now and then throughout your day can reduce the risk of getting stress headaches and muscle tension.

EXERCISE AND PHYSICAL ACTIVITY

While exercise has always been recommended for overall health, recently many researchers and physicians have been recognizing it as a wonderful way to relieve stress. Exercise helps the body eliminate the metabolic by-products of stress on our systems, and it lessens our response to any new stressors. It makes us feel good about ourselves, instills a sense of accomplishment, and improves our appearance. However, if you plan on using an exercise program as a stress-reducing method, be sure to choose a non-competitive activity, since a competitive activity itself be a stressor and only aggravate your tensions. (See Chapter 11.)

MASSAGE

If you've ever had a massage, you probably remember it as a soothing, relaxing experience. However, you may not have been aware of its potential long-term benefits in lowering stress and combating aging.

Marian Williams, a nurse at the California Pacific Medical Center, states that massage has proven enormously effective as a means of treating a wide range of hospital patients. Megan Carnarius, a nurse who worked at a nursing home, found that massage also improved the cognitive skills of her elderly patients, as well as providing them with more youthful, elastic skin. Massage can help in combating depression, and even in stimulating the growth of premature babies, suggesting that it may have some ability to encourage the release of growth hormones.

A licensed massage therapist can help you incorporate massage as an anti-stress device in your life. If you and your living partner learn to massage each other, you might be able to work even more massage sessions into your schedule!

GLUTAMINE AND STRESS

In addition to the various relaxation techniques, nutritional supplementation may also be helpful in reducing stress. One supplement in particular has been found to have not only excellent anti-aging properties but amazing stress-reducing properties as well. This supplement is the amino acid glutamine. According to the research done by Dr. Douglas Wilmore, professor of surgery at Harvard Medical School, glutamine is essential for anyone suffering from stress or stress-related illnesses.

In addition to acting as a antioxidant, glutamine has been shown to:

- strengthen immunity
- cut illness short
- aid in recovery from illness
- rejuvenate muscles weakened by stress and illness

Aging itself is a form of stress—a stress we all inevitably encounter. This makes glutamine supplementation even more critical with age. It can be taken in powder or tablet form, although the powdered form is preferrable. Studies have shown that doses as high as 40,000 mg (under a doctor's supervision) do not produce negative side effects.

STRESS AND B VITAMINS

Another group of supplements to consider taking for stress are the B vitamins. When we become stressed, these vitamins are rapidly depleted from our system. Therefore, it's necessary that we replace them daily for proper functioning.

You may have heard people say "My nerves are frazzled," or "My nerves are shot," when they talk about the stress they're under. Stress indeed affects the parts of the body related to the nervous system—especially the digestive and intestinal systems. It places the entire body under siege, also weakening the immune system tremendously. The best way to stop this attack on our body's disease-fighting center is to relax, and studies have shown that a B complex may also help significantly reduce anxiety and stressful emotions.

Although all the B vitamins aid in the relief from stress, the one that can truly help reduce stress is pantothenic acid, or vitamin B5. Also known as the "anti-stress" vitamin, B5 is a key element involved in the production of adrenal hormones, which are rapidly depleted when the body experiences stress. In addition, B5 helps convert fats, carbohydrates and proteins into energy, and it is required for normal functioning of all the cells in our bodies. It also aids in the functioning of the gastrointestinal tract—an area commonly affected and disturbed by stress. Some excellent food sources of B5 are beans, eggs, fresh vegetables and whole wheat.

If you start supplementing your diet with a B-complex vitamin, a 1 cc injection from your physician may be your best bet, since it's concentrated enough to show fast, effective results. B-complex vitamins can also be purchased in capsule or tablet form from most health food stores, in doses as low as 50 mg to as high as 500 mg per vitamin.

THINK YOUNG, LIVE LONG

All the techniques described in this chapter have one thing in common: each requires a commitment to a full and happy life, taking time for pleasure in the day as well as using hours for achievement and obligation. In the final analysis, the best way to stay young and live long is to love your life, filling it with a wide variety of challenges and joys that nourish your mind, body, and spirit. We end this chapter at a place you might begin: with the suggestion that you listen to yourself, discover what you need, and find a self-loving way to achieve it.

Chapter 15

The Longevity Test

People age biologically and chronologically. Chronological age measures the amount of time that has gone by since birth. Most of us can distinguish an elderly person from a young person. We can even categorize what age range a person might fall into. But what about a person who is 65 but looks as if he's only 45? Or a person who is 80 but functions as well as a 60-year-old? This is biological age or functional age; we all age biologically at different rates. As we have seen throughout the book, age changes affect different parts of our body at different times. These age changes occur in the DNA, tissues, organs and hormone levels, as well as in every component of the human body. This variance in our biological "clock" can help explain why one 80-year-old may be able to work during the day, go bicycling in the afternoons, and garden on the weekends, exerting more youthful qualities than another 80-year-old who may, biologically, be 80 or even 90 years old. A comprehensive battery of metabolic tests and complex laboratory analyses is necessary to accurately determine your individual biological age, a procedure that is beyond the scope of this book. However, this procedure is available at centers like the Longevity Institute International

(LII), the first of many anti-aging treatment and diagnostic centers designed to address the new healthcare specialty of anti-aging medicine. LII's program consists of extensive measurements of individual biomarkers that establish aging rates for each organ system through molecular and DNA analysis. (See Appendix C for more on LII.)

The purpose of this chapter is to emphasize how extremely useful and important it is to recognize some of the basic markers and risk factors for premature aging. Through the test presented in this chapter, you will be able to detect what changes you need to make for longevity—the period of time we can expect to live, given the best of circumstances.

The rationale for the Longevity Test is as follows:

Average life expectancy in the world's advanced countries is rapidly approaching 80 years (85 if you are a woman recently born in Japan). A recent issue of *Science* magazine reported that, with the currently expanding lifespans of modern man, all it would take for the average lifespan to reach 99.2 years is the elimination of heart disease, cancer and diabetes.

We now know what causes the majority of age-related disease. We know what mechanisms lead to almost all cases of atherosclerotic heart disease, and how to prevent it. For those with heart disease too advanced to treat by diet and lifestyle adjustment, modern methods of heart bypass, laser-created collateral blood flow, coronary sinuses, balloon angioplasty, artificial hearts and other highly developed techniques now offer a second chance for life and a healthy heart.

Cancer is slowly yielding to modern medical innovation. Ninety percent or more of all cancers are fully curable (not just five year survival rates, but a *total* cure) if detected at Stage I— usually the size of a pea or smaller. Even better, new analysis of cancer etiology shows that 80 percent of all cancers are environmental in origin. Therefore, your chances of cancer are only one in five if you don't smoke, avoid cancer promoters in food (nitrosamines, fats), and limit exposure to radiation and other environmental toxins. As you learned in previous chapters, your chances for avoiding cancer also greatly improve by supplementing your diet with antioxidants and DNA-repairing nutrients such as those discussed in Chapter 9.

Diabetes, especially adult-onset diabetes, is also coming under control thanks to improved methods of early detection and endocrine stabilization and repair. Artificial pancreas and islet cell implants have already cured dozens of people with severe insulin-dependent diabetes. In fact, new glucose control medications should soon eliminate this disease as a major overall risk factor.

Is the possibility of a 120-year lifespan far behind?

The new reality for those age 35 and younger is a healthy lifespan of 120 and beyond (assuming current advances in biotechnology, genetic engineering and medicine continue at their present rate). And 100 years is an expected average lifespan for those 55 and younger. For those over 55, researchers are cautiously only predicting an 85-year advanced lifespan (average lifespan is interpreted as meaning that 50 percent will die before the specified age and the other half will live beyond that age). Therefore, it is not unreasonable—and history may ultimately prove us somewhat conservative in our projections—for those who live the healthiest of lives and lifestyles to score a potential maximum expected lifespan of 150 on this test. Again, remember that our predictions are dependent on biomedical technology advancing with the age wave.

We recommend taking the whole test now, then taking it again in three months, when you've had a chance to integrate some of the suggestions in this book into your own anti-aging program. You can continue retaking the test every three months, as an incentive to keep yourself on the path to longevity and to see what changes you've made overall.

Allow yourself from 30 minutes to an hour to take this test. Don't mull over each question, but don't rush through anything either. Be completely honest. This is a self-test for you to learn which of your habits work toward your longevity and which do not.

The Longevity Test is an educational experience, not cold, hard, objective, scientific analysis. Regardless of what you score, chances are you can do better with simple modifications to your diet, lifestyle, environment, and mental attitude. The rewards are very significant in terms of a longer, healthier, happier and more vibrant life. Remember, it's never too early or too late to stop the clock on the aging process.

Test Tip: If you aren't sure about an answer or just don't know, the answer most likely is "no."

Good luck and long life!

THE LONGEVITY TEST

Gender

Male	−5
Female	+6

Age

0-29	+10
30-55	+5
55-65	+1
65 or older	−10

Heredity

Any grandparent lived to be over 80 (limit 4)	+1
Average age all four grandparents lived to:	
60-70	+3
71-80	+4
Over 80	+6

Family history

Either parent had stroke or heart attack before age 50	-10

-2 for a family member (grandparent, parent, sibling) who prior to age 65 has had any of the following:

Hypertension	-__
Cancer	-__
Heart disease	-__

Stroke   -‒

Diabetes   -‒

Other genetic diseases   -‒   ☐

SUBTOTAL A: ‒ + ‒ =

Family income

0-$9,000   -10

$10,000-$18,000   -5

$19,000-$30,000   +1

+1 for each additional $20,000, up to   +‒
   $200,000

Education

Some high school
(or less)   -7

High school graduate   +2

College graduate   +4

Postgraduate or professional degree   +6

Others would best describe your general
   mood/temperament as follows:
      Calm yet alert   +3

      Laid-back and passive   -3

      Angry and easily perturbed or   -10
      annoyed

Occupation

Choose one:

Professional   +3

Self-employed   +3

In health-care field   +2

Over 65 and working   +3

Clerical or support   -1

Shift work   -2

Unemployed   -3

Probability of career advancement   +1

Regularly in direct contact with   -10
   pollutants, toxic waste, chemicals,
   radiation, or carry a firearm to work.

Where you live

Large, congested urban industrial center   -4

Rural or farm area   +2

Area with air-pollution alerts   -5

High-crime area   -3
Little or no crime area   +2

Home has tested positive for radon   -2

Total commuting time to and from work:
   0-1/2 hour   +1
   1/2 hour-1 hour   0

   -1 for each 1/2 hour over 1 hour   -___

Within 30 miles of major medical/trauma   +1
   center

No major medical/trauma center in area   -1

SUBTOTAL B: ___ + ___ = ☐

Health Status

Present overall physical health:

Excellent—almost never ill, feel great   +6
   most of the time

Good—sick 10 days or less/year, feel   +4
   good most of the time

Fair—sick 11 days or more/year, feel   -2
   okay but low energy

Poor—sick 20 days or more/year, feel   -10
   average to low energy

What is your blood pressure (if measured
within the last year:
    Normal: below 140/90 mmHg   +3

    Borderline: between 140/90 and   -5
    160/95

    High: Top (systolic) reading was   -10
    above 160 and/or bottom
    (diastolic) reading was above 95

    Don't know   -5

Low cholesterol (under 200)   +5
Moderate cholesterol (200-240)   -2
High cholesterol (over 240)   -10
Don't know   -5
HDL cholesterol 29 or less   -10
    30-45   0
    over 45   +8
    Don't know   -5

Do you or close family member have
diabetes?
    Yes   -4
    No   0

Have comprehensive medical insurance   +2
    coverage

Able to use physicians of your choice   +2

Insurance limits your physician choices   -5

Have no insurance   -7

Tobacco

(1 pipe=2 cigarettes
1 cigar=3 cigarettes)
Never smoked   +7
Quit smoking   +3

Smoke up to one pack/day	-7
Smoke one to two packs/day	-10
Over two packs/day	-20

Pack-years smoked (number of packs
smoked/day, times number of years
smoked):

7-15	-5
16-25	-10
Over 25	-20

Alcohol

(Daily consumption of 1 beer or 1 glass
of wine=1.25 oz. alcohol)

No alcohol consumption	0
1.25 oz./day or less	+6
Between 1.25 and 2.5 oz./day	-4
-1 more for each additional 1.25 oz. /day	-___

Exercise

(20 min. or more moderate aerobic
exercise)

5 or more/week	+10
4 times/week	+6
3 times/week	+3
2 times/week	+1
No regular aerobic activity	-10

How many flights of stairs (of about 12
steps) do you climb each day?

1-5	0
6-10	+1
More than 10	+2
Work requires regular physical exertion
or at least two miles walking/day	+3

+1 more for each additional mile walked/
day

+___

Sedentary work/not much walking or
stair climbing

-6

After taking a brisk walk or a slow jog,
do you feel any of these symptoms:
racing heart, irregular heartbeat or
chest pain?
Yes
No
*Note: If yes, see your doctor before
continuing any exercise program.

-15

0

Need more than two pillows to sleep
comfortably because of discomfort
or breathing while lying on back

-12

Weight

Maintain ideal weight for height

+5

5-10 lbs. over ideal
11-20 lbs. over ideal
21-30 lbs. over ideal
-1 more for each additional 10 lbs.

-6
-10
-22
-___

Underweight
5-10 lbs.
11-20 lbs.

+5
-15

Determine your waist-to-hip ratio as
follows:

Measure your waist (W) and hip (H) in
inches. Divide your W measure by
your H measure. W/H=ratio

Women:
Your ratio is 0.8 or greater
Your ratio is 0.79 or less

-5

+3

Men: -12
Your ratio is 0.96 or greater
Your ratio is 0.95 or less   +2

Nutrition

Eat a well-balanced diet   +3

Don't eat a well-balanced diet   -3

Regularly eat meals at consistent times   +2

Don't regularly eat meals at consistent   -2
    times

Snack or eat meals late at night   -2

Eat a balanced breakfast   +2

Eat fish or poultry as primary protein   +5
    source (almost replacing red meat,
    once/week or less)

Eat at least 5 servings of green leafy   +3
    vegetables/week

Eat at least 5 servings of fresh fruit or
    juice a day
        Yes   +2
        No   -1

Try to avoid fats   +2
Don't try to avoid fats   -5

Fifty percent of meals consist of fried   -8
    take-out foods, prepackaged or
    precooked foods

Eat some food every day that is high in   +2
    fiber (whole-grain bread, fresh fruits
    and vegetables)

Do not eat some food every day that is   -3
    high in fiber

Take a daily multivitamin or mineral
supplement which includes at least
the following: Vitamin A/beta-carotene
(5,000 IU), vitamin E (400 mg),
vitamin B-complex (50 IU), zinc (30
mg), selenium (100 mcg) and vitamin
C (500 mg)

Yes	+10	
No		-10

Women:
Take calcium supplement   +3

Do you get colds or other infections more
than once every eight weeks?

Yes		-6
No	0	

Does it take a long time to get over a bad
infection? (For example, do your
colds typically last longer than two
weeks?)

Yes		-6
No	0	

Do you need antibiotics three times/yr or
more?

Yes		-8
No	0	

Are your lymph nodes often enlarged?

Yes		-4
No	0	

Regularly use sunscreen and avoid   +2
excessive sun

Subscribe to health-related periodicals   +2

Actively involved in a life-extension,   +5
prevention or comprehensive
wellness program

SUBTOTAL C: __ + __ = ☐

Accident control

Always wear a seat-belt as driver and passenger	+6
Don't always wear a seat belt as driver and passenger	-6
Never drink and drive or ride with a driver who has been drinking	+2
-10 for each arrest for drinking while under the influence of alcohol in the past 5 years	-__
-2 for every speeding ticket or accident in the past year	-__
For each 10,000 miles per year driven over 10,000	-1
Primary car weighs over 3,500 lbs.	+10
Subcompact	-5
Motorcycle	-10
-2 for every fight or attack you were involved in, or witness to, in the past 3 years.	-__
Smoke alarms in home	+1

Preventive and therapeutic measures

Comprehensive physical exams and blood tests (every 3 to 4 years before 50, or every 1 or 2 years over 50)	+3

Women:

Yearly gynecological exam and Pap smear	+2
Monthly breast self-exam	+2
Mammogram (35-50, every 3 yrs; over 50, every yr)	+2

Men:

Genital self-exam every 3 months	+1
Rectal or prostate exam (yearly after age 30)	+2

All:

Rectal exam and tested for hidden blood in stool (over 40, every two years; over 50, every year)	+2	
No rectal exam and test by age 50		-4

What is your menstrual status?

Still menstruating	+3	
Went through natural menopause at 41 or older	+1	
Went through natural menopause at 40 or younger		-5
Underwent total hysterectomy before 41		-8
Underwent total hysterectomy at age 41 or older		-4
Postmenopausal and take oral estrogen supplements	+5	
Well-formed bowel movements 1 or 2 times/day without difficulty	+3	
Constipation and bowel movement less than once/day		-10
Irritable bowel disorder or other problems with elimination		-7

If over 50:

Sigmoidoscopy of the lower bowel every 3 years	+2	
Have a suspicious skin lesion that hasn't healed in six weeks or that keeps growing		-10

SUBTOTAL D: ___ + ___ = ☐

Changeable Psychosocial Factors

Married or in long-term committed relationship	+10	
Not in any long-term relationship		-6
Satisfying sex life twice/week or more	+4	
Unsatisfying sex life		-10
Children under 18 living at home	+2	
-1 for each 5-year period living alone		-___
No close friends		-10
+1 for each close friend (up to 3)	+___	
Active membership in a religious community or volunteer organization	+2	
Have a pet	+2	
Regular daily routine (an orderly day, e.g., wake up at 7:00, breakfast at 7:30, work by 8:00, etc.)	+3	
No regular daily routine		-10
Hours of uninterrupted sleep/night:		
Less than 5		-5
5-8	+5	
8-10	-7	
No consistent sleep time		-5
Regular work routine	+3	
No regular work routine		-5
-2 for every for every 5 hours worked over 40 in a week		-___
Take a yearly vacation from work (at least 6 days)	+5	
No yearly vacation in past two years (at least 6 days)		-5

Regularly use a stress management
technique (yoga, meditation, music,
etc.)   +3

No stress management program   -4

SUBTOTAL E: __ + __ = ☐

Changeable Emotional Stress Factors

N=Never   R=Rarely   S=Sometimes
A=Always (or as much as possible)

	N	R	S	A
Generally happy	-2	-1	+1	+2
Have and enjoy time with family and friends	-2	-1	+1	+2
Feel in control of personal life and career	-2	-1	+1	+2
Live within financial means	-2	-1	+1	+2
Set goals and look for new challenges	-2	-1	+1	+2
Participate in creative outlet or hobby	-2	-1	+1	+2
Have and enjoy leisure time	-2	-1	+1	+2
Express feelings easily	-2	-1	+1	+2
Laugh easily	-2	-1	+1	+2
Expect good things to happen	-2	-2	+1	+2
Anger easily	+2	+1	-1	-2
Critical of self	+2	+1	-1	-2
Critical of others	+2	+1	-1	-2
Lonely, even with others	+2	+1	-1	-2

	N	R	S	A
Worry about things out of your control	+2	+1	-1	-2
Regret sacrifices made in life	+2	+1	-1	-2
SUBTOTAL F:	__+	__+	__+	__ =

Subtotals: A + B + C + D + E + F

GRAND TOTAL

Scoring

After you've added all of the subtotals together, divide the grand total by 3 or multiply by 0.333.

This is your *score*. Follow the chart for the next step. If age:

(1-30)   Age + 30 + (score x 2.0)

(31-46)   Age + 20 + (score x 1.5)

(47-61)   Age + 10 + (score x 1.2)

(62-73)   Age + 5 + (score x 1.0)

(74-82)   Age + 3 + (score x .50)

(83 +)   Age + 1 + (score x .20)

This final number is your potential estimated lifespan.

How did you do? Did you learn something about factors in your life that might be making you "old before your time" or that are sapping your youthful energy, health, and vigor?

Remember, there are no "right" or "wrong" answers to these questions. We're not suggesting that you move to the country or give up your high-powered job. And a life without at least some of the "life-stress" elements we listed would be an empty life indeed! The point is not to judge yourself, but rather to become aware of the things that may be placing a strain on your system. Then you can choose which risk factors or stressors are worth keeping and which need to be corrected.

We now know a great deal about the physical and emotional conditions for staying healthy and vigorous well into a lengthy old age and we hope you have gained a greater appreciation of how your lifespan can be significantly extended through the application of the therapeutics discussed in this book. Of course, not all the factors determining your biological age, your health, and your lifespan are within your control. But of those that are, you now have the knowledge you need to make the choices that are right for you.

Chapter 16

Pioneers of Anti-Aging Medicine and Their Personal Secrets of Longevity

Words to Live by: Some people try to achieve immortality through their offspring or their works. I prefer to achieve immortality by not dying.

—Woody Allen

We are on the cusp of a new age of medical capability. As millions of baby boomers cross the line into middle and elder age, they will be just in time for the host of new treatments now appearing on the horizon. Still as you have read, everyone can benefit from some or all of the anti-aging treatments outlined in this book right now.

Only five years ago it was impossible to say the words "anti-aging medicine" at a scientific conference without being laughed off stage. My, how quickly the times have changed! Not only has anti-aging medicine become an accepted area of medical research, but it's actually in vogue. And the next ten years will surely yield dramatic and revolutionary advances in this field.

One final word of caution. Much of the information presented in this book will allow you to treat yourself by providing sources for you to buy vitamins, minerals, and bioactive substances like melatonin and antioxidants; to devise an exercise plan for yourself; to learn methods to attain deep relaxation, and more. Other chapters concern products that you must obtain through your doctor, such as human growth hormone or DHEA. The therapies of anti-aging medicine are serious business and although most are inherently safe, remember: nothing is completely safe. We *strongly* urge you to work with a qualified physician on your own anti-aging program. If your own doctor is not interested in these new developments, find one who is. Although you can do much on your own to improve your diet and find some of the nutritional supplements you need, a qualified professional will be better able to analyze your problems, chart your course to optimum health and follow your programs with objective lab tests and medical intuition.

Here are the personal life extension programs of 28 pioneers in the new science of anti-aging medicine. These hardy souls are the founders, the leaders, the educators, the discoverers and the promoters who over the past 40 years have created the basis for the next age of health care in the new millennium.

PIONEERS IN LONGEVITY MEDICINE

See Glossary following this chapter for explanation of supplements mentioned.

Jeffrey S. Bland, Ph.D.

(Gig Habor, Washington) is an international authority and lecturer on human biochemistry, nutrition and health. He earned his doctoral degree in chemistry from the University of Oregon and was a research associate to Dr. Linus Pauling at the Linus Pauling Institute of Science and Medicine. Dr. Bland conducts an annual series of seminars for health professionals on the latest developments in nutrition and functional medicine focusing on assessment and early intervention. His monthly audio magazine, *Preventive Medicine Update* (PMU), is subscribed to by hundreds of physicians and researchers.

Personal Longevity Program

Exercise: Aerobic exercise program with weight training 45 minutes 6 times/week, includes using a stair climber and riding a stationary bike

Supplements: A multivitamin with minerals in addition to:

1,000 mg vitamin C	100 mg selenium
400 I.U. vitamin E	20 mg beta-carotene
5,000 I.U. vitamin A	100 mcg chromium
400 mcg folic acid	20 mg zinc
400 mg magnesium	

Dietary Protocol: High-fiber low-fat. Mainly vegetarian, 5 servings of fresh fruit a day, minimal amount of alcohol

Sleep: 6 hours

Relaxation: Reading and listening to music at least 1 hour/day

Stress reliever: Exercise

Personal secret: Great marriage

Best habit to cultivate: Time management

Worst habit a person can have: Sleep deprivation

Jeffrey Blumberg, Ph.D.

(Boston, Massachusetts) is a professor in the School of Nutritional Science and Policy and the associate director and chief of the Antioxidants Research Laboratory at the U.S.D.A. Human Nutrition Research Center on Aging at Tufts University. He received his doctoral degree in pharmacology from Vanderbilt University School of Medicine. He received post doctoral training in cyclic nucleotide metabolism at the Tennessee Neuropsychiatric

Institute at the University of Calgary. Dr. Blumberg has published over 100 scientific articles and serves on several professional editorial boards.

Personal Longevity Program

Exercise: Stair climbing daily for 20 minutes daily, walks 1 mile daily

Supplements: Multivitamin with minerals daily in addition to:
500 mg vitamin C   600 mg calcium
400 mcg folic acid   15 mg zinc
18 mg iron   15 mg beta-carotene
400 I.U.vitamin D
occasionally coenzyme Q10

Dietary Protocol: High fiber, low fat with moderate protein.
5 glasses of juice daily, 3-4 pieces of fresh fruit daily

Alcohol: 1-2 glasses of wine daily

Other Information: Occasionally fried foods, red meat and shell fish
No coffee and carbonated beverages

Amount of sleep: 6 hours/night

Stress reliever: Listens to music

Mental exercise: Work and problem solving

Personal secret: Enjoy your work

Best habit to cultivate: Regular exercise

Bob Delmonteque, N.D.

(Malibu, California) is an athlete, author, editor, writer, and is America's premier "senior fitness" consultant. He earned his advanced degree from the Midwestern College in Columbus, Missouri. Mr. Delmonteque is a former bodybuilder and was the personal trainer to many noted movie stars in the mid-1940s, including Clark Gable, Joan Crawford, and John Wayne. From 1962–1968, he was N.A.S.A.'s personal trainer for the astronauts including Alan Shepherd, John Glenn, and Gus Grissom.

He has had ownership of over 500 health clubs and counseled and helped set up personal training programs for over 100,000 people. Mr. Delmonteque is the senior fitness editor with Weider Publications for *Muscle and Fitness* magazine and authored the best selling book, *Lifelong Fitness: How to Look Great at Any Age.*

Personal Longevity Program

Exercise: Strenous workout for 45 minutes 3–5 times/week includes aerobics, weight training, stretching exercises
100 situps before bed nightly
Once a year trains for 6 weeks and participates in a marathon

Supplements: High potency multivitamin, multiminerals, & B complex daily in addition to:

2,000 mg vitamin C	30,000 I.U. vitamin A
450 mg ginkgo biloba, wheat grass occasionally	25 mg folic acid
1 tea bag each: sassafras tea, chamomile, fenugreek	

Dietary Protocol: 25–30% protein, 50–55% carbohydrate, 15–20% fat
About 100 ounces of distilled water, 6 pieces *only* fresh organic fruit daily

Alcohol: Seldom

Sleep: 5 hrs/day

Relaxation: Meditates 20 minutes 2x/day

Mental exercise: Problem solving and reading

Personal secrets: A good genetic background and a passion for life

Best habits to cultivate: Know that you can accomplish whatever you want and have self-confidence and self-respect.

Eric Braverman, M.D.

(Princeton, New Jersey) received his medical degree with honors from New York University and did research at Harvard University, Massachusetts General Hospital and New York University Medical School. He is the founder and director of Princeton Associates for Total Health (PATH Medical), a clinical practice that is devoted to mind and body wellness. Additionally, he conducts research on diagnosing and treating brain illness and the general prevention of medical illness and aging. Dr. Braverman has authored seven books including *The Healing Nutrients Within*.

Personal Longevity Program

Exercise: Believes in exercise rotation, for one portion of the year, likes to exercise for one to two hours three times/week, tennis, swimming, jogging and weight lifting

Supplements:

290 mg vitamin C	6.7 mcg chromium
12,233 I.U. beta-carotene	1.5 mg magnesium choline
50 mg magnesium	tryptophan or melatonin
4 mg zinc	occasionally
40 mg molybdenum	borage oil and fish oil, saw
200 mg taurine	palmetto
coenzyme Q-10	100 I.U. vitamin E
200 mg odorless garlic	500 mg niacin
50 mg vitamin B6	56.7 mcg selenium
135 I.U. vitamin D	60 mg niacinamide
6.7 mg potassium	0.35 mg boron

Dietary protocol: High protein complex and carbohydrate, protein is mainly fish, chicken and an occasional steak, trys to eat at least 2-3 pieces of fresh fruit and vegetables daily, one pitcher of water daily

Alcohol: Red wine on weekends

Other information: No fried foods, no fatty foods, tries to reduce intake of cheese and other dairy products

Relaxation: Cranial electrical stimulation, prayer and meditation

Sleep: Approximately 7 hours a day, occasional use of tryptophan or melatonin

Personal secret: Higher power as a guide to health care

Best habit to cultivate: Harmony of body, mind and spirit

Richard Cutler, Ph.D.

(Bethesda, Maryland) is a molecular biologist, president of Genox Corporation in Bethesda and formerly at the Gerontology Research Center, National Institute on Aging, National Institutes of Health. His research focuses on the genetic and biochemical basis of human longevity. This world-distinguished researcher and educator received his doctoral degree in biophysics from the University of Houston. An adjunct professor of chemistry at the University of Maryland in Baltimore, he has published over 100 articles in peer-reviewed scientific journals. He was awarded the 1994 Infinity Award for Advances in Basic Science by the American Academy of Anti-Aging Medicine.

Personal Longevity Program

Exercise: Aerobic exercise and swimming 2 hours 2 times/week, sailing and boat maintenance

Supplements: General antioxidant multivitamin with minerals daily in addition to:
500 mg vitamin C   30 mg beta-carotene

Other: 10 mg melatonin when traveling   25 mg coenzyme Q-10
Avoid iron!

Dietary protocol: Predominantly Oriental food with occasional red meat, fresh fruit in season and daily 1-2 servings of tropical fresh fruit usually on salads, daily breakfast: hot cereal with raisins

Alcohol: Occasional wine

Relaxation: Work, sailing and hobbies; e.g., piano, astronomy

Mental exercise: Problem solving on job, data analysis, reading

Personal secrets:
   1. Find a job you like, have a purpose, and be happy
   2. Be active—physically and mentally (use it or lose it)
   3. Eat a good diet with an informed nutritional basis

Best Habits to cultivate: Develop friends. A man's richness is people, particularly his true friends.

Gregory Fahy, Ph.D.

(Bethesda, Maryland) is head of the tissue cryopreservation section of the Transfusion and Cryopreservation Research Program at the Naval Medical Research Institute and the Chief Scientist of Organ, Inc. and Life Resuscitation Technologies, Inc. He earned his doctoral degree in pharmacology from the Medical College of Georgia. His areas of specialization include the mechanisms of aging, clinical intervention in the aging process, cryopreservation, the reversal of ischemic injury, and nanotechnology. He is widely published and has made numerous radio and television appearances as an expert on aging and cryobiology.

Personal Longevity Program

Exercise: Practically none due to time limitations, but occasional workouts of jogging, weights, treadmill and pushups.

Supplements: Multi-mineral supplements in addition to:

5000 I.U. vitamin A	200 mg vitamin B1
50 mg vitamin B2	175 mg vitamin B3
600 mg vitamin B5	175 mg vitamin B6
100 mg vitamin 12	25,000 I.U. beta-carotene
200 mcg biotin	

vitamin C as: ascorbyl palmitate 250 mg
               calcium and niacinamide ascorbate 1250 mg
               Acerola juice powder 300 mg

120 mg coenzyme Q-10	300 I.U. vitamin D3
800 mcg folate triglutamate	500 mg choline bitartrate
25 mg dilaurylthiodipropionate	15 mg glutathione
750-1500 mg glucosamine sulfate	3 g guar gum
250 mg inositol	150 mg lecithin
100 mg n-acetyl cysteine	500 mg taurine
25 mg thiodipropionic acid	500 mg tyrosine
Mixed plant bioflavinoids	

Drugs:

250 mg centrophenoxine	2.5 mg parlodel
2.5 mg deprenyl	topical retin A
50 mg pregnenolone	100 mg tagamet

Dietary protocol: Minimize fat and beef, almost no pork, emphasis on vegetarian meals, fish, and poultry; minimize breakfast, skip lunch, watch weight, conservative use of alcohol

Best Habit to Cultivate: Take everything in stride and minimize stress.

Philosophy: Stopping aging is something that we will achieve in the next 1–4 decades. The task for all of us in the meantime is to last another 30 years or so in reasonable condition so we can take advantage of this breakthrough.

Michael Fossel, M.D., Ph.D.

(Grand Rapids, Michigan) is a clinician, researcher, examiner for the American Board of Emergency Medicine, and author. He earned his doctoral degree in neurobiology from Stanford University and his medical degree from Stanford University. He is a clinical professor of medicine at Michigan State University. His research interests include the role of telomere biology in cancer prevention/control and the aging process.

Personal Longevity Program

Exercise: Various aerobic exercises, 1 1/2 hrs judo 3 times/week, running/jogging 2-7 miles 3-4 times/week, physical activities (playing) with children

Supplements: High quality multi-vitamin in addition to:
400 mg vitamin E   3 mg melatonin
20 mg DHEA occasionally   2 tablespoons brewer's yeast
                                     daily

Dietary Protocol: High fruit and vegetables, low meat, usually 1-2 servings fresh fruit in season

Alcohol: Minimal consumption, usually red wine with meals

Relaxation: Meditate 5-10 minutes daily, garden, cook

Stress reliever: Meditate, exercise, play with children

Mental exercise: Play chess, write, work, and read

Personal secret: Good genes and good luck

Best habit to cultivate: Learn how to relax and reduce stress

Vincent C. Giampapa, M.D., F.A.C.S.

(Montclair, New Jersey) received his medical degree from Mt. Sinai Medical School in New York City and continued his medical training at St. Luke's-Roosevelt Hospital in New York City where he specialized in plastic surgery. He also completed a year of microsurgery and hand fellowship at New York University Medical Center. He is a Fellow of the American College of Surgeons, a member of the Board of Directors and serves as Vice-President of the American Academy of Anti-Aging Medicine. Dr. Giampapa is a noted educator, researcher, and inventor. An assistant clinical professor in plastic surgery at the University of Medicine and Surgery of New Jersey Medical Center, he conducts clinical research in the areas of drug delivery systems, biomarkers of aging and facial implants.

Personal Longevity Program

Exercise: 1½ hours weight training 3 times/week, biking 25 minutes 6 times/week and karate 2 times/week

Supplements: Multivitamin/mineral daily in addition to:
2,000 mg L-glutamine   blue-green algae
phytocompounds   50,000 I.U. beta-carotene
4,000 I.U. vitamin C

Dietary protocol: High-protein, medium carbohydrate and low fat diet, a diet high in grains and vegetables with minimal red meat, 6 glasses of water/day

Alcohol: Occasional red wine

Other information: No fried foods

Relaxation: Daily meditation

Sleep: 6½ hrs each day

Personal secret(s): Four steps needed: Good genes; care for others; find work you love; and be impassioned

Best habit to cultivate: Mental calmness and mindfulness

Robert Goldman, D.O., Ph.D.

(Chicago, Illinois) is the founder and president of the National Academy of Sports Medicine and the High Technology Research Institute. An internationally published physician, Dr. Goldman received his medical degree from Midwestern University College of Osteopathic Medicine and two doctoral degrees in health sciences from Honolulu University and the other in steroid biochemistry from Institute d'Estudes Superieures L'Avenir, Brussels, Belgium. A recognized authority on androgenic steroids and high-tech sports training, he has held over 20 world records and has been listed in the *Guinness Book of World Records*. In 1980, he was inducted into the World Hall of Fame of Physical Fitness and Body Building. Dr. Goldman also is the chief medical officer for the International Federation of Body Builders (I.F.B.B.), the chair of the I.F.B.B. International Medical Commission, and a special advisor to the President's Council on Physical Fitness and Sports.

Personal Longevity Program

Exercise: 1 hr/day of aerobic exercise with light resistance training 6 times/week

Supplements: multivitamin including:

2,500 I.U. vitamin A	65 mg riboflavin
63 mg thiamin	120 mg niacin
425 mcg folic acid	100 mg magnesium
700 mg calcium	325 mg feverfew
150 mcg chromium picolinate	200 I.U. vitamin E
3 capsules odorless garlic	250 mcg vitamin B12
400 mg ginseng	200 I.U. vitamin D
4800 mg vitamin C	5 mg black currant oil

Dietary protocol: High-carbohydrate, low-fat diet, meat mainly poultry, 3 pieces fresh fruit/day, 6 glasses of water/day

Alcohol: Minimal; if any, red wine

Other information: Seldom eat fried foods, red meat and shellfish

Sleep: 4-5 hours/day

Relaxation techniques: Aerobic exercise

Personal secret: Good genetics, positive attitude. "I chose my ancestors wisely."

Best habit(s) to cultivate: Regular exercise and a "proper" diet

Denham Harman, M.D., Ph.D.

(Omaha, Nebraska) earned his doctoral degree in chemistry from the University of California—Berkeley and his medical degree from Stanford University. He is an educator, clinician, researcher, writer, editor, and administrator. He is a professor at the University of Nebraska School of Medicine. Dr. Harman developed the free radical theory of aging and expanded this theory to include the possibility that lifespan was determined by the rate of aging of the mitochondria. He is one of the founders of the American Aging Association, in addition to being a delegate to the White House Conference on Aging.

Personal Longevity Program

Exercise: Run 2-3 times/week

Supplements: Multivitamin with minerals in addition to:
1,500 mg vitamin C   1 aspirin daily
29,000 I.U. beta-carotene   400 I.U. vitamin E
every other day

Dietary protocol: High fiber low fat diet with fresh fruit 3 times/day, 5-6 glasses of water day

Alcohol: Seldom, if any red wine

Other information: Seldom eat fried foods, little red meat, no caffeine and seldom drink carbonated beverages

Relaxation: Reading, listening to music, and running

Sleep/Rest: 8 hours/day

Mental Exercise: Work

Personal philosophy: Keep working at something you enjoy and never retire. This way you will not have time to think about growing old.

Ronald Hoffman, M.D.

(New York City, New York) is trained in internal medicine and specializes in nutrition. He is the medical director of the Hoffman Center in New York City. Dr. Hoffman practices immunotherapy, focusing on the treatment of allergies and chemical sensitivities. An author of many books, including *Tired All the Time* and *Seven Weeks To a Settled Stomach*, he is a leading authority on nutrition and alternative medicine and the host of "Health Talk," a radio show on WOR that originates in New York City.

Personal Longevity Program

Exercise: 40-minute regular daily aerobic exercises including stationary bike, stairmaster, treadmill or running, strength training 3 times/week

Supplements: Multivitamin with multiminerals and antioxidant supplementation in addition to: L-glutamine, ginseng, and melatonin

Dietary protocol: Follows a salad and salmon diet that is high in phytonutrients with lean protein and mono unsaturated fats, 8 cups of water daily, 1 fruit/day

Alcohol: Organic wine and microbrewery beers

Other information: 3-6 cups of green tea daily

Relaxation: Reads novels and short stories

Stress reliever: Surfs the Internet, radio broadcasting, using kava kava

Mental exercise: Writing books and articles, reading journals

Personal Secret: Diversification

Best Habit to cultivate: Adapt to new circumstances

Worst habit a person can have: Resisting change and having fixed ideas

Gwen Ivy, Ph.D.

(Toronto, Ontario) is an internationally published researcher and educator. She received her doctoral degree in psychobiology from the University of California at Irvine. In addition to her work on the mechanisms of aging, she has done research on longevity and on health drugs, most notably l-deprenyl. Dr. Ivy is a widely published researcher who appears frequently on television and radio as an authority on longevity issues.

Personal Longevity Program

Exercise: Follows a special fitness work-out for major muscles while protecting the lower back 1 1/4 hrs 3 times/week, swim 1/2 hour 3 times/week

Supplements: multivitamin with minerals in addition to:
500 mg vitamin C　　　　　　400 I.U. vitamin E
200 mcg chromium　　　　　　100 mcg selenium
ginseng, odorless garlic and　　10,000 I.U. beta-carotene
green tea

Dietary protocol: High fiber, low fat. Diet high in fresh vegetables and seafood, fruit juices

Alcohol: Moderate amount of red wine

Other information: No fried foods

Relaxation (method and duration):   Reads mysteries

Stress reliever: Reading and/or exercising

Mental exercise: Reading and doing research

Personal secret: Learn to reduce stress and watch your diet

Best habit to cultivate: Reduce stress and be mentally and physically
active

Saul Kent

(Fort Lauderdale, Florida) is founder and president of the non-profit Life Extension Foundation in south Florida and editor of the Foundation's monthly *Life Extension* magazine. Since 1981, the Foundation has been providing its members with the latest information about (and access to) the best available life extension products and therapies in the world. Its primary goals is to achieve total control over aging by the year 2020. Mr. Kent has been involved in every aspect of the life extension movement for the past 32 years. He co-founded the first cryonics society in New York (1966), has directed numerous life extension meetings, and has appeared on many radio and television shows; and has been in the forefront of the struggle for freedom of choice in health care.

Personal Longevity Program

Exercise: 4-5 times/week, walk, jog and run on beach for 3 miles or
1/2 hour of basketball

Supplements:
8-12 capsules of multinutrient formula (has 50 ingredients)
2-4 capsules of multimineral formula

400 I.U. vitamin E	4 gm vitamin C
500 mg acetyl l-carnitine	500 mg N-acetyl-cysteine
100 mg coenzyme Q-10	1/2 cup of vegetable/herbal soup

Anti-aging therapies:

5 mg Deprenyl 5 times/week	100 mg DHEA daily
3 mg melatonin nightly	

Dietary protocol: High carbohydrate, low fat diet. High in vegetables, fruit and fruit juices, small amount (a few ounces) of meat daily, mainly fish and poultry, no fried foods

Amount of sleep: 4-6 hours/day

Relaxation: Working

Personal philosophy:
1. Don't worry about anything that's "possible"; just do it.
2. Only worry about things that are "impossible."
3. Have short- and long-term goals and work on them.

Best habit to cultivate: Good diet, regular exercise, use of supplemental nutrients, drugs and therapies for life extension, and hard work

Worst habit a person can have: Smoking!

Dharma Singh Khalsa, M.D.

(Tucson, Arizona) is the president and medical director of the Alzheimer's Prevention Foundation/Brain Longevity Institute in Tucson, Arizona. Board certified by the American Academy of Pain Management, he earned his medical degree from Creighton University School of Medicine and is a graduate of the U.C.L.A. Medical Acupuncture for Physicians program. His principal research interest is the effects of stress, conscious relaxation, nutrition, and exercise on the performance, health and longevity of the brain and nervous system.

Personal Longevity Program

Exercise: Aerobic workout 1 hour 3-4 times/week when possible, includes stair master and circuit training, also plays tennis and swims, advanced yoga and meditation—1 1/2 hour/day

Supplements: High potency multivitamin with minerals daily in addition to:

3-6 g vitamin C	l-carnitine
400 mcg folic acid	25,000 I.U. vitamin A
400 mg vitamin E	

Herbs: Ginkgo biloba, ginseng, astragalus

Other: Blue-green algae for chlorella and spirulina, and wheat grass

Drugs: 50 mg DHEA every other day

Dietary Protocol: Vegetarian with protein supplementation, fresh fruit twice day, no alcohol, little fried food, no meat, fish or eggs, 1 cup of tea/day.

Sleep: Usually 7 hours

Relaxation: Advanced Kundalini yoga, meditation and prayer daily

Stress Reliever: Go to movies and take a day off

Mental Exercise: Memorize things for cognitive exercise

Personal Secret: I love life and love the life I live. Relax and see what God has in store for you.

Best Habit to cultivate: Develop a relationship with your spiritual self

Most destructive habit a person can have: Smoking

Kenichi Kitani, M.D.

(Tokyo, Japan) is an eminent educator, clinician, editor, and researcher. Dr. Kitani received his medical degree from the Faculty of Medicine, University of Tokyo, where he is currently professor and director of radioisotopic research. For 20 years, Dr. Kenichi served as director of the clinical physiology department at the Tokyo Metropolitan Institute of Gerontology. His main research interests have been the functional alteration of the liver during aging, the effects of deprenyl on antioxidant modulation, and life prolongation in animals.

Personal Longevity Program

Exercise: Walking 2 hours/day, swimming and snorkeling when possible

Supplements: Gingko biloba ginseng, blue-green algae, odorless garlic

Dietary protocol: High-fiber, very-low fat and high seafood diet, a lot of miso soup, very little to no red meat

Drink: Green tea

Alcohol: Moderate red wine with meals

Relaxation: Meditation 30 minutes/day

Stress reliever: Walking and meditation

Personal secret: Learn how to manage stress; take stress-free vacations

Best habit to cultivate: Manage stress and follow a healthy diet

Frances A. Kovarik, Ph.D.

(Chicago, Illinois) is a reproductive endocrinologist, educator, editor, and the executive director of the American Academy of Anti-Aging Medicine. She is an adjunct professor in physiology at Oklahoma State University College of Osteopathic Medicine in Tulsa. Her primary area of research is the role of antioxidants in metabolic reactions, while other research interests include the effects of steroids on cholesterol and the relationship between lipoprotein and other biomarker blood levels and the aging process. Dr. Kovarik earned her doctoral degree in anatomy from Loyola University of Chicago. Her expertise includes curriculum development in medicine, dentistry and allied health.

Personal Longevity Program

Exercise: Aerobic exercise routine: 4-5 times/week (45-60 minutes each session), including the stationary cycle and treadmill. Flexibility exercises 20 minutes A.M. and 35 minutes P.M daily, walking, aerobic workout 30 minutes 2 times/week. Use exercise as a stress reliever.

Supplements: Multivitamin with mineral, in addition to:

1,000 mg vitamin C	100 mcg chromium picolinate
800 I.U. vitamin E	2,500 I.U. beta-carotene
800 I.U. vitamin A	600 mg inositol
niacin	100 mg choline

thiamine

1.0 mg folic acid

256 mg calcium

200 mcg selenium

25 mg L-carnitine

30 mg methionine

15 mg glutathione

Herbs: Ginkgo biloba, echinacea, ginseng every other day

Other: 50 mg/day DHEA, 3 mg/day melatonin, and 1/2 aspirin/day

Dietary Protocol: High fiber, low fat with poultry and fish and limited amount of red meat, no fried foods and no added salt, 8–10 glasses of water/day, 3 pieces of fresh fruit (in season)/day

Alcohol: Occasionally glass of wine with meal

Sleep: 5-6 hours/night

Relaxation technique: Mediate and pray 1 hour daily

Mental exercise: Exercise regimen 30 minutes twice a day, reading, research, and learning new skills/information

Personal secret: Keep a positive attitude, continue to learn and use your talents to help others

Best habit to cultivate: Exercise and stress management techniques

Hans Kugler, Ph.D.

(Redondo Beach, California) earned his doctoral degree in organophosphorus chemistry from the State University of New York at Stony Brook. He is the president of the International Academy of Alternative Health and Medicine. The author of six books on health and aging, including *Tripping the Clock,* a practical guide to anti-aging and rejuvenation. Dr. Kugler is the editor of *Preventive Medicine Update,* senior science advisor to the *Journal of Longevity Research,* and does research on fitness work and immune enhancement at Health Integration Center in Torrance, CA. Dr. Kugler is widely published and appears frequently on television and radio as an authority on longevity, health and nutrition issues.

Personal Longevity Program

Exercise: Program that alternates aerobics and weights for 1½ hrs 3 times/week, active horseback riding (cowboy events) 2 hrs 2 times/week, swimming

Supplements: B complex, multiminerals and antioxidant complex in addition to:

1,000 mg vitamin C   coenzyme Q-10
30 mg DHEA   GH-3
1 tablet calcium/magnesium

Occasionally: vanadium, glutathione, omega fatty acids

At night: 200 I.U. vitamin E, 100-200 mcg selenium, 1.5-3.0 mg melatonin and Prostat for prostate health

Twice a year: oral (sublingual) cell therapy for about 2 weeks of cell extracts from specific organ tissues, for revitalization

Cycling: 3 days on, 2-3 weeks off: Immune-enhancing substances, phycotene, DMG, sublingual thymus, echinacea, goldenseal, and specialty nutrients

Dietary Protocol: Low-fat, high-complex carbohydrates, protein at every meal. Some extra protein between meals and right before going to bed e.g. 1 tablespoon yogurt or 1/3 glass of protein shake

Alcohol: Extremely little; some beer or red wine

Relaxation: Meditation; 20 minute rest period in the late afternoon

Sleep: 7 hours/night

Stephen A. Levine, Ph.D.

(San Leandro, California) earned his doctoral degree in biochemistry from the University of California-Berkeley. He is best known for his pioneering research in antioxidant/free radical biochemistry having brought sophistication redox theory and practice to orthomolecular physicians in the early '80s. His research led to innovative nutritional formulas via NutriCology/Allergy Research Group. Dr. Levine has pioneered the introduction of products such as melatonin, germanium, buffered vitamin C and AntiOx™, along with more recent research and novel products, including Lactoferrin, and Alive and Well™. He is a researcher, writer, and administrator.

Personal Longevity Program

Exercise: Aerobic jogging and weight training generally 3 times/week, jogging 60 minutes and gym 30 minutes. Total exercise time averages about 2 hrs/wk.

Supplements: A diverse and broad spectrum ranging from vitamins and minerals to amino acids and fatty acids, use glandulars, coenzymes and metabolic intermediaries e.g., 300 mg/day coenzyme Q-10, 500 mg/day L-carnitine

This supplementation is individualized via metabolic balancing. Pro-Greens vegetable mixtures; broad range of growth factors obtained from fractionation of glandulars.

Hormones and drugs: 40 mg/day testosterone, 50 mg/day DHEA, 20 mg melatonin nightly

Dietary protocol: As specified by individualized metabolic testing including organic meats and vegetables/ balanced protein/carbohydrates

Relaxation and sleep: As much as needed, emphasizing meditation, energy balancing: sleep-enhanced stress reduction exercises; and physical exercises

Stress reliever: High doses of melatonin and kava kava

Mental exercise: Life

Personal secret: Plan for the best.

Habit to cultivate: Early to bed, early to rise

Lex, the Wonder Dog

(Chicago, Illinois) champion Airedale, mascot of the American Academy of Anti-Aging Medicine. He was featured on numerous television news shows and written about in magazines. The average lifespan for Airedales is about 11 years. At age 10, Lex was starting to fail. Dr. Ronald Klatz placed Lex on the following regime and saw startling anti-aging effects. Within 6 months, Lex had apparently de-aged to the condition of an 8-year-old dog. He was able to jump 3-foot fences, his coat returned to a dark black-brown from his senescent gray. His eyes became bright and animated, where before the therapy they were cloudy and dull. Lex ran and played vigorously with dogs 5 years his junior. Lex suffered a stroke at age 16; although he made a good recovery at age 16½ years, he developed a weakness in his hindquarters which limited his activity and the quality of his existence. Rather than have Lex suffer the infirmity of aging, he was put to sleep at an equivalent of human age 116 years.

Personal Longevity Program

Exercise: 2-3 quick walks 15–20 minutes daily, stair climbing 10 minutes daily

Supplements: 1 pediatric vitamin with meal 2 times/day in addition to:

.4 mg vitamin C	1 mg folic acid
400 I.U. vitamin E	5,000 I.U. beta-carotene
10,000 I.U. vitamin A	100 mcg selenium
vitamin B complex	100 mg coenzyme Q-10
100 mg niacin	2 capsules Acemanon
200 mcg chromium picolinate	

NOTE: Because Lex is 65 pounds, he receives one-half the dose of supplements normally prescribed for humans.

Herbs: Ginkgo biloba extract, ginseng, hydegine, garlic, green tea extract

Hormones and drugs:

PBN (mitochondrial antioxidant shown to extend lives of laboratory animals)	Growth hormone stimulating compounds
	DHEA
5 mg Eldepryl every other day	10 mg nightly melatonin

Dietary protocol: Science diet for senior dogs, 2 Kosher hot dogs/week with sauerkraut and mustard, 1 slice of low-fat pizza/week

Ralph Merkle, Ph.D.

(Palo Alto, California) is a pioneering researcher in computational nanotechnology at Xerox PARC and was the manager of the Language Group at Elxsi. He received his doctorate in electrical engineering from Stanford University. Dr. Merkle is the author of numerous publications and the holder of six patents. He is a researcher, educator, author, and administrator.

Personal Longevity Program

Exercise: Stair climber 30 minutes 5 times/week, bikes 20 miles once/week

Supplements: Multivitamin with minerals daily, no iron, additional chromium picolinate

Nutriceuticals: 1 mg/day melatonin

Drugs: ½ tablet/day aspirin

Dietary protocol: "Average American Diet," tries to avoid fried foods; fresh fruit daily, 4 glasses of water day, no alcohol

Amount of sleep: Usually 8 hours/night

Relaxation: Work, browse the Internet, bike, play video games

Personal secret: Enjoy life.

Best habit to cultivate: Thinking

Steven Novil, Ph.D.

(Chicago, Illinois) earned his doctoral degree in nutritional sciences from the Missouri College of Health Sciences. He is a clinical consultant in nutritional science to the Evanston Health Center and Director of the Evanston Nutrition Center. Dr. Novil is a nationally and internationally published author of articles relating to metabolic and eating disorders as well as weight management. His research on longevity, low blood sugar, allergies, asthma, and Oriental and American Indian medicinal herbs has been published in numerous professional journals.

Personal Longevity Program

Exercise: Walk 30 minutes 3 times/week, yoga-like exercises 40 minutes each day, calisthenics for 20 minutes 3 times/week, jogs for 30 minutes once/week

Supplements: Multivitamin with minerals in addition to:

6,000 mg vitamin C	300 mcg chromium picolinate
800 I.U. vitamin E	9 mg vanadyl sulfate
25,000 I.U. beta-carotene	50 mg zinc
500 mg proline	100 mcg selenium
500 mg lysine	1,000 mg magnesium
400 mg folic acid	1,500 mg calcium
100 mg pantothenic acid	9 mg boron
100 mg niacin	100 mg coenzyme Q-10
Ginkgo biloba	6 capsules odorless garlic
8 capsules ginseng	0.5 mg melatonin every other night
4 tablets blue-green algae	
150 mg cinnamon	25 mg DHEA every other day

Note: One day each week does not take any supplements

Dietary protocol: 90% vegetarian with no shellfish, seldom fried foods, 3-4 pieces of fresh fruit daily, 4-6 glasses of distilled water daily

Relaxation: Meditation 15 minutes, 3 times/day

Stress Reliever: Meditation, cabalistic study and physical exercise

Personal secret: Care for others and keep a positive mental attitude

Best habit to cultivate: Try to find something good in all situations.

William Regelson, M.D.

(Richmond, Virginia) is a professor of medicine at the Medical College of Virginia, Commonwealth University. A specialist in medical oncology, with joint appointments in microbiology and biomedical engineering, he has been a leading researcher in the field of aging for more than twenty years. He was formerly the director of the Fund for Integrative Biomedical Research, dedicated to research on the biology of aging. Dr. Regelson is coauthor of the best-selling book, *The Melatonin Miracle,* published by Simon and Schuster, New York, 1995. He is currently preparing a new book dealing with DHEA and anti-aging. His work in aging has been focused on hormone replacement therapy, and his prime interest involves antioxidant approaches to the prevention and treatment of age-related pathology involving cell and mitochondrial membrane integrity. This work clinically focuses on the development of novel anti-inflammatory compounds which provide cytoprotection via inhibition of phospholipases.

Personal Longevity Program

Exercise: Aerobic and anaerobic exercise 1 hour 2–3 times/week.

Supplements: Daily

50 mg DHEA every other day	occasional bioflavinoids (rutin,
50 mg niacin	quercetin); Q10
400 I.U. vitamin E (alpha-tocopherol acetate or succinate)	1 mg melatonin at bedtime
	300 mg × 2 milk of magnesia tablets
6 cc DMAE in orange juice	200 mg pyridoxine HOL
daily whey	5 mg riboflavin
Total dry cereal	almonds for magnesium

Brian Rothstein, D.O.

(Baltimore, Maryland) is a graduate of the University of Osteopathic Medicine and Health Sciences in Des Moines, Iowa. He is the medical director of the Rothstein Center for Health and Healing, which provides the largest chelation preventive medicine facility in Maryland. He is a diplomate of the American Academy for Advanced Medicine in Chelation Therapy. Dr. Rothstein served as a physician in the United States Army in human biologic research.

Personal Longevity Program

Exercise: Walks 2-4 miles daily, bike riding, hiking on week-ends and playing with children

Supplements: High-quality multivitamin with minerals daily in addition to 3-5 g vitamin C

Dietary protocol: Whole-grain, low-meat diet with a lot of filtered water

Alcohol: 3-4 times/week

Relaxation: Daily prayer (60-90 minutes/day), walking and using the hot tub

Stress relievers: Walking, hot tub, playing with children, mental exercise and cabalistic study

Personal secret: Chose parents wisely and looks to God for help

Best habit to cultivate: Balance

Joan Smith Sonneborn, Ph.D.

(Laramie, Wyoming) a leading gerontologist, was educated at Bryn Mawr College and earned her Ph.D. at Indiana University in Biochemistry/ Zoology. She did postdoctoral research at Brandeis University, University of California-Berkeley and the University of Wisconsin-Madison. Presently, she is professor and chair of the Program of Aging and Human Development at the University of Wyoming. Dr. Smith Sonneborn has been on the Executive Board and is a Fellow of the Gerontology Society of America. She was the first woman to chair the Biology of Aging at the prestigious Gordon Conference and has given over 100 presentations nationally and internationally to both the public and private sector. She has been on the Advisory Board for Government Agencies and the Alliance for Aging Research, as well as international and national scientific journals. She is an administrator, an educator, researcher, scholar, and grandmother, with a love of life and mankind.

Personal Longevity Program

Exercise: Schopp aerobic weight-lifting circuit for 40 minutes, 3 times/ week, jogging for 40 minutes, 3 times/week in fall, spring and summer, contouring exercises for 1 hour, 1–2 times/week

Supplements: Multivitamin daily in addition to:

20,000 I.U. vitamin A	400 mcg folic acid
15 mg thiamin	500 mg vitamin C
17 mg riboflavin	600 I.U. vitamin E
18 mg pantothenic acid	100 mcg iodine
21 mg pyridoxine	25 mcg selenium
15 mcg cyanocobalamin	1 mg cobalt
15 mg zinc	800 mg calcium
100 mg potassium	400 mg magnesium
18 mg iron	30 mg coenzyme Q-10
3 mg copper	500 mg carnitine
1.5 mg manganese	750 mg glucosamine sulfate

Estradiol for hormone replacement therapy

Dietary protocol: High-carbohydrate, low-fat and low-protein—mostly chicken, buffalo, wild meat, or salmon and orange roughy, 16 ounces of low-fat yogurt daily, 8 glasses water/day

Alcohol: Minimal, if any champagne or red wine

Other information: Never eat fried foods

Relaxation: Scuba diving, movies, watching TV, dancing, football and basketball games, hunting trips, fishing, also reserve "quiet time" for spiritual renewal and positive thinking

Mental exercise: Prepare lectures, read journals, attend scientific meetings, take new classes to keep current in new areas of expertise

Personal secret: Be happy. I see the "good" in myself and all those around me. I try to bring some pleasure to those I touch during the day. I grow and learn from my interaction with my students.

Best habit to cultivate: Self-discipline

Stephen Sinatra, M.D., F.A.C.C.

(Manchester, Connecticut) Dr. Sinatra is an author, clinician, educator, editor, inventor and administrator. He is board certified in internal medicine and cardiology and is chief of cardiology and director of medical education at Manchester Memorial Hospital in Connecticut and is an assistant clinical professor of medicine at the University of Connecticut School of Medicine. Dr. Sinatra has special expertise in utilizing behavior modification and emotional release as tools for healthy living particularly in heart disease with emphasis on preventive cardiology. Trained in Gestalt and Bioenergetic psychotherapy, he is a certified bioenergetic analyst. His latest book, *Optimum Health*, was released in November 1995.

Personal Longevity Program

Exercise: 40 minutes 5 times/week. Program includes: aerobic fast walk/arm swing, back and abdominal strengthening exercises, light resistance training with 10 lb. dumbbells, snow skiing and fly fishing as much as possible

Supplements: Antioxidant multivitamin with minerals in addition to:
400 mcg folic acid (anti-aging, prevents cardiovascular disease)
30 mg pycnogenol
Lipotropic factors:

600 mg choline	180 mg methionine
500 mg inositol	180 mg betaine
180 mg taurine	75 mg l-carnitine

Enzymes: Papain, bromelain, aloe vera, and acidophilus
Herbs and spices:

250 mg cayenne pepper	hawthorn berry
100 mg ginger	fenugreek
gotu kola	chamomile

hyssop, fennel, astragalus, 1-2 cloves of garlic

Other: 90 mg coenzyme Q-10, 1000 mg omega-3 oil—flax, 600 mcg melatonin with valerian root 3-4 times/week at night

Dietary protocol: Mediterranean diet that is high fiber (greater than 30 gms/day), low fat (less than 30 g/day), grains, pastas, fruits and vegetables daily, fish 1-2 times/week, occasional red meat and poultry, 8-10 glasses water/day, red wine 1-2 glasses every other day

Other: Avoid heavy metals such as copper, iron, mercury, cadmium and lead, use water filters, air filters, and full spectrum lighting, avoid prolonged exposure to sunlight, microwaves, TV, radiation, and any other electromagnetic fields

Relaxation: Prayer, cooking, reading and fly fishing

Sleep: 4-5 hours/night

Stress reliever: Play with dogs, emotional release (laughter, express anger, give myself permission to cry)

Mental exercise: Write books and newsletters

Personal secret: Be able to "surrender" and listen to the "messengers" around us. Listen to your body.

Best habit: Open my heart to love, avoid negative thoughts, create emotional support systems and maintain connections with people I care about and who care about me

Roy Walford, M.D.

(Los Angeles, California) is a professor of Pathology at the University of California Los Angeles School of Medicine. His premedical education was at the California Institute of Technology and his degree from the University of Chicago School of Medicine. He has authored four scientific monographs, including "The Immunologic Theory of Aging," and, with R. Weindruch, "The Retardation of Aging and Disease by Dietary Restriction," as well as popular science books including *Maximum Life Span* and *The 120 Year Diet*. He has received numerous awards including the Kleemeier Award of the Gerontological Society of America, the Henderson Award of the American Geriatric Society, the Research Award of the American Aging Society and the Infinity Award of the American Academy of Anti-Aging Medicine. His work includes caloric restriction studies, the molecular genetics of aging and *in vitro* senescence of immune system cells. In addition, Dr. Walford was the Southwest A.A.U. gymnastic champion and, for 2 years, captain of the wrestling team at the University of Chicago. From 1991-1993, Dr. Walford was the attending physician inside Biosphere 2 in Arizona and conducted the first well-monitored caloric restriction experiments in humans. He has had an active side career in theater, writing and video art.

Personal Longevity Program

Exercise: Body building with aerobic circuit training 1½ hours 4-5 times/week

Supplements: One multivitamin/mineral tablet daily in addition to:

400 I.U. vitamin E	0.1 mg chromium picolinate
500 mg vitamin C	25,000 I.U. beta-carotene
100 mcg selenium	20 mg coenzyme Q-10
0.5-1.0 g magnesium	

Dietary protocol: Low-caloric nutrient-dense diet, use a variety of fresh fruits and vegetables, avoid fat and eat a minimal amount of meat

Sleep: 6 hrs/day

Personal secret: Keep changing the foci of interest

Ben Weider, C.M., Ph.D.

(Montreal, Canada) is the founder and president of the International Federation of BodyBuilders (I.F.B.B.) in Montreal, Canada. I.F.B.B. now represents over 160 countries and is a member of the General Association of International Sports Federations. Since 1945, Ben Weider and his brother Joe have operated Weider Sports Equipment Co., Ltd. and Weider Health and Fitness in Canada and the United States. He was instrumental in developing the vitamin, mineral, protein, and sports nutrition industry and has been the recipient of numerous awards for outstanding leadership in the promotion of health and fitness.

Personal Longevity Program

Exercise: 1 hour/day for 30 minutes on treadmill and 30 minutes using various exercise equipment, 3 times/week

Supplements:

2,000 mg vitamin C	1,000 mg calcium
1,000 I.U. vitamin E	99 mg potassium
10,000 I.U. vitamin A	200 mcg chromium
100 mg vitamin B complex	500 mg magnesium oxide
200 mg folic acid	100 mcg selenium
1,600 mg niacin	6 mg iron
500 mg panthothenic acid	25,000 I.U. beta-carotene

1,000 I.U. vitamin D   0.66 mg copper

Herbs: 60 mg ginkgo biloba, 150 mg ginseng, 280 mg odorless garlic, 1,500 mg flax borage oil

Nutriceuticals: 3 mg melatonin, 200 mg coenzyme Q-10

Dietary Protocol: High-fiber, low-fat, medium protein with plenty of fresh vegetables daily. Four pieces of fresh fruit per day, four glasses of water daily, seldom eat fried foods and red meat—main meat eaten is poultry (white meat only), no shellfish and minimal caffeine and carbonated drinks

Alcohol: Very seldom, some red wine

Amount of sleep per day: 6-7 hours.

Relaxation: Reading, listening to music (about 1½ hrs at a time)

Stress reliever: Exercise, reading or taking a nap

Mental exercise: Reading

Other: Watching historical videotapes

Personal secret: Keep a positive outlook

Best habit to cultivate: Healthy lifestyle

Worst habit a person can have: Eating chocolate

Julian Whitaker, M.D.

(Newport Beach, California) is a respected author and editor-in-chief of the *Health and Healing* newsletter. This graduate of Emory University Medical School is the medical director of the Whitaker Wellness Center in Newport Beach, and is the immediate past president of the American Preventative Medical Association. Dr. Whitaker has practiced alternative medicine for the past 25 years.

Personal Longevity Program

Exercise: Various aerobic sports 4 times/week including biking, jogging, running, tennis, and snow skiing

Supplements: Comprehensive multivitamin with minerals in addition to:

vitamin C	aspartate
vitamin E	chromium picolinate
potassium/magnesium	arginine

Herbs: Ginseng, odorless garlic, green tea

Other: Omega-3 fatty acids, grape seed oil, melatonin, coenzyme Q-10 pregnenolone, DHEA

Dietary protocol: Low-fat/high-carbohydrate with some fish, 2-3 quarts of water/day, fresh fruit daily (4+ servings)

Alcohol: Occasionally

Other Information: No fried foods or red meat

Stress Relievers: Exercise and play with children

Sleep: 8 hours/night

Mental exercise: Research and writing

Grace H. W. Wong, Ph.D.

(South San Francisco, California) is a noted researcher in the area of gene regulation. She earned her doctorate from the Walter and Eliza Hall Institute of Medical Research, Royal Melbourne Hospital, Victoria, Australia. She has received numerous research awards. In July, 1994, Dr. Wong gave one of the invited presentations on mitochondrial disease at the Nobel Symposium 90.

Personal Longevity Program

Exercise: Aerobics 1 hour day, runs ½ hour every evening

Supplements: Multivitamin with minerals in addition to:

800 vitamin C	40-80 mcg folic acid
400 vitamin E	

Dietary protocol: Eats a little all day long (grazes) on high-fiber diet with high proteins (fish and poultry), water with added lemon throughout the day, plenty of fresh fruit, always 3 oranges and 2 lemons day

Alcohol: None

Other information: Avoids fried foods, tea, and coffee

Relaxation and stress reliever: Exercise and work

Personal secret: Think and work hard

Best habit to cultivate: Be happy and keep a positive attitude

Ronald M. Klatz, D.O.

(Chicago, Illinois) is the founder and president of the American Academy of Anti-Aging Medicine. Dr. Klatz is assistant professor of Internal medicine at Oklahoma State University and Senior Medical Editor of Longevity Magazine and contributing editor to Prime Health & Fitness magazine. He is also acknowledged as an authority in preventive/ longevity medicine and maximum human performance. A prolific inventor, Dr. Klatz holds multiple patents for advanced methods of organ resuscitation and neuroprotection.

Personal Longevity Program

Exercise: 30-minute aerobic workout including: walking, stair climbing, and weight training 5 times/week

Supplements: Daily amounts except where specified:

2,000 mg vitamin C	15 g blue-green algae + chlorella
800 mg vitamin E	10 mg melatonin, 2 times/wk as
10,000 I.U. vitamin A	a sleep aid
400 mcg selenium	0.50 grain thyroid hormone
900 mg niacin	every other day
400 mcg chromium picolinate	50 mg DHEA every other day
1 g lysine	5 mg deprenyl (eldepryl) at
500 mg l-acetyl-carnitine	bedtime
90 mg coenzyme Q-10	1/2 tablet of aspirin
gingko biloba	

Dietary protocol:

8 glasses of distilled water with lemon (for detox)

Omnivore, primarily a vegetarian. (I'd like to become a vegetarian one day but I enjoy eating "real foods" too much), limit red meat and fried food, fresh fruit twice a day.

Rest: 30-minute nap/siesta at midday about 2 P.M.

Stress reliever: Aerobic exercise program

Personal Secret: Lead a full, robust and meaningful life. Do what you love and it transforms from work to joy.

Best Habit to cultivate: Positive mental expectation of health and longevity

Philosophy: If one day you awoke in a world where no one ever told you how old you were, then how old would you be?

A LAST WORD

Having read this far, you now know more about the science of anti-aging medicine than most doctors on the planet. The real answer to aging without disease and disability starts with education—learning all you can about anti-aging science. Your destiny and health is in *your* hands. It means taking action—the time to start your own anti-aging program is *now*. And anti-aging takes determination—say "NO" to aging!

Although for centuries humankind has dreamt of long life and eternal youth, for most people on the planet, these dreams were perpetually out of reach. Now we know much and are learning more about how to prolong and maintain youth. As you explore your own anti-aging program, your path will shaped by your needs and wishes, biological inheritance, environmental circumstances, and personal preferences in diet and lifestyle. It may take some time before you find the anti-aging treatment that is right for you. But keep trying. The rewards will be far more valuable than the cost and the effort. Remember, old age is for the "other" guy. You know better, so why take it lying down? The choice is yours to be a diseased and decrepid victim or an ageless and vital winner. Join us, the members of the American Academy of Anti-Aging Medicine in our struggle against aging. The life you save can be your own.

After all, as we asked at the beginning of this book, who wants to live to be 150? You will—after you celebrate your 149th birthday.

Glossary

Acemannan A substance derived from the aloe vera plant family; functions as an immune regulating substance for autoimmune diseases and as an immune stimulator in immune deficiency disorders.

Acetyl-l-carnitine enhances energy metabolism, brain function and the immune system.

Acetyl-cysteine Protects against various toxins and pollutants.

Acidophilus (Lactobacillus acidophilus) Bacterium, part of the normal bacterial flora that help the absorption of food; enhances the immune system.

Antioxidant A substance that prevents cellular damage due to oxidation; exposure to unstable molecules called free radicals.

L-Arginine Nonessential amino acid that can stimulate the release of growth hormone; may be an effective immune enhancer; may have benefit in nutritional treatment of male infertility.

Ascorbic acid (vitamin C) Potent water-soluble antioxidant that appears to be effective in preventing diseases caused by cellular damage from free radicals, *e.g.* heart disease, cancer, and cataracts; may be an important factor in strengthening and maintaining the immune system.

Aspirin (salicylic acid) Functions as an anti-clotting agent; may help to prevent heart disease, stroke and certain forms of cancer when taken in small doses.

Astragalus Chinese herb that enhances the immune system; can lower blood pressure and may help prevent heart attack.

Betaine Helps digest fatty acids and is used in the production of RNA and DNA.

Bilberry Herb that may improve vision, particularly night vision; may aid in the prevention of vascular disease.

Bioflavonoids Potent antioxidant compounds that have anti-inflammatory and antiviral effects; are used to treat allergies and asthma; may be effective against heart disease and cancer.

Black currant oil High in gamma-linolenic acid, an essential fatty acid; involved in the synthesis of prostaglandin type 3; may protect against cancer and heart disease.

Blue-green algae Single-cell aquatic plants that contain trace minerals; may have neurostimulatory effects.

Borage oil Contains a linoleic acid that reduces the risk of atherosclerotic heart disease.

Boron Trace mineral that aids in the synthesis of steroids, particularly estrogens and testosterone; may help prevent osteoporosis and maintain strong bones; may help prevent memory loss.

Bromelain Enzyme found in fresh pineapple that helps break down protein; has anti-inflammatory and antiallergic properties.

Calcium Mineral that has beneficial effects on bone and tooth maintenance; may protect against colorectal cancer and high blood pressure. **Note:** vitamin D helps facilitate calcium absorption.

L-carnitine Amino acid that is a cofactor in mitochondrial energy production by transporting activated fatty acids across the mitochondrial membrane in cardiac and skeletal muscles; has a beneficial effect on the heart and muscles; improves stamina and endurance during exercise; may be effective in slowing down the progression of Alzheimer's disease; may help burn fat.

Beta-carotene Vitamin A precursor, an antioxidant that functions in neutralizing free radicals; may help prevent cervical cancer and atherosclerosis; is an immune system booster; appears to protect against respiratory diseases and environmental pollutants.

Cayenne pepper (capsaicin) Compound that prevents oxidation of low density lipoprotein cholesterol; may help prevent cardiovascular disease; aids in digestion by stimulating the production of saliva and gastric acid; stimulates the release of endorphins (mood enhancers).

Chlorophyll Plant compound that appears to stimulate nucleic acid (DNA and RNA) production; has well-documented detoxification and antibiotic actions; may help in the production of hemoglobin.

Choline Lipotropic factor and member of vitamin B complex family; essential for neurotransmitter production; aids in maintaining cell membranes; may slow down memory loss and help learning ability.

Chromium picolinate Mineral that protects the pancreas; a necessary co-factor with insulin to assist in the break down of sugar and metabolism of fat; may help in increasing muscle mass; helps prevent heart disease and diabetes.

Cinnamon Herb that neutralizes acidity and helps regulate blood sugar.

Coenzyme Q-10 (ubiquinone) Cellular lipid that is effective at the mitochondrial level with the production of energy; helps prevent free radical formation by inhibiting lipid peroxidation; increases stamina and may reduce heart disease.

Cobalamin (vitamin B12) Aids in the production of red blood cells, essential for the normal functioning of the nervous system; aids in the metabolism of protein and fat.

Cyanocobalamin (vitamin B12) Helps maintain a healthy nervous system and prevents anemia.

Dehydroepiandrosterone (DHEA) Hormone produced by the adrenal glands; appears to aid in the regulation and production of steroidal hormones; appears to help in reducing cholesterol levels and body fats; seems to be involved in increasing muscle mass. **Caution:** In women, it may have an androgenic effect causing facial hair growth. Available only by prescription.

Deprenyl™ Pharmaceutical approved for use in Parkinson's disease; acts as a neuroprotective agent and enhances mental function, mood and libido; has been reported in animal studies to extend both length and quality of life.

Dong qai Anti-aging herb particularly effective in women; presumed to assist in the regulation of female steroidal hormones; may aid in the regulation of blood glucose levels; may aid in lowering blood pressure in men and women.

Echinacea Herb that may stimulate the production of white blood cells; may enhance the immune system; appears to have antiviral and antifungal properties.

Fenugreek Herb that has been used to treat impotence in men; may aid in regulating estrogens and progesterone levels particularly during menopause; helps expel excess mucus from the respiratory and digestive systems; may help control blood sugar levels. **Caution:** Do not use during pregnancy.

Feverfew Herb possessing anti-inflammatory properties.

Flax oil High in alpha-linolenic acid, protective against heart disease; contains 27 anticancer compounds that may help lower the risk of breast and colon cancer.

Folic acid B vitamin that assists in the formation of red blood cells and in nucleic acids (RNA and DNA); may help prevent heart disease by controlling levels of homocysteine; may help prevent colon, rectal and cervical cancer.

Fo-ti (ho shou wu) Longevity herb used in China to help maintain hair color; may help protect against heart attack by lowering blood cholesterol levels and improving blood flow to the heart.

Garlic (odorless) Has a high concentration of allium (a sulfur-containing compound), selenium and germanium; possesses broad-spectrum antimicrobial properties; appears to reduce total cholesterol and low-density lipoproteins; due to its ability to increase natural killer cell activity, appears to be an immune stimulator and to have anticancer properties.

Genistein Isoflavone in soy and soy-based products; appears to inhibit the growth of new blood vessels any may indirectly prevent tumor growth; may aid in the prevention of heart disease.

G.H.3/procaine Analog of procaine amine; was popularized by Dr. Ana Aslan of Romania in the 1940s; believed to have diverse anti-aging effects on the cardiovascular system, the nervous system and skin.

Ginger Spice/herb containing high amounts of geraniol, which may be a potent cancer fighter; may act as an immune stimulant by helping to lower cholesterol; may prevent cardiovascular disease by inhibiting platelet aggregation; has anti-inflammatory activity.

Ginkgo biloba Herb rich in antioxidants; appears to increase the level of dopamine, producing an increase in memory retention and mental alertness; may improve circulation by inhibiting plaque deposition in arteries; appears to inhibit coagulation in blood vessels.

Ginseng Herb that may help improve mental performance; contains antioxidants that prevent cellular damage due to free radicals; may inhibit the growth of cancer cells; increases and enhances energy; appears to help the body cope with stress by normalizing body functions.

Glutathione Has powerful antioxidant properties; appears to aid in the functioning of the immune system; appears to have anti-inflammatory properties that may be effective as treatment for allergies and arthritis.

Goldenseal Herb, antifungal and antibacterial agent, effective in urinary infections.

Gotu kola (centella) Herb with antifatigue properties; stimulates memory; strengthens and tones blood vessels and may help prevent circulatory problems.

Grape seed extract Contains proanthocyanidins, unique bioflavonoids that work together with ascorbic acid; potent antioxidant and free radical scavenger; contains bioflavonoids that may inhibit the release of enzymes that promote inflammation; may aid in the maintenance of small blood vessels.

Green tea Rich source of phytochemicals that appear to help prevent cancer and heart disease; may help reduce cholesterol levels when drunk with meals.

Hawthorn berry Herb rich in bioflavonoids; appears to reduce blood pressure during exertion; has anti-cholesterol properties; has been reported to increase the contractility of the heart.

Homocysteine Amino acid which, in elevated levels, appears to be a risk factor for heart attack.

Inositol Phospholipid that is a constituent of cell membranes; may work with biotin and choline to control male pattern baldness; reported to metabolize serum lipoproteins to lower cholesterol; appears to aid in the maintanence of cell membranes.

Iron   Metal essential for red blood cell formation and vitamin E metabolism. **Caveat:** in excess, iron may be a strong catalyst in free radical production and may aid in the deposition of plaque in blood vessels.

Kava kava   Herb acting primarily as a sedative; may be used for pain control.

Licorice root   Major Chinese herb used to invigorate the functions of the heart, spleen and pancreas; contains glycyrrhizic acid that appears to block tumor growth; reported to have anti-inflammatory properties that may be helpful in treating arthritis; contains carbendoxolane that seems to be effective in treating stomach ulcers. **Caution:** Licorice should not be used by people with high blood pressure.

Gamma-linolenic acid (GLA)   Fatty acid extracted from the seeds of evening primrose or borage plants; may help prevent cardiovascular disease by lowering cholesterol levels and inhibiting blood clot formation; may help provide relief for rheumatoid arthritis through its anti-inflammatory properties.

Lysine   Essential amino acid needed for proper growth, enzyme production and tissue repair; may help stimulate the immune system; appears to have antiviral properties and may inhibit herpes virus.

Melatonin   Hormone secreted by the brain during sleep; appears to be vital for the maintenance of normal body rhythms; may play a role in many other body functions; appears to have neural antioxidant properties.

Methionine   Sulfur-containing amino acid that protects against cardiovascular disease.

Miso soup   Macronutrient soup, natural alkaline pH balancer, has a high concentration of iodine.

Niacin (vitamin B3)   Potent vasodilator; may help potentiate the effects of chromium; enhances energy production and the normal functioning of the nervous system; helps lower cholesterol; appears to function in promoting healthy skin and nerves.

Omega-3 fatty acids Contain two polyunsaturated fats; may help prevent the formation of blood clots leading to heart attacks; appear to be protective against cancer. **Caution:** Do not take omega-3 supplements, if you are taking a blood thinner or using aspirin daily, without first consulting your physician. Excessive amounts may cause bleeding.

Pantothenic acid (vitamin B5) Precursor to cortisone in the adrenal gland; appears to aid in steroid synthesis; aids in energy metabolism; an anti-stress and antioxidant vitamin; may help inhibit hair color loss.

Phytocompounds Contain trace compounds that may be protective against major diseases.

Proline Nonessential amino acid; enhances fat metabolism and aids in the production of connective tissue.

Pyridoxine (vitamin B6) Aids in metabolism of amino acids, synthesis of nucleic acids, and formation of blood cells; appears to be an important cofactor in many cellular reactions. **Caution:** Toxic in high doses; use should be monitored by a physician.

Riboflavin (vitamin B2) Has antioxidant properties; works with other substances to metabolize carbohydrates, fats and proteins for energy; works with glutathione reductase to protect against oxidative damage during exercise; appears to aid in the formation of T lymphocytes, enhancing immunity; seems to help prevent damage to the cornea.

Saw palmetto Herb that appears to aid in preventing testosterone from binding to cells in the prostate gland; may help treat the symptoms of benign prostate hypertrophy; may be useful in treating genitourinary tract problems in both sexes.

Selenium Mineral that works with glutathione peroxidase to prevent damage by free radicals; appears to be involved in the metabolism of prostaglandins; seems to protect cell membranes from attack by free radicals, giving it anticancer properties; may protect lipids from oxidation, which helps to prevent cardiovascular disease; appears to aid in the production of thyroid hormones; may protect against environmental pollutants.

Taurine Modulates neurotransmitters; aids in maintaining clear blood vessels; aids in stabilizing heart rhythm.

Thiamine (vitamin B1)   Involved in the metabolism of carbohydrates to glucose; appears to be necessary for the normal functioning of the nervous system, heart, and muscles; aids in energy production; appears to help alleviate symptoms of stress.

Tocopherol (vitamin E)   Fat-soluble potent antioxidant that works synergistically with selenium; appears to reduce the propensity of low-density lipoproteins to oxidize; may prevent the formation of blood clots; appears to help maintain normal blood glucose levels; appears to help prevent cancers of the gastrointestinal tract by inhibiting the conversion of nitrates to nitrosamines (carcinogens). **Caution:** Do not take vitamin E, if you are taking a blood thinner such as aspirin or have vitamin K deficiency, without consulting your physician.

Valerian root   Herb with effective antispasmodic properties; a nerve tonic.

Vanadium   Trace mineral that aids in the regulation of insulin metabolism.

Wheat grass   Used to protect against pollutants; excellent source of chlorophyll.

Zinc   Essential trace mineral; seems to increase the level of T cells in individuals over 70 years of age; appears to be involved in cellular division, growth and repair; may help prevent prostate gland dysfunction in older men; may help prevent vision loss due to macular degeneration and cataracts.

Appendix A

The American Academy of Anti-Aging Medicine

"The surest way to predict the future is to create the future."

THE FUTURE OF HEALTH CARE

Twelve pioneering clinicians and scientists met in Chicago in August 1993. This meeting was convened to establish a not-for-profit organization addressing the rapid growth in the new science of longevity and anti-aging medicine. The outcome of this meeting was the founding of the American Academy of Anti-Aging Medicine (A⁴M). The mission: to promote the development and dissemination of medical practices, technologies, pharmaceuticals, and processes that retard, reverse, or suspend deterioration of the human body resulting from the physiology of aging. A⁴M was founded on the premise that many of the consequences of aging that are considered diseases are biophysical processes which can be altered by medical intervention.

A⁴M's goals are to actively develop, support, and encourage educational and scientific programs concerned with the advancement of scientific knowledge and application of anti-aging techniques for the benefit of the community and the common good of all mankind.

A^4M proposes to:

1. Facilitate expeditious advances in areas of longevity medicine.
2. Make available to practicing physicians information about the multiple benefits of life-saving and life-extending technologies.
3. Facilitate the dissemination of biomedically and scientifically proven information in longevity science to physicians, scientists, and the public.
4. Assist in developing therapeutic protocols and innovative diagnostic tools to aid physicians in the implementation of effective longevity treatment.
5. Act as an information center for valid and effective anti-aging medicine protocols.
6. Establish a medical protocol review process in anti-aging medicine.
7. Develop a board certification program in the anti-aging specialty.
8. Develop funding for scientifically sound and innovative research in anti-aging medicine and biomedical technology.

A^4M members reside in 45 states of the U.S. and in 26 countries worldwide. Forty-eight percent of its members are physicians and surgeons, 31 percent are nonphysician professionals (scientists, researchers, healthcare providers, educators, etc.), and 21 percent are individuals interested in longevity science and wellness. Members include health-care decision makers from the highest levels of academia and government, with affiliations from Harvard University, Stanford University, the University of California and the University of Chicago. They are leaders in the United States Senate and the House of Representatives, and some are administrators and researchers at the National Institutes of Health, the National Institute of Aging, and the U.S. Department of Defense.

Because of the diversity of its membership, A^4M is making a significant impact on a wide range of medical arenas simultaneously. Shared accurate information about prevention, early diagnosis and treatment of age-related diseases is permitting effective changes in the way medicine is being practiced today. A⁴M's declaration that *"Aging is not inevitable"* has become the working philosophy of the leaders in medicine for the next millennium.

American Academy of Anti-Aging Medicine
7034 West North Ave.
Chicago, IL 60635
(312) 622-7401

Appendix B

Anti-Aging Specialists

The following list includes physicians who practice advanced preventive medicine and anti-aging as a subspecialty.

Arthur Balin, M.D., Ph.D.,
  F.A.C.P.
Center for Rejuvenation of
  Aging Skin
110 Chesley Campus
Media, PA 19063
(610) 892-0300

E. W. McDonagh, D.O.
McDonagh Medical Center,
  Inc.
2800 A Kendallwood Pkwy
Kansas City, MO 64119
(816) 453-5940

Allan Ahlschier, M.D.
8800 Starcrest Drive, Suite
  168
San Antonio, TX 78217
(210) 653-2708

Dharma Singh Khalsa, M.D.
Alzheimer's Prevention
  Foundation
11901 E. Coronado
Tucson, AZ 85749
(520) 749-8374

I. Stephen Coles, M.D., Ph.D.
Gerontology Research Group
5210 Fiore Terrace, Suite
  1405
San Diego CA 92122-5644
(619) 587-6667

David Steenblock, M.S.,
  D.O.
The Steenblock Institute for
  Stroke Recovery
26381 Crown Valley Pkwy
Suite 130
Mission Viejo, CA 92691

Chong Park, M.D.
Plastic Surgery Center
89 Valley Road
Montclair, NJ 07042
(201) 746-3535

Vincent Giampapa, M.D.,
  F.A.C.S.
Plastic Surgery Center
89 Valley Road
Monclair, NJ 07042
(201) 746-3535

Ronald Hoffman, M.D.
40 East 30th St., 10th Fl.
New York, NY 10016
(212) 779-1744

Gregory Keller, M.D., F.A.C.S.
 2323 De La Vina Street
Santa Barbara, CA 93105
(805) 687-6408

Stephen Sinatra, M.D.,
   F.A.C.C., P.C.
Optimum Health
483 West Middle Turnpike,
   Suite 309
Manchester, CT 06040
(860) 643-5101

L. Terry Chappell, M.D.
Celebration of Health
122 Thurman St., Box 248
Bluffton, OH 45817-0248
(419) 258-4627

Brian Rothstein, D.O.
2835 Smith Ave., Suite 208
Baltimore, MD 21209
(410) 484-2121

Barry DiBernardo, M.D.
87 Valley Road
Montclair, NJ 07042
(201) 509-2000

Chris Renna, D.O.
The Renna Clinic
2705 Hospital Blvd., Suite
   206
Grand Prairie, TX 75051
(214) 641-6660
   or

The Renna Clinic
1245 16th St., Suite 307
Santa Monica, CA 90404
(800) 460-1959

Clinic La Prairie
Ch 1815
Clarens-Montreux
Switzerland
011-964-3311

Pritikin Longevity Center
1910 Ocean Front Walk
Santa Monica, CA 90405
(800) 421-0981

Michael Perring, M.D.
Optimal Health of Harley
   Street
14 Harley Street
London W1N 1AG
0171-935 5651

Eric Braverman, M.D.
 Princeton Associates for
   Total Health
212 Commons Way, Bldg. #2
Princeton, NJ 085-40
(609) 921-1842

Jonathan Wright, M.D.
Tahoma Clinic
515 West Harrison, Suite 200
Kent, Washington 98032
(206) 854-4900

Julian Whitaker, M.D.
Whitaker Wellness Institute
4321 Birch St., Suite 100
Newport Beach, CA 92660
(714) 851-1550

* *A⁴M does not endorse physicians, medical products or services. Our list is only a reference and an educational resource. It is your responsibility to use caution and investigate all therapies mentioned in this book as many of them are new and experimental.*

Appendix C

Longevity Institute International

Longevity Institute International (LII), founded in 1996 by Dr. Vincent Giampapa, famed plastic surgeon and pioneering anti-aging physician, is the first accredited scientific anti-aging treatment and diagnostic center in the world. It is a completely unique medical, health and fitness research organization which employs revolutionary techniques designed to measure, treat and retard the aging process. The goal of LII is:

- To provide clients with state-of-the-art medical/scientific diagnostics and treatments which have been designed to provide maximum protection from the diseases and infirmities of aging.
- To provide clients with advanced regenerative therapeutics intended to restore youthful function, obtain enhanced quality of life and help the individual achieve his or her maximum potential life span.

These goals are accomplished utilizing both new and existing medical, nutritional, pharmacological and physiological intervention, making it possible to reverse, by as much as 20 years, the effects of aging related to muscle atrophy, bone demineralization, loss of strength, depressed immune system, and delayed neural reaction time. In addition, LII feels that age reversal effects due to hormonal replacement therapies can improve and rejuvenate sexual function, mental speed and clarity, skin tightness and moisture, as well as general mood and energy levels.

Extensive measurements of individual's biomarkers can establish patient aging rates on multiple levels from overall body function through molecular and DNA analysis. Biomarkers are enzymes, skin cells and biochemicals produced by the body which provide the earliest indication of when the body is approaching a critical aging juncture. Biomarkers are also predictive of the individual's risk of developing age-related diseases or infirmities.

At LII, computer analysis of this complex diagnostic data results in a customized program of biomedical interventions. Treatment regimens are adjusted and refined through periodic monitoring of results. Taken together, the elements of LII's basic program open the possibility for a comprehensive diagnostic, preventive, and therapeutic life extension program unavailable previously.

LII recognizes that aging is not a chronological event, but a complexity of specific dysfunctions affecting no two people in exactly the same combination or to the same degree. Symptoms of aging may be recognized at the organic, cellular, molecular and chromosomal levels, each of which may be targeted by an appropriate treatment strategy. The programs at LII are designed to slow the aging process specifically as it is presented in each individual client. For more information, please contact:

Longevity Institute International
89 Valley Rd.
Montclair, NJ 07042
(201) 746-4385

Appendix D

World Health Network
http://www.worldhealth.net

World Health Network ... the primary Internet resource for breakthrough, life-enhancing information and products which promote health, longevity, well-being, and nutrition.

Co-developed by the American Academy of Anti-Aging Medicine (A⁴M), the leading association for resources in anti-aging and longevity, and Caprel Consulting, a high-end Internet services provider, the World Health Network (WHN) is a forum for addressing key issues in the enhancement in people's lives.

A⁴M recognized the value of the Internet as being the perfect medium for distributing health related information to the world. Caprel Consulting saw an area in the Internet where people could easily access information about longevity, anti-aging and similar topics. And World Health Network was born.

Unlike any other web site across the Internet, WHN is dedicated to making a difference for all of mankind. Combining the discoveries and resources of A⁴M and the technology of the World Wide Web, WHN delivers breakthrough information on topics like hormone replacement therapies such as human growth hormone, DHEA, melatonin, estrogen and testosterone; provides the opportunity to learn about traditional and alternative health care practices, practitioners and associations; offers the chance for authors to contribute their works for public display; the chance to directly communicate with leaders in the health and longevity field; and much more.

The World Health Network is now hosting:

- *Advances in Anti-Aging Medicine,* Vol. 1
- *Stopping the Clock,* clinical updates
- The National Academy of Sports Medicine
- American Longevity Research Institute
- American Board of Anti-Aging Medicine
- *Health Care USA* Magazine
- *Professional Journal of Sports Fitness*

For more information, contact

Caprel Consulting
PO Box 4748
Oakbrook, IL 60522
Fax (708) 789-3556

Appendix E

Aging Research and Educational Organizations

Academy of Pharmaceutical
  Research and Science
2215 Constitution Ave., N.W.
Washington, DC 20037
(202) 628-4410
Fax: (202) 783-2351

Administration on Aging
Department of Health and
  Human Services
330 Independence Ave. S.W.,
  Ste. 4760
Washington, DC 20201
(202) 619-0724
Fax: (202) 619-3759

Advanced Medical Nutrition,
  Inc.
2247 National Ave.
Hayward, CA 94540-5012
(510) 783-6969

Aeron Lifecycles
1933 Davis St., Ste. 310
San Leandro, CA 94577
(800) 631-7900

Aeterna Pharmaceuticals
456 Marconi St.
Ste. Foi, Quebec G1N4A8
(418) 527-8525

Alcor Life Extension
  Foundation
7895 E. Acoma Dr., Ste. 110
Scottsdale, AZ 85260-6916
(602) 922-9013

Allergy Research Group
400 Preda St.
San Leandro, CA 94577
(800) 545-9960

American Biologics
1180 Walnut Ave.
Chula Vista, CA 91911
(800) 227-4473
(619) 429-8200

Alliance for Aging Research
2021 K St., N.W., Ste. 305
Washington, DC 20006
(202) 293-2856
Fax: (202) 785-8574

American Academy of
  Neurology
2221 University Ave., S.E.,
  Ste. 335
Minneapolis, MN 55414
(612) 638-8115
Fax: (612) 623-3504

Alzheimer's Association
919 N. Michigan, Ste. 1000
Chicago, IL 60611
(800) 621-0379

American Academy of Anti-
  Aging Medicine
7034 W. North Ave.
Chicago, IL 60635
(312) 622-7401
Fax: (312) 321-6869

American Aging Association
2129 Providence Ave.
Chester, PA 19013
(610) 874-7550
Fax: (610) 876-7715

American Association for
  Cancer Education
University of Alabama-
  Birmingham
Vh 700
Birmingham, Al 35294
(205) 934-3054
Fax: (205) 934-3278

American Cancer Society
1599 Clifton Road N.E.
Atlanta, GA 30329
(800) 227-2345
Fax: (312) 641-6588

American College of
  Advancement in Medicine
23121 Verdugo Dr.
Laguna Hills, CA 92653
(714) 583-7666
Fax: (714) 455-9679

American College of Clinical
  Pharmacology
300 Oriskany Blvd.
Yorkville, NY 13495
(315) 768-6117
Fax: (315) 768-6119

American Diabetes
  Association National Center
1660 Duke St.
Alexandria, VA 22314
(800) 232-3472

American Geriatrics Society,
  Inc.
770 Lexington Ave., Ste. 300
New York, NY 10021
(212) 308-1414
Fax: (212) 832-8646

American Institute for Cancer
  Research
1759 R Street N.W.
Washington, DC 20009
(800) 843-8114
Fax: (202) 328-7226

American Heart Association
7272 Greenville Ave.
Dallas, TX 75231
(214) 373-6300

American Institute of Stress
124 Park Ave.
Yonkers, NY 10703
(914) 963-1200

American Society of Human
  Genetics
9650 Rockville Pike
Bethesda, MD 20814
(301) 571-1825
Fax: (301) 530-7079

American Society of Plastic
  and Reconstructive
  Surgeons, Inc.
444 East Algonquin Rd.
Arlington Heights, IL 60005
(708) 228-9900
Fax: (708) 228-9131

Amni, Advanced Medical
  Nutrition, Inc.
2247 National Ave.
Hayward, CA 94545
(800) 437-8888

Bio Pro International,
  Unlimited
P.O. Box 890895
Oklahoma City, OK 73189
(405) 634-1310

Bio Research Institute
4492 Camino de la Plaza, Ste.
  TIJ-1063
San Diego, CA 92173-3097
(800) 291-1508

Cooper Clinic
12200 Preston Rd.
Dallas, TX 75230
(214) 239-7223
Fax: (214) 239-6649

Council for Responsible
  Nutrition
1300 19th Street N.W., Ste.
  310
Washington, DC 20036
(202) 872-1488
Fax: (202) 872-9594

The Cutting Edge
Befit Enterprises, Ltd.
P.O. Box 5034
Southampton, NY 11969
(516) 287-3813

Dana Alliance for Brain
  Initiatives
745 Fifth Ave., Ste. 700
New York, NY 10151
(212) 223-4040
  or
1001 G St., N.W., Ste. 1025
Washington, DC 20037
(202) 293-5453

Division on Aging
Harvard Medical School
643 Huntington Ave.
Boston, MA 02115
(617) 432-1840
Fax: (617) 734-4432

Doctor's Data, Inc.
170 W. Roosevelt Rd.
West Chicago, IL 60185
(800) 323-2784
(708) 231-3649

Douglas Laboratories
600 Boyce Road
Pittsburgh, PA 15205
(800) 245-4440
(412) 494-0122

Ecological Formulas
1061 B Shary Circle
Concord, CA 94518
(800) 888-4585

Eden's Secrets Corp.
423 E. Ojai Ave., #107
Ojai, CA 93023
(805) 653-5448

Emerson Ecologics
18 Lomar Park Dr.
Pepperell, MA 01463
(800) 654-4432

G & S Marketing
1442 E. Lincoln Ave.
Orange, CA 92665
(714) 539-4337

Great Smokies Diagnostic
  Laboratory
18 A. Regent Park Blvd.
Asheville, NC 28806
(704) 253-0621

Geron Corporation
200 Constitution Dr.
Menlo Park, CA 94025
(415) 473-7700

Harvard Health Letter
154 Longwood Ave.
Boston, MA 02115
(617) 432-1485
Fax: (617) 432-1506

Health & Healing Newsletter
7811 Montrose Rd.
Potomac, MD 20854
(301) 424-3700
Fax: (301) 424-5059

Health & Longevity
  Newslettter
105 West Monument St.
Baltimore, MD 21201
(410) 223-2611
Fax: (410) 223-2619

Healthmet Bioenergetics
P.O. Box 501005
Indianapolis, IN 46250
(800) 515-0030
(317) 841-1001

Heartsense Newsletter
7811 Montrose Rd.
Potomac, MD 20854
(301) 424-3700

High Tech H_2O
220 Glenwood Ct.
Danville, CA 94526
(510) 820-8829

HoBoN/HVS Laboratories, Inc.
3427 Exchange Ave.
Naples, FL 33942
(800) 521-7722
(941) 643-4636

HTN/Coral Calcium
Box 8495-269 Tramway
Incline Village, CA 89452
(800) 882-9577

International Academy of Alternative Health and Medicine
218 Avenue B
Redondo Beach, CA 90277
(310) 540-0564
Fax: (310) 540-0564

International Federation on Aging
601 E. St., N.W.
Washington, DC 20049
(202) 434-2427
Fax: (202) 434-6458

IT Services
3301 Alta Arden, #2
Sacramento, CA 95825
(916) 483-1085

Jan Marini Skin Research, Inc.
6951 Via Del Oro
San Jose, CA 95119
(408) 362-0130

Jarrow Formulas, Inc.
1824 S. Robertson Blvd.
Los Angeles, CA 90035
(310) 204-6936

J. R. Carlson Laboratories, Inc.
15 College Dr.
Arlington Heights, IL 60004
(708) 255-1600

Journal of Longevity Research
330 Washington Blvd., Ste. 900
Marina del Rey, CA 90290
(310) 577-8416
Fax: (310) 306-1058

Kare Mor International, Inc.
868 Happy Valley Circle
Newnan, GA 30263
(770) 251-1000

Keats Publishing, Inc.
27 Pine St., Box 876
New Canan, CT 06840-0876
(203) 966-8721
Fax: (203) 972-3991

Lane Labs-USA, Inc.
172 Broadway
Woodcliff Lake, NJ 07675
(800) 256-5001
(201) 391-8600

Legere Pharmaceuticals
7326 E. Evans Rd.
Scottsdale, AZ 85260
(602) 991-4083

Lifecell Technologies
International, Inc.
284 Bal Bay Dr.
Bal Harbour, FL 33154
(305) 865-2500

Life Extension Foundation
P.O. Box 229120
Hollywood, CA 33022
(800) 841-5433
Fax: (305) 989-8269

Lucas Meyers, Inc.
P.O. Box 3218
Decatur, IL 62524-3218
(800) SOY-3660

Mary Ann Liebert, Inc.,
Publishers
2 Madison Ave.
Larchmont, NY 10538
(914) 834-3100

Medic Alert Foundation Intl.
2323 Colorado Ave.
Turlock, CA 95382
(209) 668-3333
Fax: 669-2495

MetaMetrix Research
Laboratory
5000 Peachtree Industrial
Blvd., Ste. 110
Norcross, GA 30071
(800) 221-4640
(404) 446-5483

Monroe Institute
62 Roberts Mountain Rd.
Saber, VA 22938
(804) 361-1500

National Academy of Sports
Medicine
699 Hampshire Rd., Ste. 105
Westlake Village, CA 91361
(800) 656-2739 or (805) 449-
1370

National Council on Aging
409 Third St., S.W., Ste. 200
Washington, DC 20024
(800) 424-9046
Fax: (202) 479-0735

National Foundation for Brain
Research
1250 24th St., N.W., Ste.
300
Washington, DC 20037
(202) 293-5453

National Health Information
Center
P.O. Box 1133
Washington, DC 20013
(301) 565-4167
Fax: (301) 984-4256

National Health Lab
10721 Main St.
Fairfax, VA 22030
(703) 273-7311

National Institute of Mental
Health
5600 Fishers Lane, Room 7C-02
Rockville, MD 20857
(301) 443-4513

National Institute of
Neurological Disorders and
Stroke
9000 Rockville Pike
Bldg. 21, Room 8A16
Bethesda, MD 20892
(800) 352-9424

National Institutes of Health
9000 Rockville Pike
Bldg. 31, Room 8A06
Bethesda, MD 20892
(301) 496-5751

National Parkinson
Foundation
1501 N.W. 9th Ave.
Miami, FL 33136
(800) 327-4545 or (800) 433-
7022
Fax: (305) 548-4403

National Stroke Association
8480 Orchard Rd., Ste. 1000
Englewood, CO 80111
(800)-STROKES

New York Academy of
Sciences
2 East 63rd St.
New York, NY 10021
(212) 838-0230
Fax: (212) 888-2894

Nutraceutrics Corporation
600 Fairway Dr., Ste. 105
Deerfield Beach, FL 33441
(305) 725-3000

Nutrition Supply Corp.
2533 North Carson St., Ste.
2384
Carson City, NV 89706
(800) 773-7034

Odyssey Therapeutics Corp.
60 Hamilton St.
Cambridge, MA 02139
(617) 497-5100

Onco Lab
36 The Fenway
Boston, MA 02215
(800) 922-8378

Phillips Nutritionals
27071 Cabot Rd., #121
Laguna Hills, CA 92653
(714) 582-4141

Prevention Magazine
P.O. Box 7319
Red Oak, IA 51591
(800) 666-2503
Fax: (515) 246-1020

Preventative Medicine Update
218 Avenue B
Redondo Beach, CA 90277
(310) 540-0564
Fax: (310) 540-0564

Prime Health & Fitness
Magazine
21100 Erwin St.
Woodland Hills, CA 91367
(818) 884-6800
(818) 704-5734

Progressive Laboratories, Inc.
1701 W. Walnut Hill
Irving, TX 75038
(214) 518-9660

Rx Vitamins, Inc.
270 White Plains Rd.
Eastchester, NY 10709
(914) 771-9607

SpectraCell Laboratories, Inc.
515 Post Oak Blvd., Ste. 830
Houston, TX 77027
(800) 227-5227

Thorne Research Nutritionals
P.O. Box 3200
Sandpoint, ID83864
(208) 263-1337

Townsend Letter for Doctors
and Patients
911 Tyler St.
Port Townsend, WA 98368
(360) 385-0699

Tyler Encapsulations
2204-8 N.W. Birdsdale
Gresham, OR 97030
(800) 869-9705
(503) 661-5401

USANA Independent
Distributors
10504 Maria Dr.
Ft. Worth, TX 76108
(817) 246-5212

Vitamin Diagnostics/European
Laboratory of Nutrients
Route 25 & Industrial Dr.
Cliffwood Beach, NJ 07735
(908) 583-7773

Vitamin Research Products,
Inc.
3579 Highway 50 E.
Carson City, NV 89701
(800) 877-2447

ANTI-AGING FORMULARIES

ApotheCure, Inc.
13720 Midway Rd., Ste. 109
Dallas, TX 75244
214-960-6601
(800) 969-6601

Bajamar Women's HealthCare
Pharmacy
9609 Dielman Rock Island
St. Louis, MO 63132
314-997-3414

California Pharmacy and
  Compounding Center, Inc.
307 Placentia Ave., #0102
Newport Beach, CA 92663
714-642-8057

College Pharmacy
833 N. Tejon
Colorado Springs, CO 80903
(800) 888-9358

Homelink Pharmacy
2650 Elm Ave., Ste. 104
Long Beach, CA 90806
(310) 988-0260
(800) 272-4767

Medical Center Pharmacy
10721 Main St.
Fairfax, VA 22030
(703) 273-7311

International Anti-Aging
  Systems
P.O. Box 2995
London, England N10 2 NA
44-181-444-8272

Wellness Health &
  Pharmaceuticals, Inc.
2800 South 18th St.
Birmingham, AL 35209
(800) 227-2627

QUICK TELEPHONE AND ON-LINE RESOURCES

Alzheimer Web Site, http://werple.mira.net.au/~dhs/adh.html

Arthritis Information Line, Atlanta, GA (800) 283-7800

Arthritis Foundation Web Site, www.crl.com/~fredt/AF/
  arthritis.html

Arthritis Self-Management Program Web Site,
  www.netshop,net/~nsardy/dancer/shydance.html

Brookdale Center on Aging, Alzheimer's Respite Line, (800)
  648-COPE

National Center for Biotechnology Information,
  www.ncbi.nlm.nih.gov

Cancer Information Service, National Institutes of Health (800) 4-CANCER

Cancer Response Line (800) 227-2345

Endocrine Systems Cancers Web Site, cancer.mer.upenn.edu/ disease/adrenal/index.html

Phyicians Data Query, National Library of Medicine (800) 422-6237

Preview the Heart Web Site, sln.fi.edu/tfi/heartpreview.html

DHEA: The Mother Hormone Web Site, www.indra.com/ jewels/RSA/

Information by Organ Systems Endocrine/Metabolic Web Site, indy.radiology.uiowa.edu/Providers/ProviderOrgSys/ OSEndoMetab.html

National Diabetes Information Clearinghouse, Bethesda, MD (301) 468-2162

National Progesterone and Women's Health Web Site, ww.polaris.net/~health/

Fitter International Web Site, www.ipworld.com/market/fitnes/ fitter/homepage.html

International Center for Genetic Engineering & Biotechnology Web Site, www.icgeb.trieste.it/

American Institute of Nutrition. Nutrition Notes, Bethesda, MD (301) 530-7050

Human Nutrition Information Service, Dept. of Agriculture, Hyattsville, MD (301) 436-7725

Nature Made Health Line, (800) 276-2878

Your Vitamin Hotline (800) 533-8482

American Parkinson Disease Association (800) 223-2732

Parkinson's Disease Information Center Web Site, http://www.efn.org/~jskaye/pd/index.html

Parkinson's Disease Web Site, neuro-chief-e.mgh.harvard.ed/parkinsonweb/Main/PDmain.html

Stroke & Aging Research Project Web Site, www.columbia.edu/'dwd

Aminohealth Stress Management Web Site, www.haiwan.com/~fitnessa/ahealth.html

Center for Anxiety & Stress Treatment Web Site, www.cts.com/~health

National Institute of Neurological Disorders and Stroke Web Site, www.nih.gov/ninds/nindseeo.htm

World Health Network Web Site, innovative site for the latest useful information on anti-aging medicine, personal health, fitness and breakthrough technologies, http://www.worldhealth.net

References

Chapter 2

Bjorksten, J., "Crosslinkage and the Aging Process," In Rockstein, M. (ed): *Theoretical Aspects of Aging*, Academic Press, New York, 1974, p. 43.

Bjorskten, J., "The Crosslinkage Theory of Aging: Clinical Implications,". *Compr Ther* II:65, 1976.

Campanelli, Linda, C., Ph.D., "Theories of aging," *Theories and Psychosocial Aspects of Aging*,(1) 3-13.

Finch, Caleb, E., *Longevity, Senescence, and the Genome*, University of Chicago Press, 1990.

Hayflick, L., "Theories of Aging," in Cape, R ., Coe, R., and Rodstein, M. (eds), *Fundamentals of Geriatric Medicine*, Raven Press, New York, 1983.

Hayflick, L.,*How and Why We Age*, Ballantine Books, New York, 1994, pp. 222-262.

Kotulak, Ronald and Gorner, Peter, "Calorie Restriction: Taking the lifespan to its limit," *Aging on Hold*. Tribune Publishing, 1992, p. 52-57.

Martin, G. M., Sprague, C.A. and Epstein, C.J., "Replicative Lifespan of Cultivated Human Cells," *Lab Invest* 23:26, 1970.

Medvedev, Z, "Possible Role of Repeated Nucleotide Sequences in DNA in the Evolution of Lifespans of Differential Cells," *Nature* 237:453, 1972.

Review of Biological Research in Aging, Vol. 4, edited by Martin Rothstein, Wiley-Liss, 1990.

Rose, Michael R., *Evolutionary Biology of Aging*, Oxford University Press, 1991.

Rosenfeld, Albert, *Prolongevity II*, Alfred A. Knopf, Inc., New York, 1985, 247-267.

Sharma, Ramesh, "Theories of aging," *Physiological Basis of Aging and Geriatrics*, CRC Press, Florida, 1994, 37-44.

Sonneborn, T, "The origin, Evolution, Nature, and Causes of Aging," In Behnke, J,. Fince, C., and Moment, G. (eds), *The Biology of Aging.*, Plenum Press, New York, 1979, p. 341.

Warner, H.R., Butler R.N., Sprott, R.C., and Schneider, E.L., *Modern Biological Theories of Aging*, Raven Press, 1987.

Chapter 3

Cowley, Geoffrey, "Melatonin," *Newsweek*, August 7, 1995, pp. 46-49.

Hughes, Patrick, "The Hormone Whose Time Has Come," *Hippocrates*, July-August 1994.

Kane, M.A., Johnson, A., and Robinson, W.A., "Serum Melatonin Levels in Melanoma Patients After Repeated Oral Administration," *Melanoma Research* 1994; 4: 59-65.

Kent, Saul, Life Extension Reports, "How Melatonin Combats Aging," *Life Extension Magazine*, December 1995, pp. 10-27.

Lissoni, P., Meregalli, S., Barni, S., and Frigerio, F. "A Randomized Study of Immunotherapy with Low-Dose Subcutaneous Interleukin-2 Plus Melatonin vs. Chemotherapy with Cisplatin and Etoposide as First-Line Therapy for Advanced Non-Small Cell Lung Cancer," *Tumori* 1994; 80: 464-67.

McAuliffe, Kathleen, "Live 20 Years Longer, Look 20 Years Younger," *Longevity*, October 1990.

Muller, J., Stone, P., and Braunwald, E. ,"Circadian Variation in the Frequency of Onset of Acute Myocardial Infarction," *New England Journal of Medicine* 1985; 313-21: 1315-22.

Pierpaoli, Walter, and William Regelson, with Carol Colman, *The Melatonin Miracle*, Simon & Schuster, New York, 1995, pp.29-30.

Reiter, R.J. et al., "A Review of the Evidence Supporting Melatonin's Role as an Antioxidant," *Journal of Pineal Research*, Volume 18, No. 1, pp. 1-11, January 199

Reiter, Russell J., Ph.D., and Jo Robinson, *Melatonin*, Bantam Books, New York, 1995, pp. 40-41,62-69; (9),116-118.

Sahelian, Ray, M.D., *Melatonin: Nature's Sleeping Pill*, Be Happier Press, California, 1995, pp. 39-48; 77-81; 83-85.

Sahelian, Ray, M.D., "Melatonin: The Natural Sleep Medicine," *Total Health*, August 1995, Vol. 17, No. 4. p. 30 (3).

Zhdanova, I.V., Wurtman, R.J., and Schomer, D.L.,"Sleep-inducing Effects of Low Doses of Melatonin Ingested in the Evening," *Clinical Pharmacology and Therapeutics* 1995; 57: 552-558.

Chapter 4

Ben-Nathan, D., et al., "Protection by Dehydroepiandrosterone in Mice Infected with Viral Encephalitis," *Archives of Virology,* 1991; 120: 263-271.

Brody, Jane, "Restoring Ebbing Hormones May Slow Aging," *New York Times,* July 18, 1995, p. c3.

Coleman, D.L. et al., "Effect of Genetic Background on the Therapeutic Effects of Dehydroepiandrosterone (DHEA) in Diabetes-Obesity Mutants in Aged Normal Mice," *Diabetes,* 1984; 33: 26.

Coleman, D.L., et al., "Therapeutic Effects of Dehydroepiandrosterone (DHEA) in Diabetic Mice," *Diabetes,* 1982; 31: 830-833.

Cranton, Elmer, M.D., and James P. Frackelton, M.D., "Take Control of Your Aging," *Alternative Medicine Digest,* Issue 8, pps. 23-28.

Cryer, Sibyl, "New Music and Stress Reduction Technique Increase anti-Aging Hormone—DHEA—Study Says," *Institute of Heartmath,* July 19, 1995, pp. 1-2.

"DHEA Replacement Therapy," *Life Extension Report,* Vol. 13, No. 9, September 1993, p. 67.

Fettner, Ann Giudici, "DHEA Gets Respect," *Harvard Health Letter,* Vol. 19. No. 9, July 1994.

Gaby, Alan R., M.D., "DHEA: The Hormone That Does It All," *Holistic Medicine,* Spring 1993, pps. 19-22.

Life Extension Events, "DHEA Comes to the Mainstream," *Life Extension Magazine,* September 1995, pps. 1-4.

Life Extension Events, "DHEA Replacement Therapy," *Life Extension Magazine,* March 1, 1995, p. 4.

Life Extension Foundation, *The Physician's Guide to Life Extension Drugs,* 1994 Edition, pp. 46-55.

Nasman, R., et al., "Serum dehydroepiandrosterone sulfate in Alzheimer's Disease and in Multi-Infarct Dementia," *Biological Psychiatry,* 1991, 30:684-690.

Regelson, W. et al., "Hormonal Intervention: 'Buffer Hormones' or 'State Dependency': The Role of Dehydroepiandrosterone (DHEA), Thyroid Hormone, Estrogen, and Hypophysectomy in Aging," *Annals of the New York Academy of Science,* 1988, 521: 260-273.

Roberts, E. et al., "Effects of Dehydroepiandrosterone and its Sulfate on Brain Tissue in Culture and on Memory in Mice," *Brain Research*, 1987, 406: 357-362.

Sahelian, Ray, M.D., "The Fountain of Youth—The Never Ending Quest," *Muscular Development and Fitness*, January 1996, p. 48.

Sunderland, T., et al., "Reduced Plasma Dehydroepiandrosterone Concentration in Alzheimer's Disease," *The Lancet*, 1989, 2:570.

Chapter 5

"A Physician Gives His Opinion About the Entry of STH into the World of Bodybuilding," *Flex*, June 1983, p. 76.

Barbul; "Arginine and Immune Function," *Nutrition* 6(1): 53-60, (Update on Immunonutrition Symposium Supplement; Jan/Feb 1990.

Ceda, G., Valenti, G., Butterini, U., Hoffman, A.R., "Diminished Pituitary Response to Growth Hormone-Releasing Factor in Aging Male Rats," *Endocrinology* 1986;118: 2109-14.

Crist, D.M., Peake, G.T., Egan, P.A., Waters, D.L., "Body Composition Response to Exogenous GH during Training in Highly Conditioned Adults," *Journal of Applied Physiology* 65: 579-584. 1988.

Donaldson, Thomas, Ph.D., *Life Extension Report*, April 1991 Vol. 11, No. 4, p. 32.

Dr. Julian Whitaker's Health & Healing, Vol. 5, No. 7, July 1995, p. 4-5.

Howard, Ben, "Growing younger", *Longevity*. October 1992, p. 41.

Journal of the American Medical Association, March 18, 1988, Vol. 259, No. 11, p. 1703 (3).

Kelley, K. et al., "Gh3 Pituitary Adenoma Cells Can Reverse Thymic Aging in Rats," *Proceedings of the National Academy of Sciences*. Vol. 83, p. 5663, 1986, cited in "Longevity: A Fresh Shot of Life," *Omni*, Vol. 1, No. 9, July 1987, p. 85.

Lawren, "The Hormone that Makes Your Body 20 Years Younger," *Longevity*, October 1990, p. 34.

Lehrman, Sally, "The Fountain of Youth?", *Harvard Health Letter*, June 1992 Vol. 17, No. 8, p. 1 (3).

Marcus R., Butterfield, G., Holloway, L. et al. "Effects of Short-Term Administration of Recombinant Human Growth Hormone to Elderly People," *J Clin Endocrinol Metab* 1990: 519-27.

Merimee, et al., "Arginine Initiated Release of Growth Hormone: Factors Modifying the Response in Normal Men," *New England Journal of Medicine*. 280(26): 1434-38 (1969).

Rudman, D., A.G. Feller, H.S. Nograj, et al., "Effects of Human Growth Hormone in Men over 60 Years old," *New England Journal of Medicine* 323:1-6, 1990.

Rudman, D., "Growth Hormone, Body Composition, and Aging," *Journal of the American Geriatric Society* 1985;33: 800-7.

Salomon, F., R.C. Cuneo, R. Hesp, P.H. Sönksen, "The Effects of Treatment with Recombinant Human Growth Hormone on Body Composition and Metabolism in Adults with Growth Hormone Deficiency," *New England Journal of Medicine* 321:1797-1803, 1989.

Weiss, Rick, "A Shot at Youth", *Health,* Nov.-Dec. 1993 Vol. 7, No. 7, p. 38 (10).

Chapter 6

Genant, H.K., Baylink, D.J., and Gallagher, J. C., "Estrogens in the prevention of Osteoporosis in Postmenopausal Women," *American Journal of Obstetrics and Gynecology*, 1989, Vol. 161, No. 6, 1842, cited in *Office Nurse*, p. 8.

Keough, Carol (editor), "Breast Cancer," *The Complete Book of Cancer Prevention.* Rodale Press, 1988, p. 7-15.

Keresztes, P.A. & Dan, A. J., "Estrogen and Cardiovascular Disease," *Cardiovascular Nursing*, 1992, Vol., 28, No. 1, p. 1, cited in Office Nurse.

Notelovitz, M., "Estrogen Replacement Therarpy: Indications, Contraindications, and Agent Selection," *American Journal of Obstetrics and Gynecology*, 1989, 161 (6): 1832, cited in Rickert, Barbara, R.N., Ph.D., *Office Nurse*, June 1993, p. 9.

Stampfer, M.J., and Colditz, G.A., "Estrogen Replacement Thearpy and Coronary Heart Disease: A Quantitative Assessment of the Epidemiologic Evidence," *Preventive Medicine,* 1991, Vol. 20, No. 1, p. 47, cited in *Office Nurse*, p. 7.

Stampfer, M.J., Colditz, G.A., et al., "Postmenopausal Estrogen Therapy and Cardiovascular Disease: Ten-Year Follow-Up from the Nurses Health Study," *New England Journal of Medicine,* 1991, Vol. 325, No. 11, p. 756, cited in Office Nurse, p. 10.

Voigt, L.F., Weiss, N.S., et al., "Progestagen Supplementation of Exogenous Oestrogens and Risk of Endometrial Cancer," *Lancet*, 1991, Vol. 338, No. 8762, p. 274, cited in *Office Nurse*, p. 8.

Whitaker, Dr. Julian, Dr. Julian Whitaker's Health & Healing, March, 1993, Vol. 3, No. 3, p. 3.

Wallis, Claudia, "The Estrogen Dilemma," *Time*, June 26, 1995, pp. 48-53.

Williams, Dr. David G., "The Forgotten Hormone," *Alternatives for the Health Conscious Individual*, Vol. 4, No. 6, December 1991, pp. 42-51.

Chapter 7

Budenholzer, Brian R., M.D., "Prostate-Specific Antigen Testing to Screen for Prostate Cancer," *The Journal of Family Practice.*,September 1995, Volume 41, No. 13, pp. 270-76.

The Complete Book of Cancer Prevention, Keough, Carol (editor), Rodale Press, 1988, pp. 131-134.

Fahim, M.S., "Effect of Panax Ginseng on Testosterone Level and Prostate in Male Rats." *Archives of Andrology*, 1982; Volume 8, No. 4, pp. 261-263.

Horton, R., "Benign Prostatic Hyperplasia: A disorder of Androgen Metabolism in the Male," *Journal of the American Geriatrics Society*, 1984.vol. 32, no. 5, pp. 380-385.

Matsumoto, Alvin M., "Andropause—Are reduced androgen levels in aging men physiologically important?" *Western Journal of Medicine.*, November 1993, Volume 159, No. 5, p. 618-20.

Rudman, Daniel, Drinka, Paul J., Wilson, Charles R., Mattson, Dale E., Scherman, Francis, Cuisinier, Mary C., Schultz, Shiela, "Relations of Endogenous Anabolic Hormones and Physical Activity to Bone Density and Lean Body Mass in Elderly Men," *Clinical Endocrinology*,. (1994) 40, pp. 653-661.

Skerrett, P.J., "Interest in Growth Hormone May Be Shrinking," *Medical World News*. December 1992, Volume 33, No. 12, p. 26.

Tenover, Joyce S., M.D., Ph.D., "Androgen Administration to Aging Men," *Clinical Andrology*, December 1994, Volume. 23, No. 4, pp. 877-87.

Thiebolt, L..,: Berthelay , S., Berthelay, J., . "Preventive and Curative Action of a Bark Extract from an African Plant, Pygeum Africanum, on Experimental Prostatic Adenoma." *Therapie*, 1971, vol. 26, no. 3, pp. 575-580.

Chapter 8

Abraham, G.E., "Nutritional Factors in the Etiology of the Premenstrual Tension Syndromes," *Journal of Reproductive Medicine,* 1983, 28:446-464, cited in *Formulas for Life,* p. 168.

Anderson, R.A., et al., "Chromium Supplementation of Human Subjects: Effects on Glucose, Insulin, and Lipid Variables," *Metabolism,* 1983; 32: 894-899, cited in Kronhausen, Eberhard, Ed.D. and Phyllis Kronhausen, Ed.D., with Harry B. Demopoulos, M.D., *Formulas for Life,* William Morrow, New York, 1989, p. 172.

Dyckner, T., and P.O. Wester, "Effect of Magnesium on Blood Pressure," *British Medical Journal,* 1983, 286: 1847, cited in *Formulas for Life,* p. 167.

Goei, G.S. and G.E. Abraham, "Effect of a Nutritional Supplement, Optivite, a Symptom of Premenstrual Tension," *Journal of Reproductive Medicine,* 1983, 28: 527-531, cited in *Formulas for Life,* p. 168.

Riales, R. and M.J. Albrink, "Effect of Chromium Chloride Supplementation on Glucose Tolerance and Serum Lipids Including High-Density Lipoprotein of Adult Men," *American Journal of Clinical Nutrition,* 1981, 34:2670-2678, cited in *Formulas for Life,* p. 172.

Salonen, J.T. et al., "Risk of Cancer in Relation to Serum Concentrations of Selenium and Vitamins A and E: Matched CSE Control Analysis of Prospective Data," *British Medical Journal,* 1985, 290: 417, cited in *Formulas for Life,* p. 154.

Shamberger, R.J. et al., "Antioxidants and cancer. Part VI. Selenium and Age-Adjusted Human Cancer Mortality," *Archives of Environmental Health,* 1976, 31:231; Schrauzer, G.N. et al., "Selenium in Human Nutrition—Dietary Intakes and Effects of Supplementation," Bioinorganic Chemistry, 1978, 8:303-318; Mondrago, M.C. and W.G. Jaffe, "The Ingestion of Selenium in Caracas Compared with Some Other Cities of the World," *Archives of Latinoamerican Nutrition,* 1976, 26:341-352; Sakurai, H. and K. Tsuchiya, "A Tentative Recommendation for the Maximum Daily Intake of Selenium," Environmental *Physiological Biochemistry,* 1975, 5:107-118; all cited in *Formulas for Life,* pp. 152-153.

Spallholz, J.E. et al., "Anti-Inflammatory, Immunologic, and Carcinostatic Attributes of Selenium in Experimental Animals," reviewed in *Advances in Experimental Medicines and Biology,* 1981, 135: 43-62;Desowitz, R.S. and J.w. Barnwell, "Effect of Selenium and Dimethyl Dioctadecyl Ammonium Bromide on the Vaccine-Induced Immunity of Swiss-Webster Mice Against Malaria (Plasmodium Berghei)," *Infection and Immunity*, 1980, 27:87; both cited in *Formulas for Life*, p. 154.

Turlapaty, P.D. and B.M. Altura, "Magnesium Deficiency Produces Spasms of Coronary Arteries: Relationship to Etiology of Sudden Death Ischemic Heart Disease," *Science*, 1980, 208: 198; Iseri, L. T. et al, "Magnesium Therapy for Intractable Ventricular Tachyarrhythmias in Noromagnesemic Patients," *Western Journal of Medicine*, 1983, 139:823, both cited in *Formulas for Life*, p. 167.

Chapter 9

Balch, James F., M.D., and Patricia Balch, C.N.C., *Prescriptions for Nutritional Healing*, Avery Publishing Group, New York, 1990, pp. 4-12.

Borek, Carmia, PhD., Maximize Your Health-Span with Antioxidants, Keats Publishing, Connecticut, 1995, pps. 13-20.

Coles, Stephen, M.D., "CoQ-10 and Life Span Extension," *Journal of Longevity Research*,Vol. 1, No. 5, 1995.

Davies, K.J., et al., *Biochemical Biophysical Research Communications*, Vol. 107, 1982, pp. 1198-1205.

Diplock, A.T., *American Journal of Clinical Nutrition*, Vol. 53, 1991, pp. 189S-193S; Niki, E., et al., *American Journal of Clinical Nutrition*, Vol. 53, 1991, pp. 201S-205S; Di Mascio, P., et al., *American Journal of Clinical Nutrition*, Vol. 53, 1991, pp. 194S-200S, all cited in *Freedom from Disease*, p. 126.

Ebnother, Carl, M.D., "A New Theory of Heart Disease," *Journal of Longevity Research*, Vol. 1, No. 8, pp. 24-45.

Hendler, S.S., *The Complete Guide to Anti-Aging Nutrients,* Simon & Schuster, New York, 1984, p. 88; Harris, R.W.C., *British Journal of Cancer*, Vol. 53, 1986, pp. 653-659; Shekelle, R.B. et al., *Lancet*, Vol. 2, 1981, pp. 1185-1190; all cited in *Freedom from Disease*, p. 126.

Kamen, Betty, Ph.D., "Ester-C: The New Vitamin C Milestone," *Let's Live*, October 1989.

"Life Extension Update: CoQ-10 Reduces Surgical Complications," *Life Extension Magazine* March 1, 1995, pp. 4-5.

Menkes, M.S., et al., *New England Journal of Medicine*, Vol. 315, 1986, 1250-1289, cited in *Freedom from Disease*, p. 126.

Moseley, Bill, "Interview with Linus Pauling," *Omni*, December 1986, pp. 104, 106.

Roehm, J. N. et al., *Archives of Environmental Health*, Vol. 24, 1972, pp. 237-242; Mustafa, M.G., *Nutrition Reports International*, Vol. 11, 1975, pp. 475-481; Fletcher, B.L., and A.L. Tappel, Environmental Research, Vol. 6, 1973, pp. 165-175;, all cited in Sharma, Hari, M.D., *Freedom from Disease*, Veda Publishing, Toronto, 1990, p. 124.

Russell, Pauline, "Revolutionary New Form of Vitamin C," *Your Health*, October 24, 1989.

Tappel, A.L., "Measurement of and Protection From in Vivo Lipid Peroxidation," in *Free Radicals in Biology*, Vol. IV, ed., W.A. Pryor, Academic Press, New York, 1980, pp. 1-47; Dillard, C.J., et al., *Journal of Applied Physiology*, Vol. 45., 1978, pp. 927-932; both cited in *Freedom from Disease*, p. 125.

Chapter 10

Balch, James F. , M.D., and Phyllis A., C.N.C., *Prescriptions for Nutritional Healing*, Avery Publishing Group, New York, 1990, p. 211.

Dilman, Vladimir, M.D., Ph.D., D.M.Sc., and Ward Dean M.D., et al., *The Neuroendocrine Theory of Aging and Degenerative Disease*, Center for Bio-gerontology, Florida, 1992, pp. 43-92.

The Encyclopedia of Common Diseases, Rodale Press, Emmaus, Pa., pp. 294-295, cited in Langer, pp. 139-140.

Jennings, Isobel W., Vitamins in Endocrine Metabolism, Charles C Thomas, Springfield, Ill, 1970, p. 80, cited in Langer, p. 33.

Langer, Stephen E., M.D. and James F. Scheer, *Solved: The Riddle of Illness*, Keats Publishing, Inc., New Canaan, Conn., 2nd edition 1995.

Pita, J.C., Jr., et al., "Dimunition of Large Pituitary Tumor After Replacement Therapy for Primary Hypothyroidism," *Neurology*, Vol. 29, Number 8, August 29, 1979, pp. 1169-1172; Guerrero, L.A. and R. Carnovale, "Regression of Pituitary Tumor After Thyroid Replacement in Primary Hypothyroidism," *Southern Medical Journal*, Vol. 76, No. 4, April 1983, pp. 529-531, both cited in Langer, p. 141.

Spencer, J.G.C., "The Influence of the Thyroid in Malignant Disease," *British Journal of Cancer*, Vol. 8, No. 393, 1954, cited in Langer, p. 139.

Wild, Russell, Ed., et. al., *The Complete Book of Natural and Medicinal Cures*, Rodale Press, Emmaus, Pa., 1994, pp. 605-608.

Williams, Roger J., Free and Unequal, University of Texas Press, Austin, Texas, 1953, p. 19, cited in Langer, p. 11.

Chapter 11

Cooper, Kenneth, M.D., *It's Better to Believe*. Thomas Nelson Publishers Inc., Nashville, Tenn., 1995.

Kaufman, Dr. Richard Clark, *The Age Reduction System*, Rawson Associates, New York, 1986, p. 209-210.

Klatz, Ronald, D.O., and Alan Hirsch, M.D., "The Ageless Athlete," *Sports Clinic, The Professional's Journal of Sports Fitness*, Spring, 1992.

Spirduso, Waneen, W., Ed.D., *Physical Dimensions of Aging, Human Kinetics*, Champaign, Ill., 1995, p. 147.

Chapter 12

Clark, Etta, *Growing Old Is Not for Sissies: Portraits of Senior Athletes*, Pomegranate Calendars and Books, Corte Madera, Cal., 1986. This and all other profiles in this chapter have been taken from this book, except where otherwise specified.

Gallagher, Marty, "Ageless Muscle," *Muscle and Fitness*, January 1996, pp. 162-165.

Interview January 16, 1996: Richard Orenstein—associate and colleague of Jack LaLanne.

Moore, K., "The Times of Their Lives," *Runner's World*, 1992, Vol. 20, 44-47, p. 44;

Norris, Rebecca, "Heels Over Head," *American Health*, September 1995, p. 108.

Interview February 1, 1996: Bob Delmonteque.

Chapter 13

Borek, Carmia, Ph.D., *Maximize Your Health Span with Antioxidants*, Keats Publishing, New Canaan, Conn., 1995, p. 63.

Ford, *Norman, Lifestyle for Longevity*, Para Research, Gloucester, Mass., 1984, pp. 82-83.

Kaufman, Dr. Richard Clark, *The Age Reduction System*, Rawson Associates, New York, 1986, p. 125.

Mann, Denise, "GreeK Diet Promotes Longevity," December 21, 1995, p. 2.

Sinatra, Stephen T., M.D., *Optimum Health*, Lincoln Bradley Publishing Group, Tennesee, 1996, pp. 206-208.

Sultenfuss, Sherry Wilson M.S., and Thomas J. Sultenfuss, M.D., *A Women's Guide to Vitamins and Minerals*, Contemporary Books, New York,1995, pp. 173-174.

Wild, Russell, Ed., et. al., *The Complete Book of Natural and Medicinal Cures*, Rodale Press, Emmaus, Pa., 1994, pp. 28-32.

Chapter 14

Adapted from Eliot, Robert S., M.D., "The Do-It-Yourself Stress Clinic Test," *Longevity*, January 1994, pp. 45-47, 71-74.

Balch, James F., M.D., and Phyllis A. Balch, C.N.C., *Prescriptions for Nutritional Healing*, Avery Publishing Group, New York 1990, p. 298.

Cohen, Jessica, "The Healing Touch," *Longevity*, January 1994, pp. 26, 64, 66.

Eppley, K., et al., *Journal of Clinical Psychology*, Vol. 45, 1989, pp. 957-974, cited in Sharma, p. 183.

Jevning, R., *The Physiologist*, Vol. 21, 1978, p. 60, cited in Sharma, pp. 179, 182.

Levine, S.A., and P.M. Kidd, *Antioxidant Adaptation: Its Role in Free Radical Pathology*, Biocurrents Division, Allergy Research Group, San Leandro, 1986, pp. 241-242, cited in Hari Sharma, M.D., *Freedom from Disease*, Veda Publishing, Toronto, 1993, pp. 173-174.

Wallace, R.K. et al., *International Journal of Neuroscience* 16, 1982, pp. 53-58, cited in Sharma, p. 189.

Williams, Gurney, "Mind, Body, Spirit: Portable Meditation, Stress Relief for Those on the Go," *Longevity*, May 1993, p. 72.

Index

361

About the Authors

DR. RONALD M. KLATZ

 Dr. Ronald Klatz is recognized as one of the world's foremost authorities in preventive/longevity medicine and maximum human performance. Along with his many scholarly publications, he was co-author of the best selling books *Death in the Locker Room/Steroids & Sports, The E Factor, Life Extension Weight Loss* and *Deprynl—The Anti-Aging Drug.* In 1992, Dr. Klatz was appointed Senior Medical Editor at *Longevity Magazine,* the preeminent popular journal of life-extension research. Most recently, he was editor of the scientific textbook, *Advances in Anti-Aging Medicine,* vol. From 1982 to 1986, he was founder and Chief of Staff at the Pain Relief Clinic in Racine, Wisconsin, a multimillion-dollar specialty clinic providing rehabilitative medicine for the treatment of pain related conditions, sports medicine, and internal and preventive medicine. He has served as associate professor at the University of Health Sciences/Medicine & Surgery in Iowa, has been a syndicated columnist for Pioneer Press of Chicago (a division of Time-Life Inc.), hosted his own radio show, and served as an advisor to Physicians Radio Network.

Dr. Klatz is Board certified by the American Osteopathic Board of Family Practice, American Osteopathic Academy of Sports Medicine, and the Academy of Sports Physicians.

As founder and president of the American Longevity Research Institute, a not-for-profit research foundation exploring new life extension technologies, Dr. Klatz had done pioneering work in the study, treatment, and prevention of aging related degenerative diseases. He is currently a director with Life Resuscitation Technologies, Inc., a medical research and development company which, since its inception in 1989, has received numerous U.S. patents for innovative lifesaving devices and is considered the leader in the new biomedical science of human resuscitation technology. Dr. Klatz was awarded the prestigious INPEX Gold Medal in science for his groundbreaking and dedicated work in the field of brain resuscitation. In recognition of his contributions to medicine and stature within the medical community at large, his peers elected him President of the American Academy of Anti-Aging Medicine in 1993.

Dr. Klatz is co-founder of the National Academy of Sports Medicine, and co-publisher of the *Professional's Journal of Sports Fitness* and *The NASM Journal of Certified Personal Fitness Trainers*.

As a respected consultant to the medical and fitness industry, Dr. Klatz devotes much of his time to research and the development of advanced technologies for the benefit of science and humanity.

DR. ROBERT M. GOLDMAN

A noted physician and surgeon with a second doctorate in steroid biochemistry Dr. Robert Goldman has emerged as a corporate leader in the field of biotechnology and life sciences. He has spearheaded the formation, staffing, and funding of two rapidly growing corporations: Life Resuscitation Technologies, Inc. which is involved in the development of lifesaving medical devices and Organ, Inc., which is committed to the advancement of organ preservation technologies. Dr. Goldman has personally raised in excess of $8 million in private funding for both of these companies. He negotiated the acquisition of worldwide exclusive licensing rights from the American Red Cross for all organ and tissue preservation technologies developed over the last several decades and forged official strategic alliances for his companies with numerous renowned institutions.

As a scientist, researcher, entrepreneur, and businessman, he has repeatedly demonstrated the ability to bring the right teams of people together for maximum productivity. Dr. Goldman is the chair of the International Medical Commission, which under his leadership established medical committees for 160 sports federation member nations and also serves as Special Advisor to the President's Council on Physical Fitness & Sports, where he worked closely with his friend and then Council Chairman, Arnold Schwarzenegger. In 1987 he founded the National Academy of Sports Medicine (NASM), which, having established divisions on every continent, is one of the fastest-growing sports medicine organizations in the world. In 1984, Dr. Goldman founded the High Technology Research Institute, one of the premier independent laboratories analyzing health equipment and medical devices. Recognized as a world expert on drug testing and androgenic anabolic steroids, he was instrumental in establishing pharmacological dope control and collection standards for international pharmaceutical clinical laboratories.

A karate black belt and Chinese weapons expert, Dr. Goldman is a former world champion strength athlete, holding over 20 world strength records and is listed in the *Guinness Book of World Records*. In addition, Dr. Goldman was an All-College athlete in four sports, is a three-time winner of the John F. Kennedy Physical Fitness Award, was voted Athlete of the Year in 1981 and 1982, and was the recipient of the 1983 Champions' Award. In 1980. he was inducted into the World Hall of Fame of Physical Fitness. This interest in human physiology has led him to an eminent position in the field of longevity and maximum human performance and to co-found the American Academy of Anti-Aging Medicine, an organization for which he serves as Chairman of the Board. He holds specialty certifications from

numerous health organizations, such as the Academy of Sports Physicians, to which he has recently been elected a Fellow.

A medical inventor, he is the co-developer of numerous patented medical inventions, several of which have been awarded the prestigious INPEX Gold Medal for Science in 1993, Platinum Grand Prize for Medicine in 1994, and the Humanitarian Award from the International Invention/ New Products Exposi-

Dr. Bob Goldman setting the world record in handstand pushups, 321 repetitions.

tion in 1995. Dr. Goldman serves as medical advisor and is on the Board of Directors for multiple scientific organizations and publications. A consistently strong media presence, he has authored hundreds of articles, several medical texts, as well as the books *Death in the Locker Room/Steroid & Sports* (Harper/Icarus Press—1984), *Death in the Locker Room, Steroids, Cocaine & Sports* (HP Books—1987), *The E Factor/Secrets of New Tech Training* (William Morrow—1988), *Death in the Locker Room II/Drugs & Sports* (Elite Sportsmedicine Pub—1992), and has appeared on over 500 radio and television broadcasts, such as *Good Morning, America,* ABC, CBS, NBC, and CNN.

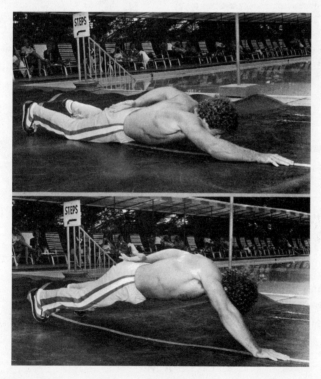

Dr. Goldman setting world record of 161 consecutive one arm extension pushups. He also set world record of 13,500 consecutive situps in 13 hours and 22 minutes.